F. Vick

ENGLISH SOCIETY
IN THE EIGHTEENTH CENTURY

ENGLISH SOCIETY IN THE EIGHTEENTH CENTURY

As Influenced From Oversea

BY

JAY BARRETT BOTSFORD

1965

OCTAGON BOOKS, INC.

New York

Originally published 1924 by The Macmillan Company

Reprinted 1965
by special arrangement with Dr. Robert Botsford and Mrs. Henry Meador

OCTAGON BOOKS, INC.
175 FIFTH AVENUE
NEW YORK, N.Y. 10010

Printed in U.S.A. by
NOBLE OFFSET PRINTERS, INC.
NEW YORK 3, N. Y.

PREFACE

While the social and economic changes of eighteenth century England have received able treatment by modern scholars, there has been no serious attempt to explain these phenomena in the light of oversea expansion. The victorious struggle for world empire proved to be a force more insistent and more powerful than tradition or local interests in reshaping the character of the individual and of the social structure of this period.

Without cessation new commodities, new ideas, and new opportunities for making wealth—all made possible by the vastness of world empire—were transforming the daily life and the thoughts and actions of millions of Englishmen. Herein the blending of a time-old heredity with a new environment produced a new type of individual. Liberated from the trammels of class convention he was a self-made man; freed from the bonds of insularity he became a cosmopolitan, a man of the world. In the new freedom which accompanied broadening trade relations one sees a blending of coarseness and refinement, of extravagance and moderation, of selfishness and philanthropy: in short, a chaotic state which seems to parallel closely the modern age. Experience acquired in the hard school of business was applied to

v

the problems of political and socal life, and one may see at the close of the century the emergence of ideals and of characteristics which we are pleased to term generically, "Anglo-Saxon."

Similarly were ramifications of world empire responsible for changes in the character and structure of the nation. Here, too, the lessons learned in business were responsible for the development of metropolitan standards, of civic and national consciousness, and of a new morality in political life. The influx of wealth eventually benefited the entire nation and happily resulted in a higher standard of living. Furthermore the pursuit of wealth which was open to all helped to break down the barriers of caste, to level class distinction and to rebuild on the foundation of the old, a social structure which was comparatively mobile and fluid. Finally the growth of a new spirit of philanthropy at home and abroad may be traced to England's awakened responsibility for the moral and religious welfare of its world empire.

As a full treatment of all phases of this subject would require more than a single small volume, the author has excluded changes which appear to be predominantly economic, intellectual or political in character. Even with the scope thus limited, consideration of topics has been brief rather than detailed, while in some cases cross references in notes must take the place of more complete treatment in the text. It should be explained that references will be found at the end of each chapter, in the hope that this arrange-

ment will serve the ends of appearance and con-
venience. A list of works and papers, following the
final chapter of the text, shows the indebtedness of
the author to a host of source and secondary material. Consultation of many of these references was
made possible by the courtesy of authorities of the
New York Public Library, the libraries of Brown,
Harvard, and Columbia Universities, and the British
Museum.

The author owes a deep debt of gratitude to Professor William R. Shepherd of Columbia University,
under whose guidance this book has been written, in
part for suggestions and criticism in questions of
interpretation, and for invaluable aid in the arduous
task of proofreading, but most of all for the unfailing
sympathy and inspiration of a scholar and a friend.
The author, too, desires to express appreciation to
his wife, Lillian Dow Botsford, for her constant
encouragement and assistance, especially in proofreading and in the preparation of the index. For
whatever errors may have survived the vigilance of
these friends, the author desires to take full responsibility.

JAY BARRETT BOTSFORD.

Providence, Rhode Island,
    April 21, 1924.

CONTENTS

ENGLISH SOCIETY IN THE EIGHTEENTH CENTURY

CHAPTER I

EIGHTEENTH CENTURY ENGLAND

IT is with a feeling of remoteness that the man of to-day looks back upon his ancestor of two hundred years ago. An age in which the telephone and wireless, the railway train and steamship, the great industrial plant and the lofty office building, the moving picture and the automobile were not yet in being seems, not two centuries, but æons of time and space away. Equally remote appears an era when man was still bound, body and soul, to tradition.

Let us see more concretely the remoteness of the early eighteenth century. It was a period when western nations were wasted and torn by suicidal dynastic conflicts, when scrupulousness in international relations was the exception; when the idea of absolute monarchy by divine right had not yet given way to the principle of popular sovereignty; when millions of workers in field and town were stifled by the paint and powder of privilege. Territorial aggrandizement was dynastic, rather than national. Europe was engulfed at first in the struggle between Bourbon and Hapsburg, later

References will be found at the end of each chapter.

1

between Hapsburg and Hohenzollern. The history of the century centred about such names as Peter the Great, Frederick the Great, Louis XIV, men whose Machiavellian policies, with their scrapping of promises and treaties on the flimsiest excuse, kept international morality at lowest ebb. England alone clung at least to the outward forms of constitutional and representative government.

Socially, even in England, the caste system proved an insurmountable barrier to progress. Clergy and nobility were to a considerable extent parasitic, in that they had political power out of all true proportion to their place in the nation. A rapidly growing middle class, vaguely desirous of recognition and consciously ambitious for a share in government, secured the adoption of favourable policies by currying favour with the party in power.[1] At any moment its investments, its plans for the future, might have been wiped out by the failure of Parliament to understand. Coming farther down the social scale, the worker in town or country was without redress from injustice, was uncared for in times of distress. In fact, his very existence was ignored except in times of national need.

Similarly, activities in economic fields were carried on with the outworn utensils of a romantic and inefficient past. Progress in agriculture was woefully hindered by the remnants of feudalism and serfdom: the open-field system, antiquated implements, faulty methods of cultivation. Industry we find restricted by the guild system, a system weakened by age and internal dissension, yet strong enough withal to limit pro-

duction and hamper progress.[2] In the seaboard nations commerce was governed by the hydra-headed
monster of mercantilism—the idea of monopoly within
a limited sphere of endeavour, on an intensely national-
istic basis.

Intellectual effort seemed to offer the sole ray of
hope. Considerably before 1700 man's mind had re-
acted favourably to the voyages of the early mariners,
to the discovery of a greater world, old and new. A
broadened horizon, a freshly awakened interest in
problems of man and universe, a real zeal for knowledge, the growth of a healthy scepticism, were all
favourable omens. As yet his search for the truth was
groping, almost blind, hampered as he was by poor
methods of organization, by poor tools (as the micro-
scope or telescope of the time), by his inherent con-
servatism, and by his lingering fear of the authority of
the church and of tradition.

And yet, in spite of multitudinous handicaps, man
continued the struggle to free himself from the worn-
out shackles of the past. His victory left him bewil-
dered, amazed, but ambitious to seize opportunity, con-
fident in his ability to succeed. Thus the end of the
century was an era removed from the beginning; momentous changes had taken place; civilization had been
brought from the gloomy night of the past to the
cheerfully lighted doorstep of the present. The development of political science brought in its wake the
scrapping of the theory of divine right and of absolute monarchy. In its stead, France, the political
missionary of the Continent, had begun to spread the

gospel of "liberty, equality, fraternity." England, in more conservative fashion, saw the fulfilment of the fruits of the Glorious Revolution, in the development of the doctrines of personal rights and the growth of a Cabinet system. Disqualification from office-holding because of religious views was lessened; while the idea of representation, advocated by the bourgeoisie, at first for its selfish interests, resulted finally in political democracy.[3]

Aggrandizement had now become national, rather than dynastic, and was of commercial as well as of territorial import. International morality was in the ascendency, in that the scrupulous observance of treaties, outwardly, at least, became a question of national honour and pride. Treaty-making was now a science, involving all the phases of national existence, and requiring the services of lawyers as well as diplomats.

Society had undergone a radical transformation. In France, revolution had swept away the worst abuses of the caste system; paradoxically, similar results were brought to the remainder of the continent by Napoleon, himself an arch-enemy of the Revolution. In England, the growing power of wealth was rapidly levelling old class distinctions. Many who became wealthy in business and trade were admitted to Parliament; some were raised to the peerage, and others were attaining a social equality hitherto denied. Nominally, opportunity was open to all, for lack of noble ancestry was no handicap to the acquisition of wealth. It must be confessed that the result was not complete social democracy, but rather the addition of a more fluid aristocracy of wealth to the one of birth.[4]

By changes of a peaceful nature, momentous in their way as those of the French Revolution, every phase of economic life was transformed. The pivot of the so-called "agricultural revolution" was the application of capital to farming, capital acquired in part from English expansion overseas.[5] It was expected that these investments would yield returns comparable with profits made in trade or manufacturing. The immediate result was the introduction of scientific methods, and particularly of implements to supplant hand-labour in the interest of efficiency and economy. Enclosures came to replace the wasteful open-field system. Such capitalist enthusiasts as "Turnip" Townshend experimented at their own expense for the benefit of farming as a whole, patronized fairs, endowed agricultural schools, and finally evolved scientific schemes of fertilization, and popularized the four-field — or Norfolk — system of rotation of crops. The government showed its kindly though perhaps mistaken interest by retaining the Corn Laws as an artificial stimulant.[6] Further stimuli to agriculture were the rapid growth of population with the subsequent rise in the price of farm products, and above all, the Industrial Revolution, with its concentration of population in factory towns. This change diverted the trend of rural industry from sheep-raising to the growth of vegetables and fruits, beef and mutton, for food.

The inability of hand-labour to supply world markets, now controlled by English capital and shipping,

proved the death knell of the old industrial organization.   The application of capital to industry offered
financial rewards as stimuli to invention, thus directing
it along practical paths.   The basic commodity for
this revolution in industry was cotton, a commodity
from overseas; the vast demand for it in cheap manufactured form called into play financial resources
accumulated from commercial endeavours.[7]   The use
of water-power, later of steam, the growth of the factory system, and improved methods of transportation
by land and water, gave the English manufacturers an
advantage over hand-workers at home, and elsewhere
in the empire, and over possible competitors on the
continent.   And so through mechanical inventions, the
use of capital, and a constant supply of raw materials,
as well as the exclusion of rivals from this supply,
England was rapidly becoming the workshop of the
world.   Those effects of the Industrial Revolution
which come within the scope of this treatise will be
considered in another connection.[8]

Still another peaceful revolution was effected, this
time in the field of commerce.   Except in England,
and even in that country until the last quarter of the
century, mercantilism was the economic policy of the
leading commercial states.   In the case of Holland,
this meant largely the exclusive spice trade with the
East Indies, and in the long run proved a failure.
Contributing causes were: corruption in the East
India Company, limitation of production and excessive
prices for products, lack of a sufficient navy to enforce
monopoly, smug content on the part of the home popu-

lation, and its disinclination to manufacture goods to exchange for Eastern products, or for those of Western nations. The Spanish empire was gradually disintegrating, and living largely on past glory. France, on the other hand, was unable to carry her well-rounded mercantilist policy to success. The interests of her monarchs were too divided, while her men and resources were diverted to the pursuit of a continental militaristic policy. The triumph of England over these rivals proceeded from the concentrated efforts of her statesmen and public, who followed but two ambitions: a well-rounded, self-sufficient commercial and colonial empire, and the increase of the trade and manufactures of the mother country.

While at first this struggle was fought under the banners of mercantilism, the reason for its ultimate success was readiness on the part of English statesmen and economists to recognize the evils of that policy and to discard it when its day of usefulness had passed. Due to the complexities of empire, it was found that regulations intended to benefit one part of the empire, for example the West Indies, served only to hurt another, in this case the American colonies; that such class measures as a protective tariff on the Corn Laws proved a menace to other industries. In short, the whole community of the nation, or of the empire, had to pay for privileges granted to some one portion of it. Moreover, it was no longer felt that one nation could succeed by monopoly alone, or that England would necessarily benefit by injuring the trade of her rivals. Gradually during the eighteenth century the abuses of mercantilism were coming to light: open corruption in Parliament to secure commercial privileges bestowed only by government, and obnoxious government regulations and interference, which led to the loss of the American colonies.

It was now that Josiah Tucker's assertion that colonies, held together under the mercantile system, had a baneful effect on the mother country became effective.[9]   The catastrophe in America led to a fear of the loss of India and the break-up of the emprise. Legislators, accordingly, paid heed to the doctrines of Adam Smith, who proposed to build up a new economy on the foundations of the old.[10]   His *Inquiry Into the Nature and Causes of the Wealth of Nations* exposed the evil effects of over-regulation on the part of government, of the artificial stimuli to trade mentioned above, and was chiefly responsible for turning economic life into the channels of free trade. For restraint and restriction, then, was gradually substituted the theory of *laissez-faire,* the encouragement of individual enterprise in all phases. Fortunately, by this time, England had triumphed over her rivals, and no longer feared serious competition.[11]

In the field of the purely intellectual we find the working out of this same doctrine of *laissez-faire.* Here individualism was usually accompanied by scepticism, leading on one hand to agnosticism, on the other, to rationalism.[12]   Exponents of the two schools were found among both French and English philosophers. The individual, not content with methods of the past, evolved new and efficient methods of experimentation and organization, and perfected better instruments for work in laboratory and field. Another offshoot of individualism was the spirit of invention, as evidenced by its application to the textile trades, and scientific research leading to discoveries in the realms of anatomy, astronomy, medicine, and geology. In his untrammeled speculations regarding religious, political and social problems, man showed signs of his escape from spiritual bondage. In his actions, however, it would seem that he had fallen under the mysterious spell of materialism — that he had simply exchanged an old master for a new one.

The changes which have been considered above took place first in England and in France, the two predominantly commercial and colonial powers of the age. It is significant that with one exception (in the philosophical field) these transformations happened first, and with greater intensity, in England, while they were felt more slowly and less strongly by her unsuccessful rival. It will be admitted that changes so radical, so far-reaching in their ramifications, would not take place without the stimulus of some outside force—a force strong enough to shake from its lethargy an entire nation, to energize and vitalize the thoughts and deeds of its people, and to drive their work and play, their very existence, along new and revolutionary channels. Such a force, the conception, the conquest, and the administration of a vast empire might well be. Just as marriage, the building of a home, the raising of a family, vitally affects the individuals concerned, so must the nation which engages in the herculean task of empire-building undergo transformation in the character of its citizenry and institutions.

What were the qualifications of England for leadership at the opening of the eighteenth century? To her geographical position she had owed isolation from continental embroilments, the training of sailors in the fishing trade, and the encouragement to merchants to sail to increasingly distant ports, and so eventually to discoveries overseas. English soil was not so fertile or varied as that of France, or her climate so equable; neither was her population superior in character or intelligence. Her chief debt certainly was to the past: to her political traditions culminating in the Glorious Revolution, to her economic stability secured by the Bank of England, founded in 1694,[13] and to the Board of Trade established two years later, to her long, successful and varied experience in commerce and trade, and most of all to her naval and colonial traditions.

During the rule of the Tudors, a few daring navigators had dared dispute Spanish claims to supremacy of the sea. Time and again, like Jason of old, English Argonauts returned home, laden heavily with a Golden Fleece. At once to heal his wounded pride and to achieve his goal of a unified Christendom, Philip II sent forth his great Armada to chastise the land of these insolent marauders. Little did he foresee that the English to a man—Protestant and Catholic—would unite in patriotism, and united, would

send to inglorious defeat the hitherto Invincible
Armada. With the collapse of the Spanish fleet, England unwittingly, but surely, dropped her century-old
policy of isolation and entered the race for commercial
and colonial empire.[14]

The seventeenth century is the story on the one hand
of adventurous merchants, a few score in number, who
secured for themselves by cajolery or bribery, when
not by legitimate means, a share of the wealth of the
Indies; on the other hand, of a few hardy men and
women, who sailed across the wastes of the Atlantic
Ocean to colonize a New England in an environment
better suited to their ideals. These pioneers in the
Old World and the New formed the vanguard of
empire. Their struggles and achievements stirred
the national pulse; their tales of strange people and
strange things fired the imagination of their countrymen; and in turning their eyes from the Continent,
Englishmen began to see their future in the wealth of
opportunity overseas.

By the opening of the eighteenth century, England
was in possession of an embryonic colonial and commercial empire: trading posts in Africa and India, a
nucleus for commerce in the West Indies, and a narrow
strip in North America, stretching along the coast from
Maine to Florida, and back to the mountains. Further aids to commerce were flourishing chartered companies—in particular, the East India and the Hudson's Bay—protected by a rigid enforcement of the
Navigation Acts.[15] In short, by 1700 England had
the promise of a well-rounded empire, favoured with a

satisfactory type of colonists, and administered according to the best traditions of mercantilism. The long struggle with France had begun, with the accession of William III (1689), which was destined to last intermittently until the downfall of Napoleon (1815). While the international situation in Europe itself undoubtedly had some influence, colonial and commercial rivalry was primarily responsible for the series of wars during that period. As a result, British power overseas was enlarged at the expense of France, just as in earlier years it had been at the expense of Spain and Holland.[16]

The commercial provisions of the treaty of Utrecht showed these phases of expansion. Great Britain gained the colonial vantage points of Acadia (later Nova Scotia) and of the Hudson's Bay territory, and in the Mediterranean, two strategic naval stations, Gibraltar and Minorca. Of importance, too, was the Asiento treaty, whereby Great Britain secured the monopoly for thirty years of the slave trade to the Spanish colonies, and the privilege of sending one ship annually.[17] This slight concession proved a bait to illegitimate commerce. Friction naturally followed; one Robert Jenkins, captain, claimed that his ear was cut off by the cruel and vindictive Spaniards. Returning home, he exhibited the severed member wrapped in cotton, and aroused his countrymen to such a state of indignation that Walpole could not refuse their clamour for war. Naturally, the powerful mercantile interests were not averse to the struggle! One practical gain from this embroglio was the recognition of

English superiority on the seas. "Before that war England was one of the sea-powers; after that, she was *the* sea-power without any second." [18]

Under the vigourous leadership of William Pitt, England emerged victorious in the gigantic mid-century phase of the struggle known as the Seven Years' War. By the Peace of Paris (1763) she received all the French possessions in the New World, with the exception of a few small islands off the coast of Newfoundland and in the West Indies. In Africa, England retained the mouth of the Senegal river. Of equal importance was the outcome of the duel with France in India. The latter country was hereby reduced from the status of empire-builder to the mere rank of trader. In short, France virtually had been ousted from the colonial field.

Soon after the middle of the eighteenth century, then, the real work of empire-building was well under way. The acquisition of land for colonization and of political control for commercial privileges, and the work of organization and administration were carried on by a group of citizens, increasing in influence and numbers.

The next conflict was an internal one, involving a struggle to escape from the bonds of mercantilism. According to this system, England was to be the emporium of trade for the empire. Colonies were valued solely in proportion to their contribution to a favourable balance of trade. India, for example, was considered a liability, early in the century at least, because of its vast exports to England, mainly of luxuries, and its scant consumption of English manufactured goods.[19] The northern colonies in America were valued largely for their exports of naval stores and other raw products to the mother country; while the southern plantations were prized for their cotton, rice and indigo,[20] and the West Indies for coffee, sugar, spices, molasses and rum, and especially for their large expenditures for slaves.[21]

As the century went on, economic pressure restricting colonial manufactures and trade, together with the growing evils of administration, contributed to the successful revolt of the American colonies.[22] The loss of these valuable possessions helped to put an end to the mercantile system,[23] and mark the adoption of a *laissez-faire* policy.[24] Freed from the stultifying influence of government regulation, British trade grew more rapidly than before. The aftermath of the struggle invigorated commercial life, restored material prosperity, and stored up a new vitality for the stress and strain of the Napoleonic Wars.

The course of development above sketched furnishes a background for the body of the present treatise. Changes so radical, so far-reaching in their ramifications, could hardly have taken place without the stimulus of some force external to England itself and to Europe at large. The writer hopes to prove that the force in this case was empire, and to show the effects of English endeavour overseas on certain phases of life and character at home.

The most obvious material result of commercial and colonial expansion was the vast influx and diversification of wealth. In this item are included profits realized from the carrying trade, from the sale of exports to colonists and to other nations, and the sale of goods of all descriptions to the home population. To enterprise overseas are to be attributed investments in companies like the East India and the South Sea, as well as fortunes made, or lost, in the Stock Exchange. In what manner, by what code of ethics, was this wealth acquired? How was it distributed? What readjustment of social classes, and of social life followed? If this wealth was created in the main by oversea enterprise, how did its use affect the life, customs and character of individuals and the nation?

In this connection a factor of great importance was the introduction and use of oversea commodities. Most of them had been brought to England prior to 1700; by this date they were no longer curiosities. The question with regard to the eighteenth century, then, is largely one of extent of use: of increased importations and lowered prices, which tended to make imported articles available to an increasing percentage of the nation. For example, tea and sugar, at one time luxuries, had become by the close of the century objects of common consumption. A few examples may serve, at this point, to demonstrate the extent and variety of such contributions from overseas. Among them were potatoes, rice, corn, sugar, molasses, tobacco, tea, coffee, chocolate, lime-juice, and rum. Other articles, some of them imperative for a self-sufficient mercantilist empire, included naval stores and timber, dyes, and the products of American fisheries.

Articles of adornment embraced furs, cotton, silk, gold, jewelry, canes and fans. Other commodities were chinaware and pottery, bric-a-brac, and household pets. Nor may the profits accruing from the negro-slave traffic be left out of account. How did these acquisitions from the Old World and the New World tend to make life more comfortable, varied and inter-esting, by concealing the mere mechanism of existence? What effect did they have on the social graces, on mak-ing the art of private living more attractive?

Finally, from overseas came the valuable contribu-tion of new ideas. True, the world had by now recovered from the dazing effects of the first dis-coveries. Credulity had developed into healthy curiosity. Intellectual enthusiasm, thoroughly aroused, sought an outlet in scientific experimentation. Contact with lands and peoples strange and distant continued to furnish inspiration. Their ways of living and think-ing, their food and drink, their institutions, were of absorbing interest, and helped to produce theories of social betterment suggestive of a possible transforma-tion of European life. The fascination of the Orient in particular held the English mind under its spell, and played no small part in moulding the operation of Eng-lish thought.

In considering the introduction and the increased adoption of such commodities from overseas as have been listed above, as a necessary part of the diet and clothing of the English nation, we have dealt in the main with concrete facts. In spite of mercantilist philosophy, however, it would be unfair to presume that the effects of the growth of world empire were wholly materialistic, or that the sole interest of Englishmen was confined to maintaining a favourable balance of trade. While the field of purely intellectual interest lies beyond the scope of the present treatise, certain aspects of it can hardly be left out of consideration. If the axiom, that the characteristics of human nature remain constant, be admitted, it is certain that the growing knowledge of the lands and people, of their ideas and philosophies, of the animals, birds and plants, of British possessions overseas, must have fired the imagination of people at home in countless ways, devious and subtle; that a realization of the extent, of the character and of the responsibility of empire, must have affected in a manner certain, though intangible, the thoughts and actions of all those who came under its spell. And the spell of empire was by no means confined to the commercial classes and the gentry. Every sailor in the service of His Majesty, or of the East India Company, could spin thrilling tales of adventure, or recount strange customs or sights from lands afar to his family at the fireside, or to his cronies at the tavern. Similarly, the returning clerk, or official, or merchant, or West India planter, could remove the stigma of insularity from his own circle of friends. Countless pamphlets and books on travel furnished food and stimulus to the intelligence of those who could read.

With the imagination thus aroused, there came an insistent and consistent demand for intelligent travel and for authentic accounts of experiences. Dr. John-

son urged Warren Hastings to observe carefully everything of interest in the Orient, to extend his patronage
especially to experimental knowledge and natural history.   In this way alone could conjectures and super-
stitions about India be dispelled, and acquaintance with
the arts and sciences be obtained by the English.[25]

The complaint—though in this case the complaint
was without justification—of those who sought exact,
scientific knowledge was, that so far the majority of
travellers had been either merchants or missionaries,
who were "influenced either by motives of commerce
or piety; and their accounts are such as might reasonably be expected from men of a very narrow or very
prejudiced education."[26]   The ideal traveller would
be a man of philosophical nature, whose mind was
tinctured with miscellaneous knowledge, and whose
manners were humanized by contact with his fellow-
men.   Such a contact, too, would develop friendly
relations with foreign peoples, for it "would in some
measure repair the breaches made by ambition; and
might show that there were still some who boasted a
greater name than that of patriots, who professed
themselves lovers of men."[27]

Real enthusiasm was aroused by the expedition completed in 1700, when Edmund Halley published his
chart of the variations of the compass.[28]   Of more
widespread significance was the publication of the story
of Captain Dampier's travels,[29] which furnished the
background for the popular combination of fact and
fiction of *Robinson Crusoe*.   The wildest dreams were
inspired, too, by Anson's voyage in the *Centurion* to

the islands of the Pacific and China (1740-1744),
when upon his return the prize money captured from
Spanish galleons was carried to London in thirty-two
wagons to military music.[30]   To satisfy in some measure the demand for scientific exploration, Byron was
sent forth in 1764 to investigate the truth as to the
Patagonian giants.[31]   Two years later, Wallis and
Carteret made their celebrated trip to the South Seas,
returning with a collection of weapons used by sav-
ages.[32]   The crowning achievements of eighteenth century exploration, however, are found in the voyages
of Captain Cook, who was first sent (1767) by the
Royal Society to the South Seas, to observe the transit
of Venus over the disk of the sun.   Accompanied by
an astronomer, naturalists, and a painter, this explorer
gave to the world a thorough knowledge of "Georgia,"
or the western coast of North America, and a practic-
able chart for navigators sailing about Cape Horn.[33]
On the first voyage, Cook rediscovered New Zealand
(neglected since 1642) and, in reaching Botany Bay,
gave England title to a new continent.   Considerable
ignorance of these new-found lands remained to be dispelled, if Cowper be taken as criterion:

> .   .   .   Even the favoured isles
> So lately found, although the constant sun
> Cheer all their seasons with a grateful smile,
> Can boast but little virtue: and, inert
> Through plenty, lose in morals what they gain
> In manners, victims of luxurious ease. . . . [34]

His colleagues completed the true functions of
exploration by describing completely the new races with

whom they came in contact, and by returning with a collection of plants and flowers.   In the second voyage (1772), Cook, now raised to the rank of commander, discovered New Caledonia, and in the last voyage, where he met his death at the hands of natives, he discovered Cook's Islands and the Sandwich Islands.[35] Accounts of the novelty, variety and grandeur of these scenes, compiled by his associates, destroyed prejudice and preconceived theories, it was said at the time, and they revived the spirit of discovery which had lain dormant since the sixteenth century.[36]   By refuting fanciful theories, every nation that sent a ship to sea would partake of the benefit, but naturally Great Britain herself, with her boundless commerce, must take the lead in reaping the full advantage of her own discoveries.[37]

In other respects these voyages proved of inestimable benefit.   Future unprofitable researches were thereby discouraged, and the dangers that followed ignorance made for increased safety of future navigation.   According to one enthusiastic critic:

How many nautical observations have been collected and are now ready to be consulted, in directing a ship's course along rocky shores . . . amidst perplexing currents and dangerous shoals.   But above all, what numbers of new bays and harbours and anchoring-places are now, for the first time, brought forward, where ships may be sheltered, and their crew find tolerable refreshment.[38]

With this increased knowledge, the old fear of protracted voyages was now removed.   Men realized that they could be away from home for as long as three or four years, and could retain their health in any change of climate.[39]   Finally Cook proved that the discovery of a northwest passage, while rational in theory was not possible in fact; and, as a contemporary put it: "perhaps this is the last voyage that will ever be undertaken for the purpose." [40] Inspired by the travels of these explorers, their example was followed on a limited scale by others of their countrymen. Their objective, of course, was the continent, rather than lands overseas.   It was said that for one Englishman who travelled during the reigns of the first two Georges, ten embraced the glories of the Grand Tour, in the time of George III.[41]

Finally, the travels of Mungo Park to Africa furnished another spur to the imagination. The account of his experiences [42] was "seized with avidity by any one who reads at all," largely because it contained a mixture of the unknown and the marvellous which finds an echo in every bosom, and too commonly, a large portion of actual personal suffering and danger, which is of all subjects of the most painful and fascinating interest."[43]

Its widespread appeal was but the culmination of the popularity of works of travel, which had been growing from the early part of the century. Public interest in experiences of travellers was best satisfied by the thrilling account embodied by Defoe in his immortal *Robinson Crusoe*. This was, indeed, the best-seller of the early century, running through four editions in the first year of publication. Scarcely less popular was Swift's *Gulliver's Travels,* an exotic panorama of strange foreign lands, combined with brilliant

satire, and exciting incident.[44]   Dr. Johnson sold four
thousand copies of his *Journey to the Hebrides* during
its first week,[45] thus satisfying public curiosity by a mere
trip to Scotland.   In fact, in speaking of Hawkes-
worth's compilation of the voyages to the South Seas,
Dr. Johnson remarked, that anything which pertained
to travel or exploration would probably achieve financial success.[46]   The publication of Raynal's *Histoire.
Philosophique et Politique des Etablissements et du
Commerce des Européens dans les deux Indes,* satisfied
the demand for a scholarly account of a region destined
to become the heart of the British Empire.

"This work," wrote Horace Walpole, "tells one everything
in the world; how to make conquests, invasions, settlements,
fortunes, commerce, navigation, tea, coffee, china, mines, salt,
spices . . . of rice, of camels, ginghams, and muslins; of millions of livres, pounds, rupees, and cowries. . . . It has made
me learned enough to talk about Mr. Sykes and the Secret
Committee (on East India affairs), which is all that anybody
talks of at present." [47]

The growing popularity of works on travel is perhaps best illustrated by that mirror of public opinion,
the *Annual Register*.   Its early numbers contain but
few references to travel overseas, but the volume for
1773 reflects a rapidly growing interest in this subject.
The following statement by the editors is significant:

Books of travel are read with as much relish as ever, though
the number of publications of that sort might well be supposed to have long since satiated the public curiosity. . . .
Polite education, the love of variety, the pursuit of health, have
rendered foreign objects and foreign customs familiar to our

countrymen of the higher ranks. The immense extent of our commerce has communicated a considerable share of the same knowledge to all degrees. . . . This accounts for the reception of books of travels, to which they are multiplied, and the sameness of the objects which they describe.[48]

The very exigencies of travel served to stimulate speculative and inventive genius. Considerable thought was demanded, for example, as to the best means for preserving health and safety. In the preparation of "Useful Hints to Sailors and Sea-Faring Men," are found the beginnings of the science of personal hygiene. Men were advised to bathe frequently in sea-water, to take with them a plentiful supply of linen (more probably, cotton), to be temperate in the consumption of hard liquors, to wash their teeth, and include fruit-juices in their diets.[49] To these admonitions an English physician, himself an extensive traveller in the Persian Gulf, added advice intended to "preserve persons from the perniciousness of dews in hot climates." [50] The century abounds in attempts to provide passengers and crews with fresh drinking-water for long voyages. For the mitigation of accidental death by wreck or storm, English seamen found bamboo sticks tied about the body most valuable. This idea, adopted in 1730, was later developed into the modern life-preserver.[51]

Furthermore, the interest in objects of nature and the desire to return with specimens fit for purposes of exhibition and study stimulated inventive genius to discover satisfactory methods of preservation. Dr. Hill, for one, gave minute details of a new method of preserving birds, "with their elegant plumes unhurt," and "in their original shape and colors." [52]   Other schemes were evolved, such "as the supplying our colonies with the seeds of useful plants; in order to have their produce imported from thence into England, instead of the places of their natural growth in Europe, Asia, and Africa, as we do at present." [53]

Full directions for the achievement of this laudable purpose followed.[54]   When the introduction of new crops from overseas brought in its wake a swarm of new insects and vermin—as with Indian corn, the corn butterfly—man's ingenuity sought, and discovered, methods of extermination.

The examples cited above serve at least to indicate the varied source of mental stimuli.   In comparing the American savage with the European, philosophers found the solution to real happiness in a return to nature, in a release from the shackles of a complex and artificial civilization.   In the life of the individual, this feeling was expressed in a growing love of outdoor recreation.   In thought, blind adoration of authority gave way to rationalism, to self-assertion by the individual.   Science replaced magic, and sought to supplant faith by understanding.   If scepticism, or even atheism seemed to reign, it meant little more than a healthy sign of intellectual unrest, of dissatisfaction with things as they were.   Astronomers, botanists and chemists, with imaginations fired by the vastness of the universe, were already making their contributions to a better conception of the well-ordered mind of its Maker.   The researches of Sir Hans Sloane in

Jamaica transformed the science of medicine, and his collections formed the nucleus of the British Museum.[55] Nor in the field of pure science was oversea influence lacking. The studies and writings of Benjamin Franklin gave him a high reputation in the scientific world, and his discovery of the lightning conductor opened a wide vista for scientific research.[56]

If it be admitted that necessity is the mother of invention, the obvious need and opportunity for a prosperous England gave countless outlets for the products of inventive genius. Most impressive of all was the ambition to make England a great cotton manufacturing country. The possibilities which underlay this oversea commodity were responsible, as will be shown,[57] for the Industrial Revolution, an event which transformed the economic and social life of England, and eventually of the entire civilized world. Other materials from distant stretches of empire soon came to serve as fodder for the new machinery; through the variety and inexhaustibility of her resources, England was assured of industrial supremacy for at least a century to come. Even in minute processes the pressure from overseas, the desire for a self-sufficient empire, transferred work from the laboratory to the shop or factory. The refinement of saltpetre and of borax, for example, brought independence for England from Asia, America, and competition in Europe.[58]

For no long stretch of time, then, was the imagination allowed to languish for want of stimulus from overseas. In travel itself, in the narration of experiences by pen or speech, and in the privacy of his home, the Englishman was reminded of the vastness of the universe, and was ever urged to appreciate, if not to solve, its mysteries. The truth is that he had already discovered and realized the importance of empire to his own life and the life of his country. Addison was perhaps the first to appreciate the insufficiency of England, and her dependence on abroad:

If we consider our own country in its natural prospect, without any of the benefits and advantages of commerce, what a barren uncomfortable spot of earth falls to our share! Natural historians tell us that no fruit grows originally among us, besides hips and haws, acorns and pignuts, and other delicacies of like nature; that our climate of itself, and without the assistance of art, can make no farther advances towards a plumb than a sloe, and carries an apple to no greater perfection than a crab: that our melons, our peaches, our figs, our apricots, and cherries, are strangers among us, imported in different ages, and naturalized in our English gardens; and that they would all degenerate and fall away into the trash of our own country, if they were wholly neglected by the planter, and left to the mercy of the sun and soil. Nor has traffic more enriched our vegetable world, than it has improved the whole face of nature among us. Our ships are laden with the harvest of every climate: our tables are stored with spices, and oils, and wines: our rooms are filled with pyramids of china, and adorned with the workmanship of Japan: our morning's draught comes to us from the remotest corners of the earth: we repair our bodies by the drugs from America, and repose ourselves under Indian canopies. My friend Sir Andrew calls the vineyards of France our gardens; the spice-islands our hot-beds; the Persians, our silk-weavers; and the Chinese, our potters. Nature indeed furnishes us with the bare necessaries of life; but traffic gives us a great variety of what is useful, and at the same time supplies us with everything that is convenient and ornamental. Nor is it the least part of our happiness that whilst we enjoy the remotest products of the North and South, we are free from those extremities of weather which give them birth; that our eyes are refreshed with the green fields of Britain at the same time that our palates are feasted with fruits that rise between the tropics.[59]

The same realization of the significance of empire is expressed in a lighter vein by that most characteristic of eighteenth century men, Horace Walpole:

I am heartily glad that we shall keep Jamaica and the East Indies another year, that one may have time to lay in a stock of tea and sugar for the rest of one's days. I think only of the necessaries of life, and do not care a rush for gold and diamonds, and the pleasure of stealing logwood. The friends of government, who have thought on nothing but reducing us to our islandhood and bringing us back to the simplicity of ancient times, when we were the frugal, temperate, virtuous old England, ask how we did before tea and sugar were known. Better, no doubt; but as I did not happen to be born two or three hundred years ago, I cannot recollect precisely whether diluted acorns, and barley bread spread with honey, made a very luxurious breakfast.[60]

REFERENCES TO CHAPTER I

[1] See below, Chapter VII.

[2] In France, Colbert's efforts to rehabilitate industry by the sovereign remedy of the day, minute and intensive government regulation, were largely nullified by the chauvinistic policy of his master.

[3] This ideal was not achieved until the nineteenth century, with the passage of the Reform Bill of 1832, and of subsequent legislation.

[4] See below, Chapter VI.

[5] "Manufacture and foreign commerce together have given birth to the principal improvements of agriculture." Smith, Adam, *Inquiry into the Nature and Causes of the Wealth of Nations*, I, p. 340.

[6] Material for this paragraph was obtained from Hammond, *The Village Labourer*, Cunningham, *The Growth of English Industry and Commerce*, and Prothero, *English Farming, Past and Present.*

[7] The vast increase of foreign and colonial trade, bringing imports of raw materials, "has been in part the cause, in part the consequence of the wonderful development of manufacturing energy apparent in our country during the last hundred years or so." Fox Bourne, *English Merchants*, II, p. 8.

[8] See below, Chapters II and VI.

[9] Tucker, *Cui Bono* (1781), p. 14.

[10] He held that under the mercantile system "all the European colonies have, without exception, been a cause rather of weakness than of strength to their respective mother countries." Smith, A., *op. cit.*, I, p. 460.

[11] The French Revolution and the Napoleonic Wars, following the earlier struggles of the century, prevented France from becoming a serious rival.

[12] Lecky, *History of the Rise and the Influence of the Spirit of Rationalism in Europe in the Eighteenth Century.*

[13] Craik, *History of British Commerce*, II, p. 126.

[14] *Ibid*, II, p. 123. See also below, Chapter VI and Chapter VII.

[15] See Willson, *Ledger and Sword*, and *The Great Company.*

[16] This was recognized by economists of the eighteenth century. Adam Smith, for example, writes: "The latest War (the Seven Years' War) was altogether a colony trouble. . . . The Spanish War, which began in 1739, was principally a colony quarrel. Its pretended purpose was to encourage the manufactures and to increase the commerce of Great Britain." Smith, *op. cit.*, I, p. 480.

[17] Anderson, *History of Commerce*, III, p. 55.

[18] Mahan, *The Influence of Sea Power upon History*, 1660-1783, p. 225.

[19] *The Country Journal or Craftsman,* 20 July 1728.

[20] See below, Chapter II.

[21] "The labour of these slaves is the principal foundation of our Riches there upon which account we should take all proper measures to bring them upon easy terms. . . . Slaves are the first and most necessary material for planting; from whence follows that all measures should be taken that may produce such a plenty of them, as may be an Encouragement to the Industrious Planter." D'Avenant, *On the Plantation Trade, in Works,* II, pp. 37-38.

[22] Especially annoying and stultifying were those acts which prevented free trade between the colonies in certain articles. In 1705 molasses and rice were banned, a few years later naval stores, and in 1722, copper and furs. The "Molasses Act" of 1733 placed prohibitive duties on foreign sugar, molasses, and rum. Egerton, *A Short History of British Colonial Policy;* Anderson, *op. cit.,* III, passim.

[23] It should be remembered that Canada was still regarded as a barren waste, and Australia, but recently rediscovered, was not yet explored. The real possibilities of India were hardly realized.

[24] See above, pp. 7-8.

[25] *Letter from Dr. Johnson to Warren Hastings,* 30 March, 1774. Hastings himself urged the introduction of the study of the Persian language into English education. Boswell, *Life of Johnson,* IV, p. 69. See also *Letter of Walpole to the Earl of Hertford,* 6 Feb., 1764.

[26] *Annual Register,* 1762, p. 157.

[27] *Ibid,* p. 159.

[28] Cunningham, *A History of England in the Lives of Englishmen,* IV, pp. 60-61.

[29] Dampier, *A Collection of Voyages:*

    1. *Capt. Dampier's Voyages around the World.*

    2. *The Voyages of Lionel Wafer.*

    3. *A Voyage round the World by W. Funnell.*

    4. *Capt. Cowley's Voyage round the Globe.*

    5. *Capt. Sharp's Journey over the Isthmus of Darien, and Expedition into the South Seas.*

    6. *Capt. Wood's Voyage through the Streights of Magellan.*

    7. *Mr. Robert's Adventures and Sufferings among the corsairs of the Levant; his Description of the Archipelago Islands, etc. Illustrated with maps and dr ughts: also several birds, fishes and plants.*

[30] Traill, *op. cit.,* V, p. 221.

[31] *Ibid,* V, p. 222.

[32] *Ibid,* V, p. 223.

[33] It should be remembered that the voyages of the Spaniards ofttimes served to bewilder, rather than to instruct, navigators of other nations.

[34] Cowper, *The Task*, I, le., 620-626.

[35] For detailed accounts of these voyages, see, *An Authentic Narrative of a Voyage performed by Capt. Cook, and Capt. Clarke, in H. M.'s Ships, the Resolution and the Discovery, during the Years 1776, 1777, 1778, 1779, and 1780, in search of a Passage between the Continents of Asia and America. Including a faithful Account of all their Discoveries, and the unfortunate death of Capt. Cook; illustrated with a Chart, and a Variety of Cuts.* By W. Ellis, Assistant Surgeon to both vessels. 2 v., London, 1782. And, *A Voyage to the Pacific Ocean, undertaken by the Command of H. M. for making Discoveries in the Northern Hemisphere, to determine the Position and Extent of the West Side of North America; its Distance from Asia; and the Practicability of a Northern Passage to Europe; performed under the Direction of Capts. Cook, Clarke, and Gore, in H. M.'s Ships, the Resolution and Discovery, in the Years 1776-1779.* 3. v. London, 1784.

[36] *European Magazine*, June, 1784, p. 428.

[37] *Ibid*, p. 429.

[38] *Ibid*, p. 428.

[39] Anderson, IV, p. 319.

[40] *European Magazine*, Apr., 1782, p. 269.

[41] *Letters concerning the present State of England*, p. 240.

[42] Park, *Travels in the interior Districts of Africa*, 1795-1797.

[43] *Annual Register*, 1799, p. 594.

[44] Cunningham, *Lives*, IV, p. 126 f.

[45] *Letter from Miss H. More to Mrs. Gwatkin*, 1775, in Roberts' *Memoirs of the Life and Correspondence of Mrs. Hannah More*, I, p. 32.

[46] Boswell, *op. cit.*, II, p. 247-248.

[47] *Letter of Walpole to the Countess of Aylesbury*, 20 Dec. 1772.

[48] *Annual Register*, 1773.

[49] *Ibid*, 1761, pp. 139-140.

[50] *Ibid*, 1760, pp. 120-121.

[51] *Ibid*, 1761, p. 141.

[52] *Ibid*, 1763, pp. 105-107.

[53] *Ibid*, 1760, p. 127.

[54] *Ibid*, p. 131 f.

[55] Leadam, *History of England*, pp. 498-499; see also Gardner, *History of Jamaica*, p. 205.

[56] Lecky, *op. cit.*, III, p. 377.

[57] See below, pp. 39-45.

[58] *Ann. Reg.*, 1763, pp. 121-122.

[59] *The Spectator*, 19 May, 1711.

[60] *Letter of Horace Walpole to Sir Horace Mann*, 15 Nov., 1779.

CHAPTER II

EMPIRE AND THE BALANCE OF TRADE: ARTICLES FOR
THE MAINTENANCE OF NATIONAL LIFE.

PRIOR to the eighteenth century, England had witnessed the entry of numerous products from lands overseas; but most of them had been limited in quantity and beyond the reach of the average purse.[1] The turning point came shortly after 1700. Then their importation began to increase by leaps and bounds, and their prices to fall. From being luxuries many of them became necessities, part and parcel of the nation's life, and of the daily lives of its citizens. Although incoming commodities were responsible for vital changes in the life and character of England and Englishmen, it should be remembered that, according to the doctrines of mercantilism, the criteria of imperial success were the stimulation of home industries and the excess value of exports over imports, *i.e.*, a favourable balance of trade. Strictly, then, trade should be encouraged only with those areas which could show a profit on the balance sheet of importations and exportations.

Statistics scarcely do justice to the phenomenal increase of imports from lands overseas during the eighteenth century. In some commodities, as tea and coffee, excessive excise and customs duties served to double, or even to treble the amount which was smuggled.[2]　For one reason or another clerks and accountants found it convenient or profitable to offer juggled figures for public consumption.　Certain commodities also arrived indirectly through other lands, such as spices from Holland.　In spite of their incompleteness and inaccuracy, statistics show a steadily increasing stream of goods from across the waters; a volume even more impressive when the decline in price of many articles is considered.

During most of the period England's possessions in America were considered the most valuable part of empire, with the West India islands as the chief member, and the southern plantations increasing rapidly in favour.　In the latter half of the century the loss of the Thirteen Colonies and the gradual dropping of mercantilism turned more attention to India, resulting in an enormous increase in Indian imports.　In the final decade a new interest developed in the southern part of the United States, largely because of the introduction and development of sea-island cotton, and Eli Whitney's cotton-gin, which combined to provide raw material for the mills of England.　Finally, there was the contribution to national and private economy of Africa and Canada.

The following tables bear witness to the increasing volume of oversea trade.　It should be borne in mind that these statistics, which leave out of consideration legitimate trade, are by no means complete:

Year	Value of Imports
1720	£ 6,090,083
1730	7,780,019
1740	6,703,778
1750	7,772,039
1760	9,832,802
1783	11,651,281
1789	37,784,000
1798	42,261,000
1802	31,400,000[2]

Year	Value of Exports
1705	£ 5,308,966
1709	5,913,357
1711	5,962,988[4]
1713-5 (average)	7,696,573
1728-38 "	7,891,739
1749-51 "	12,599,112
1755-7 "	11,708,515
1762-3 "	14,693,270
1775-6 "	17,492,515
1783-5 "	22,641,982
1790-2 "	31,464,800
1796-7 "	38,506,771
1802 "	41,400,000[5]

The most obvious change in the volume of imports and exports took place in the trade with Africa and the Orient. Slow to gain headway, it became, before the close of the century, the main basis of England's foreign interests, despite the fact that during the greater part of the century, the capital employed in the East India trade was but one-fourth that invested in West India commerce. While the trade with Africa totaled but £154,573 in 1700, and £189,798 in 1750, it increased in value in 1772 to £810,024 and in 1781 to £835,423.[6] Finally, in 1793, it passed the million mark, where it remained for the rest of the century.[7] A greater bulk of trade was carried on, however, with the East Indies.

TRADE OF GREAT BRITAIN WITH EAST INDIES.

Year	Imports	Exports	Total
1700-1	£ 167,382	£ 149,644	£ 317,026
1719-20	931,441	83,811	1,015,252
1734-5	1,297,400	186,375	1,483,775
1749-50	1,104,180	508,654	1,612,834
1762-3	1,059,335	887,083	1,946,418
1767-8	1,507,963	1,156,082	2,664,045
1772-3	1,933,096	845,707	2,778,803
1781	2,526,339	595,131	3,121,470
1784-5	2,703,940	1,153,532	3,856,572[8]

The next decade witnessed a continuance of this steady upward trend, in 1793 reaching £5,000,000.[9] By 1798, goods carried to and from Asia were valued at more than £10,000,000.[10]

Aside from the factor of volume, it is interesting to note the commodities which were sent to England in exchange for manufactured goods of the latter country. In one year (1787) Africa exported goods valued approximately at £117,817.[11] In the list were included gum arabic, gum senegal, camwood, ebony, red-wood, elephants' teeth (ivory), ostrich feathers, bee's wax, and a negligible amount of cotton. From Asia, a trade-area which included India and China, there was shipped to England in the year 1800, a most varied assortment of goods, including

books, canes, drugs, gums, oils, indigo in large quantities; cochineal, China-ink, galls, turmeric, seed-lack, shell-lack, stick-lack, ivory, fans, cane-mats, cinnamon, cloves, mace, nutmeg, pepper, cayenne pepper, ginger, sago, sugar, tea, a little rice, coffee, preserved fruits, mother-of-pearl shell, and spoons made of it, saltpetre, arrack, cotton, cotton yarn, raw silk of Bengal and China, calicoes and muslins, cassia, ebony, sandal, satin and sapan woods.[12]

To them are to be added porcelain, some of which was adorned with figures of European design, japanned cabinets, tables, chairs, boxes, and other ornamental furniture, artificial flowers and "other toys," skins of tigers and panthers, besides rubies and other precious stones,[13]—surely an array sufficient to transform the home, and the industrial life of a nation.[14]

In respect to their articles of export, the West India islands and the southern plantations of the Thirteen Colonies belong in the same group. In 1731 Jamaica and Barbados sent to England, sugar, cotton, indigo, ginger, pimento, rum, lime-juice, cocoa, coffee, molasses, logwood, hardwood, and many drugs.[15]

TRADE OF GREAT BRITAIN WITH WEST INDIES.[16]

Year	Imports	Exports	Total
1700-1	£ 537,473	£ 289,675	£ 827,148
1729-30	1,149,978	304,529	1,454,507
1759-60	1,550,469	1,004,362	2,554,831
1784-5	2,964,826	965,414	3,929,240

Virginia and Maryland sent among other things, "not only what Tobacco we consume at Home, but very great Quantities for Re-exportation, which may properly be said to be the surest way of enriching this Kingdom."[17]   In 1772-3 for example 55,929,957 pounds of this commodity reached Great Britain; of this amount all but approximately five million pounds were re-exported.[18]   In addition to tobacco, the Carolinas contributed rice and Indian corn. Of the former commodity 457,122 cwt. were imported in 1772-3, while 361,334 cwt. were re-exported,[19] thus proving a considerable source of profit according to mercantilist theory.

TRADE OF GREAT BRITAIN WITH THE SOUTHERN COLONIES.[20]

Year	Imports	Exports	Total
1700-1	£ 252,711	£ 213,591	£ 466,302
1729-30	498,562	215,716	714,278
1762-3	939,129	850,431	1,789,570
1772-3	1,138,836	788,197	1,927,033

On the other hand, the northern colonies furnished England chiefly with iron, timbers for shipbuilding, staves and hoops, pitch, tar and turpentine, and a few drugs, as sassafras and sarsaparilla.[21] Nova Scotia and Newfoundland sent in addition, codfish, oil, and seal skins,[22] while Canada exported, largely through the Hudson's Bay Company, pelts of all kinds: beaver, otter, cat, fox, black-bear skins, and the furs of wolverines and martins.[23] As is evidenced by the character of these commodities, the volume of trade fluctuated according to the demands of fashion. Their increased popularity is shown by their importation in 1731 to the amount of £6,000,[24] while in 1782, the Canada sales of furs and peltry netted £189,000.[25]

TRADE OF GREAT BRITAIN WITH THE NORTHERN COLONIES.[26]

Year	Imports	Exports	Total
1700-1	£ 56,423	£ 130,235	£ 186,658
1734-5	108,973	318,334	427,307
1767-8	294,896	1,334,834	1,629,730
1772-3	237,522	1,242,717	1,480,239

From the time of the American Revolution to the close of the century territorial changes require a re-grouping of exports to Great Britain. From the following table it may be gathered that the Revolution proved far from disastrous to trade; while the enhanced exports of the United States after the conclusion of peace were due largely to the supply of cotton for the mills of England.

TRADE OF GREAT BRITAIN WITH AMERICA.

Source	Year 1790 [27]	1796 [28]	1798 [29]
United States	£1,403,388	£1,997,374	£1,627,710
Canada	229,562	238,512	273,010
West Indies	3,479,298	4,298,532	3,461,020

As already observed, in accordance with the doctrines of mercantilism English colonies were also valued in proportion to their ability to contribute towards a self-sufficient empire. Of utmost importance were those colonies which furnished commodities essential for the security and protection of empire. In this group were certainly to be included a curious list of articles considered as "naval stores." As early as 1716 practically every product listed in this group, heretofore obtainable only from Russia, Prussia, or elsewhere in the Baltic region was discovered to exist in the American colonies.[30] Their vast forests furnished timber in limitless quantities, not only for masts and ships of the Royal Navy, but for exportation to Portugal and Spain. This intercourse was considered even more profitable,[31] for the cutting down of forests made way for farm lands, while the very bulk of lumber employed a large number of ships and sailors in its transportation.

Pig-iron was a commodity no less essential, for which Great Britain, in 1731, was spending abroad no less than £200,000 annually.[32] "Now if Encouragement was given for making Pig-Iron in our Plantations . . . then all the Places in this Kingdom where there is water enough, and a sufficient Quantity of Wood, might have Forges erected upon them." [33] In fact, pig and bar iron first began to be manufactured in the province of Virginia in 1714. Later, Pennsylvania took the lead in turning out products of first quality, to the detriment of this manufacture at home. [34] In this group, too, are classed hemp and flax, the former for cordage of all sorts, the latter for making sail-cloth. [35] In addition, the woods of America furnished abundant supplies of turpentine, pitch, and tar, a condition made possible by government subsidies. [36] The shortage of tar (in 1776) occasioned the discovery of a substitute, when "some gentlemen of Bristol set up works for extracting the oil from pit-coal, used for making lamp-black. . . . It possesses all the qualities of tar, for half the price." [37] Until this time, however, there were no complaints of the lack of these importations from the colonies. [38]

Another essential for warfare was saltpetre, the base of explosives used at the time. In 1730 the East India Company sent to England 682,000 pounds of this commodity, which is limited to certain favoured portions of the earth's surface. By the close of the century the annual importations of saltpetre were valued at £178,321. [39] Other goods classed among naval stores were pearl-ash and potash. In 1731 it was said that their importation "has never yet been undertaken, tho' doubtless our Plantations, if once got into the right Way of making it, would sufficiently supply us

with all that we want." [40]   This prophecy was more
than justified: before the close of the century, not only
New York and Pennsylvania, but Nova Scotia, Newfoundland and Canada furnished a surplus for re-exportation.[41]   Without doubt, the fact that England
was no longer dependent on foreign countries for these
supplies of war caused a new feeling of power and independence to develop in the hearts of English people.

During the last two decades of the century the
maintenance of industrial life, particularly of the new
manufacturing system achieved by the Industrial Revolution, was even more vital to the existence of the
Empire, than a supply of naval stores from the colonies.   To be sure, several of the articles enumerated
above were assets as well to industrial progress.   Still
other oversea commodities, however, satisfied England's new needs: various hardwoods used in the construction of the new machinery, a constant supply of
raw cotton to feed its spindles and looms, and finally
a brilliant assortment of dyestuffs to popularize the
finished product.

The transformation in the technique and the organization of manufacturing known as the Industrial Revolution owed its inception to oversea expansion.   The
change centred in the new cotton industry.   As we
shall see, the introduction of East India cottons created
an insatiable demand for cheap goods of this material
—a demand which could only be met by radical changes
in methods of manufacturing.   Under the protection
of a benign government, the infant industry prospered
until, late in the century, English manufacturers could

produce a product superior to the imported, and one which sold at an appreciably lower price.   Aside from capital, moreover, accumulated in oversea endeavour and available for manufacturing on a large scale, England could obtain all necessary raw materials within the confines of her own empire, as well as a limitless supply of cotton dyestuffs, and hard-woods to be used for the new machinery.

From ancient times, Indian artisans had manufactured cotton goods of unrivalled excellence. Behar had become famous for its handkerchiefs, table-cloths of superior quality came from Patna, and the best sort of basinets were made in the north of India.[42]   In any case Indian calicoes, muslins, and chintzes had besides the attraction of beauty the added attraction of cheapness; before 1700, their popularity had so threatened the English woollen manufacturers that the law forbade the introduction of Indian silks and calicoes for domestic use or furniture, under penalty of £200.[43] Even this threat failed to check the desirable new commodity; for similar acts, with intent to prohibit, were passed soon afterwards.[44]   In spite of this legislation, and of the frantic efforts of the vested woollen interests to stem the tide, English manufacturers were beginning surreptitiously to imitate the coarser East Indian fabrics.[45] By the Manchester Act of 1735, the Calico Acts were interpreted as not meaning to include the coarsely woven fabrics made in England. As home industry improved, an increasing number of weaves were exempt from penalties.[46]

With the manufacture of cotton now an accepted fact, it too became a "vested interest," and under the protection of a kindly government. In his tour of Great Britain (1727) Defoe commented on the "grand manufacture of cotton of all varieties" in Manchester;[47] while another writer, twelve years later, stated with conviction that

the manufacture of cotton, mixed and plain, is arrived at so great perfection with these twenty years that we not only make enough for our own consumption but supply our colonies and many of the nations of Europe. The benefits arising from this branch are such as to enable the manufacturers of Manchester alone to lay out above of thirty pounds a year, for many years past, on additional buildings.[48]

The repeal of the Calico Act (1774) removed the last restraint from progress.[49] Shortly after this came the epoch-making inventions of Crompton, Arkwright, and others, which transformed this industry to one of large-scale production, setting an example for others desirous of satisfying growing markets. By 1787 it was estimated that it furnished employment for about 100,000 men and women, and 60,000 children—most of the latter taken from different parishes and hospitals in Great Britain—who turned out an average of about 500,000 pieces a year, a production which reduced the price of cotton far below that of wool or linen.[50]

Statistics of the growing importations of cotton bear graphic witness to the increased use of cotton, and of its place in British industry: [51]

Year	Quantity of Cotton Wool Imported	Value in Pounds of Exports of British Cotton Goods
1702	1,976,359	£ 23,253
1710	715,008	5,698
1720	1,972,805	16,200
1730	1,545,472	13,524
1741	1,645,031	20,709
1751	2,976,610	45,986
1764	3,870,392	200,354
1771-5	4,764,589	....
1776-80	6,766,613	2,000,000

The lack of fine, raw material hampered the natural progress of this industry. Widespread cultivation of sea-island cotton in the United States, however, and the timely invention of the cotton-gin by Eli Whitney (1793) filled this need.[52] In 1787, the importation of cotton jumped to 22,600,000 pounds,[53] in 1790 to 31,447,605 pounds, and in 1800 to 56,010,-000 pounds.[54] The value of cottons exported by England in these same years shows an increase equally remarkable: £1,101,457, £1,1662,369, and £5,406,501 respectively.[55]

During the above period of experiment and change inventors, such as Arkwright, Crompton, and Cartwright, found satisfactory material for their machinery in the hard woods brought from overseas. Hard pine, mahogany, logwood, ebony and lignumvitae were easy to manipulate to a high degree of accuracy, and proved sufficiently resistant to the wear and tear of parts. In 1787, importations of ebony were valued at £3,504, lignumvitae at £2,497, logwood at £81,225, and mahogany at £57,786.[56] In 1799 importations of mahogany sold for £162,772.[57] It is interesting, too, that these commodities furnished profitable employment for many English cabinet-makers.[58]

Lands overseas also furnished invaluable accessories to the textile industries—not only to the infant manufacture of cotton, but for linen and wool as well—in a generous assortment of dyestuffs. Indigo was at once most common and the most highly esteemed of these. For centuries India had supplied the world with this dyestuff, and as late as the seventeenth century this product constituted a considerable part of its exports. The various species of plants producing indigo were indigenous to India, China and Java,[59] despite the claim of patriotic West Indians who asserted that their own islands had produced indigo for a considerable time.[60] While it is not certain whether this dyestuff was introduced into the New World by the Spanish or the French, in the early eighteenth century Jamaica and the Carolinas became the chief centres of production. In 1747 the latter colonies shipped to England about 200,000 pounds of indigo; [61] but by 1763, they could dispatch no more than 249,000 of it across the seas.[62] The failure of nineteen out of twenty plantations in Jamaica indeed was laid to the impossibility of profit from the cultivation of indigo, after payment of excessive duties. By 1787, the total exports of that commodity from the western world had declined to a paltry 34,000 pounds,[63] a statement which bears out the current belief that "a manufacture once destroyed can never be revived again." [64] With this abandonment of indigo culture by the West India planters, the East India Company again took it up in its own territory, to "insure a regular supply of an article so essentially necessary to the most important British manufacturers, independent of foreigners." During the first few years heavy losses were obvious, when exports amounted to but 24,317 pounds (in 1781) and 25,575 pounds in the following year.[65] The efforts of the Company, however, were amply rewarded soon after, both from a patriotic and from a financial point of view, as is shown by the amount of indigo sold. From a scant 245,000 pounds in 1786, bringing £61,533, importations increased to 2,923,848 pounds in 1796, with a market value of £505,878, and three years later to 4,571,420 pounds, bringing a purchase price of £1,024,983.[66]

Next in importance, perhaps, was cochineal, a scarlet dye obtained from the dried body of an insect indigenous to both the East and the West Indies.[67] Plentiful were materials for yellow dyes: fustick, a yellow dyestuff from the wood of a West Indian tree; turmeric, from the root of an East Indian plant, which yielded a deep yellow colour, while perhaps the most convenient to use was gamboge, a gum from the East Indies, which "requires no preparation, but dissolves immediately on rubbing it with the addition of water. It is a fine transparent yellow." [68]

Sandal wood (or, as it was called, Sanders Wood or Saunders Wood) which was indigenous to the tropics of both hemispheres, was responsible for saunders red, which imparted an extremely deep shade to textiles.[69] Used in conjunction with indigo, sandal wood created a popular shade which became known as saunders blue.[70]   Other dyestuffs included sticklack and orchil (archil, or archelia). The former dyestuff, red in colour, came from the incrustation of insects on certain trees indigenous to the Orient.[71] Orchil, obtained from lichens which grew on the shores of various Mediterranean islands, Madagascar, Zanzibar, Angola, etc., imparted a violet tinge to articles treated with it.[72] India ink, also invaluable to textile manufacture, was still imported from the Far East in 1800, although the greater part was now manufactured in England.[73]

Gum arabic, another oversea commodity, was the usual solvent for mixtures of dyestuffs.[74] In 1787, the value of gum arabic, imported from Africa, was £6,388; in 1773, £160,245; in 1782, £104,216; while in 1799 it had reached the slightly higher figure of £204,660.[75] The task of evolving delicate and attractive tints from these chemicals became an art. A single contemporary recipe will perhaps serve to demonstrate methods, and at the same time to show the influence of oversea commodities in this branch of industry. For purple:

take eight ounces of logwood, an English pint of rain-water, an ounce of alum; infuse them well over a slow fire in a glazed pan or earthen pot, for about twenty-four hours; add a quarter of an ounce of gum arabic, let it stand for a week, strain it through a piece of fine cloth, and keep it close. But the richest purple is made by blending cochineal and indigo.[76]

All the ingredients in the process except the rain-water, the fire, the pan and the pot, were exotics.

REFERENCES TO CHAPTER II

[1] Gillespie, *Influence of Oversea Expansion on England to 1700*, p. 32 ff.

[2] See below, pp. 67 and 178.

[3] The statistics for 1720-1760 are cited from Macpherson, *Annals*, III, pp. 116, 160, 227, 283 and 339 respectively; for 1783, from Cunningham, II, p. 695; for 1789 and 1798 from Rose, *A Brief Examination into the Increase of the Revenue, Commerce and Manufacture of Great Britain*, p. 8; for 1802, from Ogg, *Economic Development of Modern Europe*, p. 80.

[4] Chalmers, *Estimate*, pp. 89-90.

[5] Figures given for 1713-1763 are from Chalmers, *Estimate*, pp. 90, 105, 112, 116 and 132 respectively; from 1775 to 1797, from Macpherson, *Annals*, IV, pp. 154, 170, 535 and 604, respectively; for 1802, from Ogg, *op. cit.*, p. 80.

[6] These figures are from Anderson, IV, pp. 30, 40, 170 and 535 respectively.

[7] Macpherson, *Annals*, IV, p. 288.

[8] These figures are from Macpherson, IV, pp. 30, 34, 37, 40, 43, 126, 170, 361, and 604 respectively.

[9] Rose, *op. cit.*, p. 8.

[10] Edwards, *History of the British Colonies in the West Indies*, III, p. 248.

[11] Macpherson, *Annals*, IV, p. 154.

[12] *Ibid*, IV, pp. 545-546.

[13] See Chapter IV for social uses of these articles.

[14] Macpherson, IV, p. 367.

[15] See, *The Importance of the British Plantations in America*, p. 31; Gee, *The Trade and Navigation of Great Britain Considered*, p. 20.

[16] The above figures are taken from Macpherson, *Annals*, IV, pp. 30, 36, 42 and 604, respectively.

[17] Gee, *op. cit.*, p. 21.

[18] Macpherson, IV, p. 447.

[19] *Ibid*, IV, p. 448.

[20] These statistics are taken from Macpherson, IV, pp. 30, 36, 43 and 170, respectively.

[21] Gee, pp. 24-26.

[22] Macpherson, IV, p. 542.

[23] Anderson, III, p. 167.

[24] Craik, *op. cit.*, II, p. 205.

[25] Anderson, IV, p. 441.

[26] These figures are from Macpherson, *Annals,* IV, pp. 30, 37, 126 and 170, respectively.

[27] *Ibid,* IV, p. 214.

[28] *Ibid,* IV, p. 399.

[29] *Ibid,* IV, p. 466.

[30] Gee, p. 48; Anderson, III, p. 70.

[31] It was estimated that in 1731 about 500 trees a year were imported from the plantations, particularly from Maine, Massachusetts and New Hampshire. Gee, pp. 53-54.

[32] *Ibid,* p. 68.

[33] *Ibid,* p. 71.

[34] Wood, *Survey of Trade,* p. 51.

[35] As early as 1730, 50 cwt. of hemp were sent to England from the Carolinas. *Ibid,* p. 62. After the loss of the American colonies, the East India Company began to import hemp from Bengal at a cost of about two-thirds that of Russian hemp. Macpherson, *The History of the European Commerce with India,* p. 241.

[36] This step was taken because of Sweden's arbitrary refusal, in 1703, to sell these products to England, except under unfavourable terms. Wood, p. 55.

[37] Anderson, IV, p. 260.

[38] Gee, p. 90; in 1763, the Carolinas alone exported to England, 3,110 barrels of pitch, 1,119 barrels of tar, and 751 barrels of turpentine. Anderson, IV, p. 7.

[39] Wood, p. 76; Macpherson, *Annals,* IV, p. 504.

[40] Gee, p. 90.

[41] The average importation to England, for three years preceding 1799, of pearl-ash was £137,900, of potash, £141,946. Macpherson, *Annals,* IV, p. 504.

[42] See Ure, *The Cotton Manufacturing of Great Britain Investigated and Illustrated,* I, p. 104.

[43] Acts 11 and 12, Wm. III, c. 10.

[44] 10 Anne, c. 19; 12 Anne, c. 9.

[45] Baines, *History of the Cotton Manufacture in Great Britain,* p. 103; Cunningham, II, p. 130.

[46] Usher, *Industrial History of England,* p. 285.

[47] Defoe, *Tour of Great Britain,* I, p. 76.

[48] *Gentleman's Magazine,* March, 1739.

[49] Usher, *op. cit.,* p. 286.

[50] Anderson, IV, p. 655.

[51] Baines, *op. cit.,* pp. 109, 215. It was estimated that in 1766, the annual value of all British-made cottons was £600,000. Postlethwayt, *Universal Dictionary of Trade and Commerce,* p. 52.

[52] Without this invention sea-island cotton would have been considerably dearer, and consequently its manufacture would have been

seriously retarded. Baines, p. 300. The importation of raw cotton from the United States jumped from 189,316 pounds in 1791, to 17,789,803 pounds, in 1800. *Ibid,* p. 302.

[53] Macpherson, *Annals,* IV, p. 133; also Edwards, *op. cit.,* III, p. 99.

[54] Baines, p. 215. He also classified British cotton manufactures for 1787 as follows: Calicoes and muslins, 11,600,000 lbs.; fustians, 6,000,000 lbs.; mixtures, 2,000,000 lbs.; hosiery and cambrics, 3,000,-000 lbs. p. 216. Their value was estimated at £7,500,000. Anderson, IV, p. 656.

[55] Baines, p. 215; for slightly different estimates, see Edwards, III, p. 99.

[56] Macpherson, *Annals,* IV, p. 504.

[57] Anderson, IV, p. 663.

[58] See below, pp. 105-106.

[59] Crace-Calvert, *Dyeing and Calico Printing,* pp. 140-145.

[60] Edwards, III, p. 100.

[61] Anderson, III, p. 262.

[62] *Ibid,* IV, p. 7.

[63] *Ibid,* IV, p. 159.

[64] Edwards, III, p. 110.

[65] Macpherson, *Commerce with India,* p. 202; Anderson, IV, p. 395.

[66] Macpherson, *Commerce with India,* p. 416.

[67] Murphy, *A Treatise on the Art of Weaving,* p. 337.

[68] *Ibid.*

[69] Crace-Calvert, *op. cit.,* pp. 128-131.

[70] *Ibid.*

[71] *Ibid,* p. 222.

[72] *Ibid,* p. 228.

[73] Macpherson, *Annals,* IV, p. 652.

[74] Murphy, *op. cit.,* p. 341.

[75] These statistics are cited from Anderson, IV, pp. 154, 449, 450, and 540 respectively.

[76] Murphy, p. 339.

CHAPTER III

THE NATIONAL DIET

A SIGNIFICANT effect of the increased importation of oversea products in the eighteenth century is found in the changes which took place in the daily fare of the English people. Up to the end of the seventeenth century cookery books, with few exceptions, contained recipes only for foodstuffs native to the British Isles. The upper classes, for whom such books were written, were probably acquainted with the spices of the Orient and the fruits of warmer climes, but these were luxuries too expensive for the purse of the average citizen. In 1683 the condiments necessary to prepare a cod's head, according to a recipe in "The Young Cook's Monitor" cost nine shillings, while the head itself cost but fourpence.[1] Towards the end of the century, when sugar was becoming more plentiful, there was an increasing vogue for sweet pastry, but it was not until the Hanoverian era that we find more than a few recipes for sweets.[2] Beef, lamb, veal, deer, rabbits, native fish, fowls and vegetables, washed down by beer and ale made from English hops, were the usual food of even the gentry. Russia supplied some of the wheat for bread, but Asia and America had not yet begun to pour their riches upon England's shores. The Englishman of 1700 was a true product of his three or more stupendous meals a day: slow of thought, unimaginative, stolidly self-contented. But as the century progressed, new concoctions on the plate and in the glass before him awakened him to a new *joie de vivre*. From the morning cup of tea or coffee to the bit of confection at the soirée, products from lands overseas subtly moulded and mellowed British character.

One of the first of the new articles of diet was the potato, a common enough vegetable now, but at one time a curiosity and a luxury. Throughout the seventeenth century, its struggle for popularity was handicapped by prejudice, as well as by its scarcity and high price.[3] Before 1800, however, it had become "a constant outstanding Dish, at every meal, breakfast excepted, at the table of the Rich as well as the Poor."[4] A visitor to England in 1748 remarked that "potatoes are now very much used together with the roast meat."[5] In the north, particularly, the potato had become a staple article of food throughout the rural districts, and, after the Industrial Revolution, factory workers in town welcomed it because of its sustaining qualities and low price.

The growing popularity of the potato early in the century is attested by the following newspaper advertisement:

Mr. Jonathan Hubbard of Richmond offers to deliver potatoes from 1000 pounds to 100 tons at ½d. a pound. Will contract with H. M.'s Navy, or others who think them fit provision for the Sea, to be delivered next year, and they shall be all Scarlet, Pink, or White, if the contract be made before the time of planting.[6]

Versatility in preparation added to the virtue of the tubers. In the south it was commonly roasted or boiled, and eaten with butter. In the north it was usually

boiled (sometimes with the skin on, and sometimes with it taken off), chopped into small pieces, and with butter (either cold or melted), or bacon fried. . . . The principal way in which this useful root is dressed in the North by labourer's families, is, by being peeled, or rather, scraped raw; chopped, and boiled together with a small quantity of meat cut into very small pieces. The whole of this mixture is then formed into a hash, with pepper, salt, onions, etc., and forms a cheap and nutritive dish. No vegetable is, or ever was, applied to such a variety of uses in the North of England, as the potatoe.[7]

On the other hand, prejudice still lingered in the hearts of the labourers of the south, who rejected soup made of this vegetable even in a famine year, with the outcry that "this is washy stuff, that affords no nourishment: we will not be fed on meal and chopped potatoe, like hogs."[8]

Its general adoption, however, is made clear by certain copious directions for its preparation for the table, which appeared in periodicals and essays of the time. One recipe, "on the boiling of Potatoes, so to be eat as bread," advised that they should be nearly the same size, should be boiled from thirty to seventy-five minutes, with a little salt thrown in, and when ready, eaten with a little salt as bread. "Nothing but experience can satisfy any one how superior the potatoe is, thus prepared, if the sort is good and mealy. . . . With a little butter, or milk or fish, they make

an excellent mess." [9]   A final point in favour of this
vegetable was its supposed self-sufficiency.   "It is also
a fact, and one of great importance, that potatoes and
water alone, with common salt, can nourish men completely." [10]

Indian corn, or maize, proved less successful in combating prejudice.   It was thought that the English
climate would prevent its successful cultivation from
an economic point of view: that too seldom was the
English summer long enough or hot enough to ripen
it fully.[11]   Some, however, believed that it might become a profitable domestic commodity,[12] and an
additional unit for crop rotation.

Although maize did not become a staple of English
agriculture, directions for its use were not lacking.
This cereal was suggested as a partial substitute for
wheat, and as such was considered superior to rye,
barley or oats.[13]   Reference was made to the negro
slave's allowance of three barrels of corn annually, and
to the fact that he was fed almost solely on dry bread,
called Pawn, or Poan, and also to the fact that the
blacks "regale themselves with another mess, also made
of Indian corn, called homony." [14]   The imports of
maize from the New World hardly sufficed to supply
more than the seed used for its cultivation in England.
It is significant, though, that in a single year of need
(1795), it served as a low-priced substitute for
wheat.[15]

A compendium, published late in the century, gives
instances of other cereals, which were used principally
as the bases for desserts.

"Sago," it states, "is a farinaceous substance, prepared from the pith of a palm tree, which grows in the East Indies, and to which Botanists have given the name of Cycas circinalis. An inferior sort, from a different tree, is produced in the West Indies. Tapioca is another of the mucilaginous and mealy substances, which may be obtained from the palm tree . . . and is brought from the West Indies and South America. Both tapioca and sago are highly nutritious, and require no other preparation than to be moistened with hot water, or to be boiled in water. A little sugar and spices, or wine, are palatable and wholesome additions to them. They may be made with milk into thick pottage. Tapioca is often used in puddings in the same manner as rice." [16]

During the reign of George III, rice was admitted free of duty until 1783, in order to encourage its use.[17] In 1795, it served as an alternative for home-grown grain, which was scarce and sold at an exorbitant price. The children of the Foundling Hospital were given rice pudding twice a week as a means of saving flour, and it was then found that rice could be used as an ingredient in making bread.[18] In the same year, the East India Company imported large quantities of rice. It was remarked that now, for the first time, India, "which in all ages had supplied the western world with articles, rather of ornament and luxury, than of use, sent to Europe an article necessary for the support of life." [19]

Since the early part of the century, the southern plantations of America had raised and exported this product on a large scale. In 1733, the Carolinas alone exported 36,584 barrels of rice, though we are told that the major portion of this found its way to lands other than the mother country.[20] Within forty years, however, imports to England bear witness to the frequent use of this cereal in her homes.[21] Another proof of its growing popularity is furnished by a comparison of a cook-book published in 1734 with one that appeared at the end of the century. In the former no recipes for the preparation of rice are given, while in the latter there are twenty-two.[22]

Throughout the eighteenth century the tomato, or "love apple," a distinctive product of the New World, continued to ornament the gardens of England, with its round, red fruit. As late as 1819, it continued to be cultivated for the singularity of its appearance.[23] It is uncertain who first dared solve the mystery of its edibility, though before 1800, a few souls must have appreciated its luscious flavour. Phillips, writing in 1820, tells us:

that this fruit has long been used by the wealthy Jew families in this country; and within these last few years it has come into great use with all our best cooks, as it possesses in itself an agreeable acid, a very unusual quality in ripe vegetables, and which makes it quite distinct from all garden vegetables that are used for culinary purposes in this country. . . . Love-apples are now to be seen in great abundance at all our vegetable markets, but I do not find that they are used by the middle or lower classes of English families, who have yet to learn the art of improving their dishes with vegetables.[24]

Like the tomato, the peanut seems to have been a curiosity, rather than an article of food. In 1769, a paper was read before the Royal Society to explain this vegetable substance to the learned members. Specimens which had been sent from North Carolina were exhibited, as well as samples of peanut oil. It was recommended that the latter be used as a substitute for imported olive oil. The recommendation evidently had little effect.[25]

New varieties of asparagus and spinach, which are not mentioned by earlier culinary authorities, were in common use by 1723, when John Nott, cook to the Lord-Lieutenant of Ireland, wrote his "Cook's and Confectioner's Dictionary." [26] The latter vegetable was discovered to be an anti-scorbutic by Captain Cook on his first voyage to New Zealand in 1772.[27]

Various members of the gourd family also added variety. The small gourd, or squash, "when young and properly boiled and dressed with butter and black pepper, is a delicious vegetable." [28] Vegetable marrow, however, found particular favour with the English epicure, though it is doubtful whether this vegetable found its way into the markets before 1819.[29] On the other hand, the pumpkin, a native of the Levant, failed to equal in England its popularity in America, where "this fruit has lately been raised in the neighbourhood of London to an extraordinary size, weighing nearly 200 weight. These are sold in the shops of the metropolis more as a curiosity than for use." [30] Rhubarb, which had long since found its way from western China and the Volga region to England, continued to be used not only for medicinal purposes, but as a vegetable.[31]

The products mentioned above, added variety to the table of the Englishman of average taste, as well as of the epicure. Oft-times, too, fruit from lands overseas brought new charms to the later courses of a meal. And if repartee seemed to sparkle as the eighteenth century waxed and waned, it was doubtless not hindered by the influence of these lighter, and more inspiring desserts. In the reign of Queen Anne, fruit was a rarity, and was "brought only to the tables of the Great, and of a small Number even of them." [32] Throughout the century, dates remained a luxury enjoyed only by the few, partly because of their scarcity and high price, partly because they were considered hard of digestion, and a cause of headache and loss of teeth. [33] Fig-trees were first brought to England in 1745, when trees planted by John Long of Sussex proved so productive as to form the principal support of a large family. By the close of the century, figs, which were considered nourishing and easy of digestion, were enjoyed by "refined palates of the higher order of society," though neglected, and even the subjects of derision, by the middle and lower classes. [34] Both dates and figs, natives of the Near East and Northern Africa, were now imported largely from Turkey, Italy, and Spain. [35]

On the other hand, lemons and oranges made a far wider circle of friends. Early in the century, "Lisbon, China Oranges, and Sower Oranges" were sold for two pence each at the foreign fruit market at Billingsgate. [36] This price permitted their occasional enjoyment even by those of slender means. These fruits, natives of the Orient and transplanted to America, were imported chiefly from the Mediterranean countries, after several attempts proved their inability to survive the long trip across the Atlantic.[37] No doubt it added to their popularity that officers and crews of Captain Cook's expeditions found lemon and orange juice of great benefit in warding off attacks of scurvy. This experience was shared by Commodore Anson's men in their trip around the world.[38] Physicians recognized the merit of oranges in combating excessive doses of narcotics, and prescribed orangeade, "an agreeable drink of orange juice, water and sugar to people in the height of a fever." [39] Lemon juice and coffee were used as "dissolvents of the stone," by a certain Dr. Lobb.[40] But medicinal purposes were not the only ones for which the fruits were used. They were evidently common items of diet, for the *Compleat Housewife* (1734) has no less than thirteen recipes for lemons, and nineteen for oranges. In 1799, the value of the importations of the fruits was estimated at £101,987.[41]

Limes, in part because they came from the British West Indies, were more esteemed than lemons, especially for cold punch. A beverage known as "shrub" was made from lemon and lime juice, added to rum.[42] This concoction proved a popular embellishment of mixed gatherings of the time. The watermelon, a native of Egypt, China and the East Indies,[43] was appreciated in England for its grateful coolness a... delicious flavour. Here it was principally used as dessert and "was eaten with sugar, ginger, pepper, or salt, agreeable to the taste." [44]

Bananas, too, which were transplanted from the tropics of the Old World to the New, were considered a wholesome fruit, nor was their use hindered because of large shipments from Jamaica. This fruit was also served for dessert, or as the basis for punch or marmalade, and was considered equally delicious baked in tarts or boiled in dumplings. The peach, probably indigenous to China and India,[45] was soon cultivated with much success in North America. Being easily perishable, it could not be transported across the ocean, and the cool English summer prevented its growth there, except in hothouses.[46] On the other hand, the Virginia strawberry was brought to England as early as 1629, while a larger variety from Chili arrived in 1727, via France. The crossing of these berries with each other and with native varieties produced the "fruits enormes, d'une saveur excellent," [47] for which England has become famed.

The fruit from overseas which eventually became most popular was slow in winning favour. The pineapple, which grows abundantly in South America and the hotter islands of the West Indies, especially Jamaica, was practically unknown in England in the seventeenth century.[48] As late as 1716, that distinguished traveller, Lady Mary Montagu, wrote from Constantinople of the pineapple as if she had never before seen or heard of it. Before 1733 it was cultivated in English hothouses, but for some time its high cost confined the fruit to the tables of the rich. Late in the century, however, it was served as an ice in popular outdoor places of amusement.[49] Not until 1820 did the first commercial shipment of 400 pineapples arrive from Bermuda, with the hope of a regular supply for the future.[50]

During the eighteenth century, sugar ceased to be classed as a luxury, and was considered a necessity by wealthy and poor alike.[51] Its use was varied and universal: for sweetening the morning or afternoon cup of coffee or tea, or their equally popular colleague, punch; as well as for cooking purposes of all descriptions.[52] Its low price even made popular simple confections. In 1732, white sugar candy sold from 12d. to 17d. the pound, while brown sugar candy with its less æsthetic appeal, sold as low as 6½d. the pound.[53] Loaf sugar, double refined, was worth 9d. the pound, while the less discriminating could purchase brown sugar from 60 to 70 shillings the hundred-weight.[54]

"One of the most pleasant and useful Things in the World," a contemporary calls it, "for besides the advantage of it in Trade, Physicians and Apothecaries cannot be without it, there being near three Hundred Medicines made up with Sugar; almost all Confectionery Wares receive their Sweetness and Preservation from it, most Fruits would be pernicious without it; the finest Pastries could not be made nor the rich Cordials that are in the Ladies' Closets, nor their Conserves; neither could the Dairy furnish us with such Variety of Dishes, as it does, but by their Assistance of this noble Juice." [55]

Another declares that it "tempers the crudities of fruits, and gives a relish to many a wholesome mess, whether of peeled barley, oatmeal, grots, rice, or milk." [56] Statistics of home consumption tell in large part the story of sugar's increasing popularity: [57]

Year	Home Consumption of Sugar
1720	581,508 cwt.
1721	497,540 cwt.
1722	616,893 cwt.[58]
1731	722,445 cwt.[59]
1748	668,468 cwt.[60]

This sugar was valued, wholesale, at about £15 the hogshead of 1200 pounds. In fact, imports remained practically at these figures until 1759, when they reached the total of 1,030,066 cwt.[61] From now on until the close of the century the total imports of sugar remained above the million mark. In 1772-3, 1,586,-179 cwt. of sugar were consumed in England,[62] in 1781-2, 1,229,849 cwt., and in 1787, 1,727,343 cwt.[63] Figures for the rest of the century are incomplete. In the three years, however, from 1788 to 1791, there were imported into England from the West Indies, over seven million cwts. of sugar, an average of 2,564,-428 cwt. per annum. Surely this is indisputable evidence of the increasingly widespread use of this commodity.[64]

It is difficult to list the tempting and dainty dishes which chefs concocted with the aid of sugar, or the added zest which they imparted, not only to the jaded appetite of the rich, but to the poor who never before had been able to include delicacies in their menu. But, as is the case with all innovations, there were criticisms as well as praise for the new foodstuff. One critic asserted:

If sugar abounds with salts, it must consequently be productive of the scurvy. This is frequently seen among West Indians, who are fond of sweetmeats; boys in grocer shops; and what is more remarkable, men who break sugar for the grocers, are observed to be more than commonly afflicted with this distemper."[65]

Sugar, too, he believed to be bad for young persons, "especially such as drink wine and malt liquors." And above all, said he, "I must take this opportunity to inform you that it would be greatly to the commercial interest of the nation, if we consumed less sugar ourselves, and sold more to foreigners." [66] In this last statement undoubtedly lay the germ of his criticism, and of the school which followed his lead.

From overseas, also, came materials for beverages to suit every palate and purse. Throughout the seventeenth century chocolate had lent itself admirably to the exotic leisure of milady's boudoir-breakfast. The introduction of coffee was responsible, among other things, for the novel institutions bearing its name. Tea was about to gain a popularity which was to link its name inseparably with that of England. The devotees of these beverages found in their favourite drink a new and pleasurable satisfaction for the palate. A certain psychological value might also be attached to the leisure which attended informal meetings at the coffee-house, or to the refined setting of five o'clock tea. Perhaps inspiration might follow even a temporary relief from the routine of business or social life. During the seventeenth century whatever advantage these beverages afforded was confined to a favoured few. In the following decades, however, chocolate, coffee and tea became available for an increasing number. The barriers of price, scarcity and prejudice were largely removed—all who wished might enjoy them.[67]

Of the three, chocolate, so much liked in the preceding century, was now less popular. In 1702, there were only five chocolate houses in London;[68] of these but two were of importance. The beverage could be obtained, however, at the majority of coffee-houses for twelve pence a quart, or two pence the dish—a price just double that of coffee or tea.[69] As Addison informs his readers, the fashionable lady relied on it for her morning drink.[70] Why chocolate gave way to the cheaper and more readily digested tea,[71] is easy to understand. As the cultivation of the tree producing it declined in the English West India islands, mercantilism, patriotism and the force of public opinion came to prefer the latter beverage. By 1768 cocoa was no longer a commodity to be regarded.[72] Chocolate now came to be favoured in cake or tablet form, sold in shops as a confection, or for preparing it as a drink at home.[73] If newspaper advertisements are a criteria, its sale was considerable, though its quality was dubious. Early in 1703 it was announced that a "world traveller has an Invention to grind up Chocolate and fine loaf Sugar and best Vanello 12d. a pound cheaper than some of the foul Stuff with which London is crowded; cheaper and better than people could make at home."[74] Two months later the author of this scheme offered to sell his cakes from 3s. 8d. to 4s. 8d. apiece according to quality, and the same without vanilla, from about 6d. less a bar. Further, he advises his patrons, that after his patent has passed the seal, "he will set many Persons to work, that he may furnish All Persons of Quality, and Others, with as great a Quantity as they please, according to his former Proposal of returning their Money if misliked." [75] During the next decade, prices of chocolate ranged from 1s. 8d. to 3s. the pound. These prices remained practically without change during the first half of the century, when the advertisements ceased.[76] The chocolate tree is believed to have been cultivated in English hot-houses as early as 1739.[77]

Coffee, too, found the public a fickle mistress. This beverage, is most famed, perhaps, as the raison d'être for that epoch-making institution, the coffee-house, which reached its zenith of popularity in the reign of Queen Anne. Of these rendezvous for business and social relaxation, Misson writes: "The Houses, which are very numerous in London, are extreamly convenient. You have all Manner of News there: You have a good Fire, which you may sit by as long as you please; You have a Dish of Coffee, you meet your Friends for the Transaction, and all for a Penny, if you don't Care to spend more." [78] In fact, the attempt to raise the price of a cup of coffee from 1d. to 1½d. met with such vigorous protests that it was soon abandoned.[79] In public sale coffee showed great fluctuation, reaching the low-water mark in 1707, when it sold for 5s. the pound.[80] Five years later, "the strongest body'ed Coffee, roasted by a fine new Method," could be purchased for 5s. 6d.[81] In 1728, it evidently found buyers at 11s. 6d. the pound,[82] although the news sheet for 8 January, 1732, in which it was advertised, fails to list coffee among groceries.

For almost the next half century, this beverage lost its popularity in favour of tea. So low, indeed, had it fallen as to be ignored by the bitter and far-searching reformers of the mid-century. A turning point in the history of coffee came with its introduction into Jamaica.[83] In 1732, the Council of Jamaica reminded the government that excessive duties had ruined the cocoa trade, and desired that coffee should be encouraged by "bounty, importation, or otherwise." [84] In reply, England reduced the import duty on this commodity from 2s. to 1s. 6d. the pound.[85] The effect of the change, however, was not felt until the last quarter of the century, when a further cut in duties was reflected in increased imports.[86] Now the hitherto despised American berry was considered the equal of Java coffee; and indeed was often sold as such in the markets.[87]

A treatise on coffee, written in 1785, states succinctly what its status was. Until recently, its use had been confined to a few individuals. With them it had been a luxury, and as such not of public concern.[88] With the reduction of the duty on coffee, together with the vast imports, it was now brought within the reach of "almost every description of people." [89] Moreover, coffee was not so easy a victim of adulteration as tea. The tonic and invigorating qualities of this beverage were dwelt upon at length: especially its effect if taken clear when the stomach is overloaded with food or nauseated; moreover, it aids digestion and "diffuses a genial warmth that cherishes the animal spirits." [90]   It was considered valuable, and in fact preferable to the use of opiates, for the relief of headache; and in the case of intellectual persons, long watching and intense study were "wonderfully supported by coffee without the usual ill-effects of the lack of sleep." [91]

The author of these opinions concludes with suggestions for the preparation of coffee:

It has long been a custom with many people among us, to add mustard to their coffee. . . . The Eastern nations add either cloves, cinnamon, cardamons, etc., but neither milk, or sugar. Milk and sugar, without the aromaticks, are generally used with it in Europe, America, and the West India islands. [92]

Another writer (in 1784) affirmed that coffee was a satisfactory beverage for breakfast, if taken without sugar. [93]   As late as 1820, it was a common complaint that Englishmen made their coffee too weak, and took it with too much sugar. [94]

Tea, on the other hand, now most favoured by Englishmen, was slower in making its influence felt. In 1664, the East India Company, desiring to present the king with a rarity, gave him two pounds of it. [95] In 1678, the Company glutted the market by importing less than five thousand pounds of tea; in the next six years, it brought in but 410 pounds. [96] From 1697 to 1699, the average annual imports of tea were less than 20,000 pounds. In the eight following years, they rose to an average of more than 60,000 pounds. It was not, however, till 1721, that imports exceeded for the first time one million pounds. During this period prices were correspondingly high. In 1707, "very fine Green and Bohea Tea" sold at 16 shillings, a pound, "the best Green Tea" at 20 shillings, and "Bohea Tea" at 26 shillings.[97] Five years later the best Bohea tea sold at 18 shillings, with inferior grades at from 10 to 14 shillings the pound.[98] In 1727, Bohea was selling for 13 shillings.[99] By 1732, Bohea had dropped to 11, Congo to 12 and Pekoe to 14 shillings the pound, while the luxurious Hyson variety brought 35 shillings.[100] The introduction of Chinese green tea about 1715 was largely responsible for increased consumption after that date. From 1717 to 1726, the average annual importation of tea was estimated to be 700,000 pounds, whereas in the decade 1732 to 1742, it exceeded 1,200,000 pounds.[101]

Statistics for the second half of the century leave no doubt as to the growing popularity of tea, or that its use had descended to the "plebeian order." From a mere four million pounds, sold for home consumption at the Company's warehouses in 1762, the amount increased steadily, until in 1785 it reached 10,856,578 pounds, and five years later the huge total of 15,035,722 pounds.[102] And now it was sold at prices fitted for every purse. In 1766 it was estimated that the nation spent £1,250,000 on this commodity; with prices ranging from 2s. 6d. to 20s. the pound, and the average price somewhere near 5s. the pound.[103] Statistics, compiled for 1787, show Bohea as the most popular variety.[104]

Yet these figures, impressive as they are, hardly

picture the extensive use of tea, for that commodity had long since been a bonanza of the smuggling trade. Early in the century one hears of tea arriving through underground channels:

So great a Quantity of Tea brought up at Ostend, and in Holland, at very low Rates, by our honest Smugglers, and so many new, clever, and successful ways found of bringing it in Custom free, that our East India Company need not be at the Trouble to bring any more from China.[105]

In spite of efforts to check this evil, the escape from excessive government duty offered attractive bait to illicit trader and to consumer. In 1766, practically seven million pounds of illegally imported tea reached England.[106] By 1784, it was believed that from eight to nine million pounds were smuggled into England annually.[107] In this same year the traffic received a serious blow, when all existing taxes on tea were repealed, and in their place a flat rate of 12½% substituted.[108] This fact accounts in large part for the great increase in imported tea shown in the statistics given above.[109] In addition to the duties payable on real tea, the government was further cheated when several million pounds of leaves of sloe, ash, and other trees were used annually to adulterate the genuine article.[110]

By the mid-century, then, in tea drinking at least the labourer and mechanic were able to ape the lord. Even in the huts of peasants, "Misery itself had no power to banish Tea, which had frequently introduced that Misery. . . . It took its rise from Example. . . .

The business depends entirely on the example of ladies of rank in this country." [111]   It is an interesting fact, moreover, that tea became popular in spite of, or perhaps because of, the barbed shafts of its critics, which blamed not only physical ailments but national ills, on this beverage.   These laments, which pervaded much of the earlier literature of the century, may be best summarized in Jonas Hanway's *Essay on Tea*.   This noted traveller and philanthropist's first complaint was that "there is not quite so much beauty in this land as there was.   Your very chambermaids have lost their bloom by sipping Tea. . . . I am persuaded we shall not enjoy a blooming health whilst we continue the use of Tea." [112]   The beverage was a cause of scurvy, "by enervating the powers of Nature, and disabling her to throw off what is pernicious." [113]   Tea and other hot liquids prevented sleep, and had a harmful effect on the teeth, as well as weakened digestion.   The prevalence of paralytic and nervous disorders was due to tea, which was considered especially disastrous to the fair sex.[114]   Its use was alleged even to threaten the future of England, which, "as a wise, active and warlike nation, would least desire to imitate the most effeminate people on the face of the Earth—the Chinese, who are at the same time the greatest sippers of tea." [115]   With such arguments, and lacking their one deadly weapon, ridicule, the reformer met his usual fate, and tea remained unrivalled as the national drink. The beverage from China, accordingly, had its champions and panegyrists.   Many doubtless approved the sentiments expressed in a poem of 1761:

With joys I see, in ages yet unborn,
Thy votaries the British Isles adorn,
With joy I see enamour'd youths despise
The goblet's lustre for the false one's eyes;
Till rosy Bacchus shall his wreaths resign,
And Love and Thea triumph o'er the vine.[116]

Further recognition of its service to the cause of temperance was shown after the reduction of the duties in 1784, when it was stated that

tea has become an economical substitute to the middle and lower classes of society for malt liquor, the price of which renders it impossible for them to procure the quantity sufficient for them as their only drink. . . . In short, we are so situated in our commercial and financial system, that tea brought from the eastern extremity of the world, and sugar brought from the West Indies and both loaded with the expense of freight and insurance . . . compose a drink cheaper than beer.[117]

The following generation seems to have appreciated still more the value of tea in this respect:

Perhaps it would not be easy to find a better evidence of the advancing refinement as well as comfort of the great body of the people than is furnished by this steadily extending preference for what may be called the temperate man's wine—"the cup that cheers but not inebriates." [118]

Tea also was absolved of responsibility for scandal-mongering, unless it be asserted that "as almost every person in the kingdom drinks tea, almost every person talks scandal, a position that is false in every respect."[119]

The growing tendency towards temperance, however, found an opponent in another beverage from overseas—Jamaica rum. This species of alcoholic tonic found a ready welcome among its users, for no critic dared accuse them of effeminacy. Nor on the other hand did rum, a British imperial product, have to withstand the shafts levelled at its equally potent, but foreign cousin, gin.[120] Statistics show a steadily increasing demand for it for the second half-century. Importations rose steadily from 607,074 gallons in 1750 to 1,809,908 gallons in 1794.[121] To these figures should be added an equal amount of illicit liquor, for in 1795, the duty on rum amounted to but £31,000. Furthermore, it is impossible even to estimate the quantity of imported molasses which was used for purposes of distillation.[122]

Upon oversea commodities were largely dependent the milder beverages of punch and shrub. Usually rum was the chief ingredient in these drinks, and was used in ample proportions. Since they were intended for feminine consumption as well, their alcoholic potence was reduced as their pleasantness of taste was enhanced by the the juice of limes, oranges, or lemons, with dainty slices of pineapple or banana, and a liberal use of sugar.[123]

From the New World, also, came what is often regarded as man's greatest solace: his inspiration in work, his companion in play, tobacco. In the opinion of an anonymous rhymester of the early part of the century, it is

> Divine Tobacco! which gives Ease
> To all our Pains and Miseries;
> Composes Thought, makes Minds sedate,
> Adds Gravity to Church and State;

Courted by Kings, and Men of Conscience,
The Throne's Perfume, the Altar's Incense;
Arch-Bishops, Bishops, Priests and Deacons,
Most reverently can Fire their Beacons.
When Rheums, Catarrhs, and Colds molest us,
Doctor Tobacco must assist us.
Divine Tobacco! Indian God!
The Courtier's Feast, the Poor Man's Food;
In Summer cool, in Winter warm,
Julep and Cordial for each Harm.[124]

By that time its use in England had become general
and accepted.[125]   In 1709 it was estimated that the
annual consumption of tobacco for the previous ten
years averaged 11,260,659 pounds.[126]   In 1730
Maryland and Virginia alone sent to Great Britain
30,000,000 pounds of tobacco.[127]   While in 1744-1746,
the annual importations averaged 40,000,000 pounds,
the average home consumption had sunk temporarily
to the low figures of seven million pounds.[128]   In the
year before the American Revolution, Virginia and
Maryland sent across the water 96,000 hogsheads, of
which only 13,500 were consumed at home.[129]
Strangely enough, during the lean war years the use
of tobacco showed a marked increase, for in 1779
Englishmen consumed over ten million pounds, in
1781 eight and a half million.[130]   Eighteen years
later, when tobacco was valued at 5d. the pound,[131] the
importations were appraised at £1,024,266.   To the
above figures must be added a liberal estimate for
smuggling; since tobacco, as other heavily taxed commodities, suffered from illicit trade.[132]

Tobacco continued to be smoked in pipes, in which

form it was highly favoured by men who frequented the coffee-houses. Others, like Sir Andrew Freeport, enjoyed a comfortable smoke at home, where from ten to twelve, he indulged in three pipefuls.[133] It was no longer fashionable for women to smoke, though many of the old country women still clung to their clay pipes.[134]

Following the seizure of Spanish shipping at Vigo (1702), when several thousand barrels of fine snuff were acquired, tobacco in that form rapidly gained favour among the élite. Indeed, they alone were able to afford it, for as late as 1707, "neat, superfine Brazile snuff," sold at four guineas the pound, or 6s. the ounce, with "finest Portugal Lisbon Snuff" selling at 2s. the ounce.[135] Five years later, a more widespread use was made possible, when plain Spanish snuff, "right and fine in Tin Pots," sold at 5s. the pound, though the finest Brazil snuff sold at 3s. the ounce.[136]

Steele complained that this "impertinent custom" had been adopted by the women.[137] In fact the social status of a person was determined by the grace and elegance with which he performed the rites of this practice. At the shop of Charles Lillie the perfumer, where the best snuff could be purchased, instruction in the social etiquette of its use could be obtained.[138] With the decrease in price, the use of snuff spread among the lower orders; and there is evidence that tobacco, for a time anyway, acted as a social leveller:

The custom of taking Snuff is grown so monstrous, that 'tis descended from the Quality to the Oyster Girl, and the Beau is only to be distinguished from the Link-Boy, by the Grandeur of his Box, and the Excellence of his Snuff. I was not a little surpriz'd the other Day, when passing by Whitehall, to see one Boy cleaning a Gentleman's Shoes, and his Consort, at the Instant a little out of Employment, managing his Snuff-Box with an air of Quality.[139]

The practice continued throughout the century.

While snuff took its place among the cure-alls of the time, undoubtedly it proved as satisfactory as the less pleasant, and oftimes dangerous, quack medicines. Most beneficial was

the True Imperial Golden Snuff; which Thousands of People have found to be the most effectual Remedy ever known, for all Distempers of the Head and Brain; it immediately cures the Headache, be the Pain ever so violent; instantly removes Drowsiness, Sleepiness, Giddiness and Vapours; it is most excellent against Deafness and Noise in the Ears; cures Stoppages or Cold in the Head, etc; and far exceeds all other Snuff for all Humours in the Eyes and Dimness of Sight, and certainly prevents Appoplexies and Falling Sickness.[140]

From lands overseas, moreover, came many important contributions to materia medica. Their need was real, for at the close of the seventeenth century doctors were none too versed in the knowledge of their craft; often, indeed, their ignorance made prospective patients turn to traditional and home-made medicaments.[141] Quacks profited by this dissatisfaction and by the human desire for a quick, harmless, painless and sure cure. These gentry, then, were first to commercialize the gifts of distant regions.

Early in the century the patent-medicine calling was in full popularity. One of its nostrums was "the true

Balsam of Cathay, being the most effectual Remedy
ever brought into Europe for giving immediate Ease in
the Gout, and all Gouty and Rheumatick Pains, prevailing against those Distempers even to a Miracle." [142]
If this failed, the gullible were next exhorted to try
"Balm of Gilead, right and true, lately imported, direct from the East Indies."[143] Lest partiality be
shown, the "Powder of Paraguay" was regarded by its
modest sponsor as the "most effectual medicine ever
brought to Europe (or indeed ever known in the
World) for rheumatism, etc." [144] So great was its
success that a few years saw it dignified with the re-
sounding title of "Stoughton's Great Cordial Elixir,"
that medicine "which saved the Lives of so many at
Jamaica a while ago." [145] Then there was "the incomparable India Dentissick Roots—6d. each root.
To be pounded up and cooked in water to preserve
Teeth. Not offensive to Taste or Smell." [146] The
greatest hoax of all, perhaps, was the "volatile Spirit
of Bohea Tea . . . the first of this kind that was
ever made in England, which hath been found the most
absolute Cure for Consumptions, inward Wastings,
and all other Decays of Nature, incident to Mankind,
being infinitely more Balsamick, healing to the Lungs,
and attuning to the whole Constitution than the Infu-
sion of the Leaf in Water." [147]

Fortunately the drugs of the New World and the
Old did not find their sole outlet in patent medicines.
Rather did they furnish inspiration and material for
the advancement of the science of medicine. For some
time quinine—Peruvian bark or Jesuit's bark—had

been used in the New World for the breaking up of
malarial and other fevers. In England it came to be
the most valued and valuable of agencies in curing
agues, chills and fevers.[148] From the North American colonies, in particular Pennsylvania and New
York, came various tonics, such as snake-root and sarsaparilla, restorative medicines in complaints arising
from poorness of the blood, and the aromatic bark
of the sassafras tree.[149] The aloe epatica, from Mexico and Central America, was used to relieve liver
complaints.[150] Camphor, however, seems to have
found its chief value at the time in the manufacture
of India-ink. From bitter almonds was extracted
prussic acid; essence of almonds was used for confectionery and perfumery, although considered highly
dangerous.[151]

From the white poppy were derived opium and
laudanum. In an age when their soothing and sedative
qualities were mistaken for curative ability their abuse
was common. Narcotic intoxication by smoking, too,
was prevalent in the East, whence it spread to some
extent in England. By administering an opium deriv-
ative to patients, physicians unwittingly inflicted an
unfortunate habit upon many of them. Papers refer
to death by laudanum poisoning, for the most part
accidental.[152] Clive for one met his fate, either by a
self-inflicted over-dose of this drug, or by one administered by his physician.[153] An even more insidious
evil was its use in patent medicines, where it subtly
lulled the patient into a feeling of false security.[154]

To exhaust the subject of drugs and medicinal ingredients, or to trace the growth of medicinal science, lie beyond the scope of this treatise. The following items, however, culled from the list of imports for 1786, give some idea of their variety: aloes cicotrina, aloes epatica, antimonium crudum, asafætida, camphire (camphor), cantharides, cassia lignea (used for adulterating cinnamon), cardamons, cortex Peru (quinine), cream of tartar, gambogium, gum arabic, jallap, opium, sarsaparilla, sassafras, senna, sumac.[155] A correspondent of Hannah More's, speaking of these drugs, truly asked, "What were the battles of Bunker's Hill and Long Island, compared to these?" [156].

From limited areas of the earth's surface, and from times immemorial, have come the precious spices. Allspice, cloves, cinnamon, nutmegs, and above all, pepper, continued to offer both first and last aid to the prodigal, or the economical, cook. In 1796, for example, pepper was imported to the value of £254,-194;[157] in 1799, importations of this commodity brought £295,712.[158] And yet several factors were at work to lessen their raison d'être: new vegetables, both from the continent, and from overseas; better meat, with less need for disguising it, due to improved methods of stock-breeding; the growing appreciation of natural vintages, rather than of spiced wines; and finally the addition to the culinary repertoire of such necessities as sugar, chocolate, and vanilla.

The consumption of spices in Europe, formerly so prodigiously great as to render the possession of the countries which produced them the great fountain of the vast wealth and power of the Dutch East India Company . . . has of late (1796) fallen off so much, that the monopoly of the trade is no longer worth preserving at the enormous expense of keeping the islands.[159]

Some of the uses of oversea spices may be discovered by culling from the pages of a contemporary cook-book. Ginger was frequently used in preparing fowls.[160] Anchovies were employed as seasoning.[161] Caraway seeds were used to make cordials.[162] A drink called "aqua mirabilis" was made from cubebs, cardamons, galengal, cloves, mace, nutmegs, cinnamon, and certain domestic herbs.[163] The old-fashioned still mixed ambergris and musk with wine.[164] The following recipe for making a "strong mead," gives in quaint phrases of the age, the method of mixing a typical spiced wine:

Take of spring water what quantity you please and make it more than blood warm, and dissolve Honey in it, till 'tis strong enough to bear an Egg, the breadth of a Shilling; then boil it gently near an Hour, taking off the scum as it rises; then put to about nine or ten Gallons, seven or eight blades of *Mace,* three *Nutmegs* quartered, twenty *Cloves,* three or four Sticks of *Cinnamon,* two or three Roots of *Ginger,* and a quarter of an ounce of *Jamaica Pepper;* put these Spices into the Kettle to the Honey and Water, a whole *Lemon,* with a sprig of Sweet-briar, and a sprig of Rosemary, etc.[165]

As early as 1728, it was felt that pimento, a new importation from the West Indies, was lessening the consumption of the older spices.[166] From 1793 to 1807, an average of 1,767,500 pounds of pimento per annum was shipped from the West Indies.[167] From the same source came vanilla, too, with its grateful aromatic qualities, and used for flavouring candy, perfumery, or even for medicinal purposes. Ginger, long popular as a far Eastern product, now became a considerable export from the West Indies.[168] In 1787, they sent to the mother country, 616,444 pounds of pimento, and 105,470 pounds of ginger.[169] While the older spices were not completely superseded,[170] it is clear that the substitution of new and milder flavourings, in conjunction with varied fruits, vegetables and beverages from overseas, made possible for the Englishman a lighter and more healthful diet.[171]

REFERENCES TO CHAPTER III

[1] Hazlitt, *Old Cookery Books and Ancient Cuisine*, pp. 71-79.

[2] *Ibid*, p. 84.

[3] Gillespie, *op. cit.*, p. 44; Hazlitt, *op. cit.*, p. 65.

[4] Eden, *The State of the Poor*, I, p. 501.

[5] Kalm, *Account of His Visit to England*, p. 15.

[6] *The Post-Boy*, 17/19 Jan., 1712.

[7] Eden, *op. cit.*, I, p. 501.

[8] *Ibid*, I, p. 533.

[9] Rumford's *Essays, Political, Economical and Philosophical*, p. 277. A popular cook-book, written about the end of the century, gives recipes for preparing potatoes in no less than twelve ways: boiled, broiled, roasted, fried, mashed, potato cheesecakes, pastry, pudding with meat, plain potato pudding, potato rolls. Rundell, *A New System of Domestic Cookery*.

[10] *Report of the Board of Agriculture, concerning the Culture and Use of Potatoes*, p. 84.

[11] DeCandolle, *L'Origine des Plantes Cultivées*, p. 317.

[12] "If it be true, as we are confidently told it is, that Maize will thrive and succeed, as well in England, as it does in the United States of America, and in many of the circles of Germany, it is not easy to assign a good reason for its not being more generally cultivated. On land equally good, with but equal skill and labour, the increase is said to be greater than wheat, and the saving of labour in the in-gathering, during the busy season of harvest, is of very serious moment." Eden, I, p. 524.

[13] *Ibid*, I, p. 527.

[14] *Ibid*, I, p. 524.

[15] Importations of maize from 1771 to 1790, inclusive, totalled but 32,000 quarters. Anderson, IV, pp. 233-234; Macpherson, *Annals*, IV, p. 217. After the banner year, 1795, when 20,586 quarters were imported, the average importation of maize fell to an average of approximately three thousand quarters a year. *Ibid*, IV, p. 534.

[16] *An Enumeration of the Principal of Vegetables, etc., that may be Substituted in Place of Wheat, and other Bread-corn* (1796), pp. 22-23.

[17] 23 Geo. III. c. 56.

[18] *Annual Register*, 1796, p. 110.

[19] Macpherson, *Annals*, IV, p. 362.

[20] Anderson, III, p. 183.

[21] Importation of rice to England in the late century ran as follows: in 1772-1773, 457,122 cwt., *Ibid*, IV, p. 448. In 1791, 226,381 cwt.; in

1793, 231,864 cwt.; in 1795, 144,859 cwt.; in 1797, 116,395 cwt., and in 1800, 304,914 cwt. Macpherson, *Annals*, IV, p. 534.

[22] Smith, E., *The Compleat Housewife* (1734); Rundell, *op. cit.* (1808, 3d ed.).

[23] Phillips, *Pomarium Britannicum*, p. 238.

[24] *Ibid*, p. 240.

[25] *Annual Register*, 1770, p. 109.

[26] Hazlitt, p. 84.

[27] Smith, J., *A Dictionary of Plants*, p. 388.

[28] Phillips, *op. cit.*, p. 183.

[29] *Ibid*, p. 184.

[30] *Ibid*, p. 321.

[31] Smith, J., *op. cit.*, p. 353.

[32] Misson, *Memoirs and Observations in his Travels over England*, p. 34.

[33] Dates of inferior quality were used, and highly prized for medicinal purposes, especially to "assuage all immoderate fluxes of the stomach, coughs, and vomitings." Phillips, p. 151.

[34] *Ibid*, p. 166.

[35] Candolle, *op. cit.*, p. 241.

[36] Ashton, *Social Life in the Reign of Queen Anne*, I, pp. 195-6.

[37] Anderson, III, p. 298.

[38] Phillips, pp. 231, 278.

[39] *Ibid*, p. 279.

[40] *Annual Register*, 1761, pp. 125-126.

[41] Macpherson, *Annals*, IV, p. 504.

[42] Phillips, p. 233.

[43] *Ibid*, pp. 248-249.

[44] *Encyclopaedia Britannica*, art. "melon."

[45] Candolle, pp. 243-246; Phillips, p. 306.

[46] Candolle, pp. 178-179; Phillips, p. 285.

[47] Candolle, p. 163; Phillips, p. 335.

[48] Gillespie, *op. cit.*, pp. 51-53.

[49] Phillips, p. 297.

[50] *Ibid*, pp. 299-300.

[51] *Ibid*, p. 300. This author prophesied that within the next half-century, "We shall have African gardens of great extent on the Thames, and pineapples cried through our streets two for a crown." *Ibid*, p. 301. He predicted also popular use of the "aki, the avocade pear of the West Indies, the flat peaches, the mandarine orange, and the Litchi of China, the mango, the mangostan, and the durien of the East Indies." *Ibid*.

[52] Before sugar came in quantities from the West Indies, it cost four times its price in 1772. Oldmixon, *British Empire in America*, I, p. 18.

[53] *Read's Weekly Journal or British Gazetteer,* 8 Jan., 1732.

[54] *Ibid;* see also Hazlitt, p. 55.

[55] Oldmixon, *op. cit.,* II, p. 159.

[56] Hanway, *Letters on the Importance of the Rising Generation of the Labouring Part of our Fellow Subjects,* II, p. 185.

[57] In 1747, Hannah Glasse published her "Complete Confectioner." In the introduction, she said there was nothing else available for reference or consultation. See Hazlitt, p. 155. Hazlitt also says, that beginning with Nott's *Cook Book* (1723), there is more frequent mention of "Marmalades, blanc-manges, creams, biscuits, and sweet cakes." p. 84.

[58] Gee, p. 46. This author states (1732): "It is said, before the War, that 10 or 12 Millions of Pounds was as much as we spent at Home annually; but of late our Consumption has been about 60 Millions of Pounds (for Sugar)."

[59] Anderson, III, p. 265, and IV, p. 320.

[60] *Ibid,* III, p. 265.

[61] *Ibid,* IV, p. 320.

[62] *Ibid,* IV, p. 445.

[63] *Ibid,* IV, p. 660.

[64] Macpherson, *Annals,* IV, p. 263. In 1794, London alone received shipments of sugar to the extent of 1,809,908 cwt. *Ibid,* IV, p. 364.

[65] Hanway, *Essay on Tea* (1766), p. 218.

[66] *Ibid,* p. 221.

[67] For the effects of these beverages on manners and customs, see below, Chapters VI, VII and VIII.

[68] Ashton, *op. cit.,* p. 221.

[69] *Daily Courant,* 4 Jan., 1703.

[70] "Wednesday. From eight to ten. Drank two Dishes of Chocolate in Bed, and fell asleep after them." *Spectator,* 11 Mar., 1712.

[71] Mrs. Delany, *Autobiography and Correspondence,* I, p. 74, mentions the increased cost of chocolate in 1727.

[72] Phillips, pp. 74-75. Also "about a century ago (1693), the choclate-nut was a principal article of export from Jamaica. Now, it is believed, there is not one plantation of it in the island." (1793).

[73] Oldmixon, II, p. 396.

[74] *The Daily Courant,* 11 Jan., 1703.

[75] *Ibid,* 15 Feb., 1703.

[76] *The Post-Boy,* 1/3 Jan., 1712; *Mist's Weekly Journal,* 20 July, 1728.

[77] Phillips, p. 77.

[78] Misson, *op. cit.,* p. 28.

[79] *The Daily Courant,* 8 Aug., 1712.

[80] *The Post-Man,* 3/5 July, 1707.

[81] *The Post-Boy,* 1/3 Jan., 1712.

[82] *Read's Wkly. Jl.,* or *Brit. Gaz.,* 6 Jan., 1728.

[83] By Sir Nicholas Lawes, in 1728. Gardner, *History of Jamaica,* p. 111.

[84] *Read's Wkly. Jl.,* or *Brit. Gaz.,* 19 Feb., 1732.

[85] Anderson, III, p. 183.

[86] Importations of coffee to England from the West Indies:

Year.	Pounds.	
1772	449,880	Anderson, IV, p. 451.
1774	654,700	Macpherson, *Annals,* IV, p. 217.
1780	735,392	*Ibid.*
1788	1,035,369	*Ibid.*
1790	1,783,740	*Ibid.*

[87] "In the year 1752, the export of coffee from Jamaica was rated at 60,000 lbs. . . . in 1808, the exports of Jamaica were 29,528,273 lbs." Phillips, pp. 114-115. In 1799, there were 686 coffee plantations in Jamaica (Edwards, III, p. 113), totalling 30,000 acres in a highly prosperous condition. Gardner, p. 321.

[88] 23 George, III, c. 79.

[89] Mosely, *A Treatise Concerning the Properties and Effects of Coffee,* p. 32.

[90] *Ibid,* p. 37.

[91] *Ibid,* p. 41. It is interesting that even in the nineteenth century coffee was regarded as having restorative, if not actually medicinal qualities, and was recommended for headache, for gout, against overdoses of opiates, and for other troubles. Phillips, p. 117 f.

[92] Mosely, *op. cit.,* p. 54.

[93] Dr. Fothergill, *Observations on Diet,* in *European Magazine,* July, 1784.

[94] Phillips, p. 121.

[95] Macpherson, *Commerce with India,* p. 131.

[96] *Ibid.*

[97] *The Post-Boy,* 31 July, 1707.

[98] *Ibid,* 21 Dec., 1712.

[99] Mrs. Delany, *op. cit.,* I, p. 74.

[100] *Read's Wkly. Jl.* or *Brit. Gaz.,* 8 Jan., 1732.

[101] Hanway, *An Essay on Tea,* p. 216.

[102] Macpherson, *Annals,* IV, p. 336; for another estimate of importations see Rose, pp. 45-46.

[103] Hanway, *op. cit.,* p. 268.

[104] The total for this year of 18,852,675 lbs., included 6,493,816 of Bohea, 4,366,136 of Congo, 1,113,900 of Souchong, 5,355,251 of Singlo, and 1,623,572 of Hyson. This table includes tea destined for reexportation. Anderson, IV, p. 667.

[105] *Applebee's Original Weekly Journal,* 19 Aug., 1721.

[106] Raynal, *op. cit.,* V, ii., p. 139.

[107] Anderson, IV, p. 551.

[108] 24 Geo. III sess 2, c. 38.

[109] See above, p. and n. 104.

[110] Hanway, *Letters*, etc., II, pp. 179, 181.   For smuggling, see Ch. VII.

[111] Hanway, *Essay on Tea*, p. 245.

[112] *Ibid*, pp. 222-223.

[113] *Ibid*, p. 218.

[114] "How many SWEET CREATURES of your sex, languish with weak digestions, low spirits, lassitudes, melancholy, and twenty disorders, which in spite of the Faculty have yet no names, except the general one of Nervous Complaints?   Tell them to change their Diet, and among other Articles, to leave off drinking Tea, it is more than probable the greatest part of them will be restored to health."   *Ibid*, p. 220.

[115] *Ibid*, pp. 208, 213.

[116] *Annual Register*, 1761, p. 262.

[117] Macpherson, *Commerce with India*, p. 132, n. 1; see also Eden, *op. cit.*, I, p. 532.

[118] Craik, II, p. 215; see also Chapter IX.

[119] Anon, *A Sunday Ramble* (1807), p. 72.

[120] See below, on temperance, Ch. X.   Gin was accused of being a vile creature, and a "Vampyre" to the nation, but was tolerated because her friends, "Mr. Rum and that moderate Lady, Mrs. Punch," could hardly under the circumstances be abandoned.   In fact, "great intercession was made in particular for Mr. Rum and Mme. Punch; it being alleged in their Behalf, that our Sugar Colonies and several other Branches of our Trade depended very much upon them."   *The Country Journal, or the Craftsman*, 5 June, 1736.

[121] Macpherson, *Annals*, IV, p. 364; Anderson, IV, p. 452.

[122] These figures are given in Anderson, IV, p. 452.

[123] Kalm, *op. cit.*, pp. 119-120.

[124] *The Humours of a Coffee-House*, 30 July, 1707.   Cowper's eulogy to tobacco, in *The Pipe and the Snuff Box*, is strikingly similar.

[125] For the history of tobacco in England prior to the eighteenth century, see Gillespie, p. 105.

[126] Anderson, II, p. 34.

[127] Statistics of home consumption are not given for this date.   *The Importance of the Brit. Plant. in America* (1731), p. 37.

[128] Anderson, III, p. 265.   Its value at this time was estimated at 6s. the pound, although the retail price was considerably higher.

[129] *Ibid*, IV, p. 187.

[130] *Ibid*, IV, p. 453.

[131] Before it was cultivated on an extensive scale, tobacco cost from 4s. to 16s. a pound to the consumer.   By 1768, it had dropped to 17d. to the merchant.   Oldmixon, I, p. xxii.

[132] In 1787 Pitt complained that 700,000 pounds of tobacco were annually smuggled into England. Macpherson, *Annals,* IV, p. 189.

[133] *The Spectator,* 4 March, 1712.

[134] Misson, *op. cit.,* p. 62.

[135] *The Daily Courant,* 22 Aug., 1707.

[136] *The Post-Boy,* 1/3 Jan., 1712.

[137] The coquetry of the fair sex is wittily described in *Spectator,* 4 April, 1712; see also *Tatler,* 29 Mar., 1709/10.

[138] *Spectator,* 8 Aug., 1711.

[139] *The Weekly Jl.,* or *Brit. Gaz.,* 11 June, 1720; Walpole, *Letters to Sir Horace Mann,* 21 July, and *to the Countess of Aylesbury,* 13 June, 1761.

[140] *The Daily Courant,* 30 Dec., 1707.

[141] For recipes used in compounding home-made medicines, see Smith, E., *op. cit.,* pp. 269-348.

[142] *The Post-Man,* 16/18 Feb., 1703.

[143] *The Daily Courant,* 30 Dec., 1707.

[144] *The Post-Man,* 21/23 Oct., 1703.

[145] *Ibid,* 3/5 July, 1707.

[146] *The Daily Courant,* 30 Dec., 1707.

[147] *Ibid,* 30 Dec., 1707.

[148] Brown, Thos., *The Dispensary,* passim. During the first part of the century, this supply came from surreptitious trade with Spanish colonies or with the less surreptitious seizure of Spanish galleons. In 1762, for example, 122 serons of quinine, weighing 200 pounds each, were acquired in this manner. Anderson, IV, pp. 7-8.

[149] Macpherson, *Annals,* IV, p. 542. The sassafras tree is believed to have been first introduced into Kew Gardens in 1782, when it attained a height of forty feet. Smith, J., *Dict. of Plants,* p. 370.

[150] *Ibid,* p. 12; Chambers' *Encyclopaedia.*

[151] Smith, p. 11, pp. 81-82; Chambers' *Encyclopaedia.*

[152] *Read's Weekly Jl.,* or *Brit. Gaz.,* 1 Aug., 1732.

[153] *Letter of Walpole to Sir Horace Mann,* 24 Nov., 1774.

[154] For medicinal uses of opium and its derivatives see *British Apollo,* 6/8 Mar., 1710; *Annual Register,* 1763, p. 116; *European Magazine,* Jan., 1785.

[155] Macpherson, *op. cit.,* IV, pp. 664-665.

[156] *Letter of Mr. Langhorne to Hannah More,* 19 Dec., 1776.

[157] Macpherson, *Annals,* IV, p. 426.

[158] *Ibid,* IV, p. 504.

[159] *Ibid,* IV, pp. 371-372.

[160] Smith, *Compleat Housewife,* pp. 350-352.

[161] *Ibid,* p. 3.

[162] *Ibid,* pp. 233 and 236.

[163] *Ibid,* p. 229.

[164] *Ibid,* p. 230.

[165] *Ibid,* p. 208.   Commodities of oversea origin are in italics.

[166] Boyer, *Political State of Great Britain,* xxv (Feb., 1728) ; Edwards, III, p. 148.

[167] Gardner, p. 322.

[168] Smith, J., *Dict. of Plants,* p. 425.

[169] Macpherson, *Annals,* IV, p. 159.   For the decrease in ginger importations at the close of the century, see Edwards, III, p. 140 ff.

[170] Macpherson, *op. cit.,* IV, p. 426.

[171] In 1732, spices sold at these prices:

    cinnamon, 7s. 9d. the pound.
    cloves, 9s. 1d. the pound.
    mace, 15s. 6d. the pound.
    nutmegs, 8s. 6d. the pound.
    pepper, 14s. 2d. the pound.

Drugs were sold as follows:

    balsam of Peru, 16s.
    cardamons, 3s. 4d.
    camphire (refined), 18s.
    crabs' eyes, 22d.
    jallop, 3s. 9d.
    manna, from 1s. 6d. to 3s. 6d.
    mastic (white), 4s. 6d.
    opium, 11s.
    balsam Coprava, 2s. 10d. *Read's Wkly. Jl., or Brit. Gaz.,* 8 Jan., 1732.

CHAPTER IV

CHANGES IN PERSONAL AND HOUSEHOLD ADORNMENT

The Fan shall flutter in all Female Hands,
And various Fashions learn from various Lands,
For this shall Elephants their Iv'ry shed;
And polish'd Sticks the waving Engine spread;
His clouded Mail the Tortoise shall resign,
And 'round the Rivet pearly Circles shine.
On this shall Indians all their Art employ,
And with bright Colours stain the gaudy Toy;
Their Pain shall here in wildest Fancies slow,
Their Dress, their Customs, their Religion show,
So shall the British Fair their Minds improve,
And on the Fan to distant Climates rove.
Here shall the Chinese Dame her Pride display,
And silver Figures gild her loose Array;
She boasts her little Feet and winking Eyes,
And tunes the Fife, or tinkling Cymbal plies;
Here cross-legg'd Nobles in rich State shall dine,
When on the Floor large painted Vessels shine,
For these, O China, shall thy Realms be sought,
With these, shall Europe's mighty Shops be fraught,
Thy glitt'ring Earth shall tempt their Ladies' Eyes,
Who for thy brittle Jars shall Gold despise.

Thus wrote John Gay in his whimsical treatise of
1714,[1] depicting various alterations in costume and
furbelows brought about by intercourse with distant
lands overseas. Literally the lands of the seven seas

were combed for articles of personal adornment. The Orient furnished the most delicate silks and satins, and later the finest varieties of cotton goods, such as calicoes, muslins and crepes.[2] From lands overseas came gold, silver, diamonds, rubies, pearls, amber, ivory, tortoise-shell, as well as cosmetics and perfumes. "I consider woman as a beautiful and romantic animal," said Addison,[3] "that may be adorned with furs and feathers, pearls and diamonds, ores and silks. The lynx shall cast its skin at her feet, to make her a tippet; the peacock, parrot and swan shall pay contribution to her muff, the sea shall be searched for shells and the rocks for gems; and every part of nature furnish out its share towards the embellishment of a creature that is the most consummate work of it." The eighteenth century man was no less gorgeous than his mate, and Addison's words might have been applied to him with equal truth.

While Versailles continued to set the fashion for the beau monde,[4] England depended on its own activities overseas for a large part of fashion's materials. The unwillingness of the mercantilist to decrease his balance of gold in favour of France made him more zealous of a British empire, self-sufficient in regard to luxuries as well as necessities. Indeed the gentry and nobility were not loath to alter the decrees of Versailles, if a favourable balance of trade might be secured thereby. Since the days of Charles II costume seems to have had little or nothing of royal patronage, and the ever-changing goddess of fashion owed her mode and eccentricities largely to the more

influential nobility and commoners.[5]   The vast increase
in oversea commerce, therefore, served at once to enlarge the stocks of materials and articles of personal
adornment, and the numbers of those able by their
newly acquired wealth to follow fashion's dictates.[6]

It is evident that for the first half of the century
London alone set the fashions, and with changes of
such rapidity that the country gentry were unable to
follow the pace.   As a result, the visitor to the country

finds as great a Variety of Garbs and Habits in the Persons
he converses with. . . . If instead of running after the Mode,
they would continue fixed in one certain Habit, the Mode
would some time or other overtake them, as a Clock that
stands still is sure to point right once in twelve Hours.[7]

The town citizen from the beginning aped the man
of fashion.   As the "Female Tatler" observes:

If anything can equal the contempt which a man of fashion
has for a citizen, it is that which the citizen has for the man
of fashion; only with this difference, that the man of fashion
is uniform and consistent in his contempt, and that the citizen
is so far otherwise that he attempts to imitate those very customs and manners which he affects to contemn.[8]

As the century waned, one observes a growing uni-
formity in dress.   Even at the time of Misson's visit
(1719), it was said that "every tradesman is a merchant, every merchant a gentleman, and every gentleman one of the *noblesse*." [9]   In fact, it became impossible to distinguish the aristocracy from the middle
classes, as far as dress was concerned.   According to
a statement of the time: "Dress, fashion and affectation have put all upon an equality; so that it is diffi-

cult to tell the milliner from her ladyship, my lord
from the groom, or his grace in Pall-Mall from the
tallow-chandler in Wapping." [10]

By the close of the century, class distinction in dress
had disappeared—a fact which was made possible by
the cheapening influence of cotton.[11]   As a contemporary put it:

> The very servant not only apes but rivals her mistress in
> every specie of whim and extravagance.   All sorts of people
> are consequently confounded or melted down into one glaring
> mass of superfluity or absurdity.   The lower orders are entirely
> lost in a general propensity to mimic the finery of the higher;
> and every woman we meet would seem by her gesture and
> apparel to possess at least an independent fortune.[12]

Even in rural districts one finds similar complaints
of an unpleasing similarity in clothes:

> The next figure I saw, 'twas a milliner's maid,
> A high cap and pink ribbons adorning her head,
> She stalked like a peacock, when waving her fan,
> And used an umbrella upon a new plan;
> Her elbows she lean'd on her hoops as on crutches,
> And wagged her silk gown with the air of a duchess.[13]

This would indicate that the country was now following more closely the trend of town fashions.[14]
"Fifty years ago," said a writer in 1761, "the dress
of people in distant counties was no more like those
in town than Turkish or Chinese.   But now in the
course of a tour you will not meet with a high-crowned
hat or a pair of red stockings." [15]   Here again the
popularity of cotton and the increased production and
cheapened price made possible by the Industrial Revo-

lution were important factors in bridging the gap between country and town.

It is the province of the present chapter to note, not the constant changes of fashion, but rather the dependence of fashion on lands overseas. One may realize this dependence by a perusal of the advertisements of stolen clothing. In 1711, for example, there were purloined from the house of a Mr. Peter

1 Isabella Colour Gown flowered with Green and Gold, 1 Silver Lace half an Ell deep, 1 Silver Orrice, ¼ Yard deep a large Parcel of black and silver Fringe, 1 purple and gold Atlas Gown, 1 scarlet and gold Petticoat edged with Silver 1 black Velvet Petticoat, 1 white Sattin Gown lined with black Silk, 1 Petticoat, strip'd with green, gold and white, 2 silver Laces each ¼ Yard deep, 1 yellow Chintz Gown and Petticoat, 1 Pair Shoes and Clogs lac'd with Silver, 1 dark colour Cloth Petticoat, with a Silver Orrice, 1 White Damask Lining for a Gown, 1 Silver Tankard about a Pint, 1 wrought Silver Cup about a Pint, 4 Silver Spoons.[16]

In the advertisement quoted above, as well as in these items which follow, it is only necessary to notice the universal use of silk and satin,[17] the prominence of gold and silver trimmings, and the variety of shades and colours made possible by new dyestuffs from overseas.[18]

The ladies of 1719 must have presented a colourful appearance, if one is to judge by this description:

Behold one equipped in a black silk Petticoat with red and white calico border, cherry-coloured Stays trimmed with blue and silver, a red and dove-coloured damask Gown flowered with large trees, a yellow Satin Apron, trimmed with white persian, and muslin Headclothes with crowfoot edging, double Ruffles with fine edging, a silk-furbelowed Scarf, and a spotted Hood.[19]

A lady's riding-dress, advertised for sale was "of blue Camblet, well-lac'd with silver, being a coat, waistcoat, petticoat, hat, and feather," [20] while the costume of a Mrs. Beale, lost in 1712, was fully as rich.

Nor was men's costume less ornate. The loss suffered by Mr. John Osheal in 1714, furnishes several items of a gentleman's wardrobe:

A scarlet suit, laced with broad gold lace, lined and faced with blue; a fine cinnamon cloth suit, with plate buttons, the waistcoat fringed with a silk fringe of the same colour; and a rich yellow flowered satin morning-gown, lined with a cherry-coloured satin, with a pocket on the right side.[21]

From about 1740 to 1760, claret-coloured, as well as light-blue, cloths were considered handsome suits. Both of these shades were made possible by new dye-stuffs. Silver button-holes and silver garters were fashionable adjuncts to such costumes.[22] Women continued to wear many-coloured and beflowered silk gowns, and petticoats with gold or silver nets.[23] Fashion called for diamond-buckled shoes for both sexes.[24] In fact the wearing of jewels was a serious demand, of feminine fashion at least.[25] The nabobs' ladies were especially favoured; and they appeared at the fashionable watering-places and at social functions in town resplendent in diamonds, rubies and pearls, grotesquely draped about their persons.[26] Queen Charlotte, wife of George III, wore on her wedding day a stomacher worth £3,000, and a tiara of diamonds.[27]   It was the custom, too, for women to borrow jewels of each other, and to appear at social functions glittering with all the brilliance of another's glory.   Even the Queen was guilty of the practice.[28]

In passing, it may be interesting to note the influence of the American Indian on dress.   Philosophers of the time, who compared unfavourably the sordidness of an artificial civilization with the happiness of the savage, urged a "return to nature."   This sentiment was accepted by the public in its adoption of a new fad in landscape gardening and in various outdoor recreations.[29]   The simplicity of clothes, which marked the close of the century, was possibly another material result of this process of reasoning.[30]   It was felt that the loose, comfortable, and commodious garb of the savage was far more agreeable than the "compressive ligatures of modern drapery," as well as more conducive to health.[31]   In the matter of head-dress, this influence was marked.   Cuts of the period (1775-1795) show a marked resemblance between the English head-dress and that of the American Indian.   Hannah More wrote to her sister in 1776, that women were wearing four or five ostrich feathers of different colours at the back of their perpendicular caps.[32]   In fact, till the close of the century, the use of from three to seven feathers for decorating the head, was popular.[33]

Fur was another valuable adjunct to dress.   Creators of fashion and mercantilists alike favoured many uses for skins, large importations of which came annually to England.   During the reign of

Queen Anne, hats of black and white beaver were worn
by ladies of fashion, and plain, broad-brimmed ones
by women with less expensive tastes.[34]   They remained
in style well into the third decade, when they were
edged with coloured silks, and trimmed with gold and
silver lace.[35]   Men, too, adopted this expensive luxury
for their head-gear, although it must have proved
rather warm for comfort.[36]   Statistics show in general
the increased popularity of furs, but their use declined
at times according to the dictates of fashion.   In
1731 Craik reports that £6,000 worth of peltry was
imported annually from America.[37]   About 1750, the
popularity had diminished so much that it was feared
the trade might disappear.[38]   Towards the close of
the century importations had reached large proportions, for in 1782, the sales of furs and peltry in
London amounted to £189,000.[39]

Likewise, in the time of Queen Anne, it was fashionable for beaux to wear beaver muffs, a fashion
gently satirized by Addison.[40]   Muffs of leopard skins
were preferred by the fair sex.[41]   Ermine rivalled silk
as the popular material for petticoats.[42]   With the
adoption of bear-skin caps by George III for his
army the uses of fur during the eighteenth century
have been duly chronicled.

A substantial revolution in dress was made possible
by the introduction of that new commodity from overseas: cotton.   In spite of legislation which sought
to prohibit the importation of articles of this material,
their use continued to increase.[43]   The extent of
damage to woollen manufactures caused by the lessened

consumption of them is made clear by contemporary writers.[44]   Steele blamed this decline upon

a tawdry, pie-spotted, flabby, ragged, low-priced thing, called callicoe; a foreigner by birth; made the Lord knows where, by a parcel of heathens and pagans that worship the devil and work for a half-penny a day. . . . The fashion is the grievance, because it is a fashion; it is in the ladies' power at once to make it odious and abhorred all over the kingdom. . . . If the women in England will but set their hands to this work, not a callicoe, not a piece of linen printed or stained, shall be sold in England.[45]

Fashion and women, however, decreed otherwise. A contemporary states that muslin was popular in 1756, and again in 1760 affirmed that nothing else was talked of at Bath, but "crapes, bombazeens, thick muslins." [46]   Fifteen hundred yards of crepe were sold in one shop during one night.[47]   Calico had come to stay, and England showed its usual adaptability in making later the manufacture of it and cotton in general a mighty industry of its own.[48]

A great change in wearing apparel, then, was the substitution of cotton for wool and silk.   As early as 1700 handkerchiefs had become a necessity in the days when snuff-taking was at its height.[49]   Among the members of the fair sex handkerchiefs of Flanders lace brought as high as £10, while Turkey handkerchiefs fetched half that price.[50] The value of calico and other cotton handkerchiefs must have been high, for they were regarded as prize-hauls by pickpockets.[51] Cotton, too, was in demand for the hooped petticoat.[52] Printed calicoes were favoured materials for gowns for day-time wear, as well as for dressing-gowns and night-gowns for both sexes.[53]   Beau Brummel and his colleagues utilized the new material, and fresh "linen" became synonymous with "gentlemen." In pursuit of this ambition the beau often used three shirts a day.[54] The wearer of an untidy shirt was immediately dubbed a country lout, who was known to change his linen but twice a week. The famous running-footmen of the thirties owed their tidiness to the wearing of cotton garments, undoubtedly following their fastidious masters in this respect.[55] By 1745 printed calicoes were in demand for bedroom furnishings, replacing rich and dusty velvet.[56] This change added both charm and cleanliness to the third of man's life which, till now, had received little consideration. Certainly before the close of the century the craze for muslins, chintzes and printed calicoes was so pronounced and so permanent as to make them usurp the place of silks, satins, woollens and velvets. With the adoption of the cheaper grades by the people of the new manufacturing centres England became a country more attractively garbed. Because of the cheapness of the materials, frequent change was now possible, resulting in a higher standard of personal hygiene. Nor can the psychological effect of new, clean and attractive garments on the wearer be overestimated.

From the Orient, too, came another fashion—the daily cold bath—which, though now an established English custom, was not of western origin. From the manner in which Hickey writes of his visit to Canton, China, in 1769, it seems evident that Englishmen as yet had not adopted the custom of cold tubbing daily:

Bob . . . told me the old gentleman regularly every morning between six and seven o'clock used a cold bath, in which after remaining near an hour, he rolled himself in a loose gown and lay down upon a couch, where the men I saw shampooed him. This is a prevalent custom in China, as well as every part of India. . . . Many Europeans (*i.e.,* those resident in the Orient) are extremely fond of it.[57]

From this passage it may be inferred that by the end of the century something so pleasant as to make Europeans "extremely fond of it" had found its way to England. The matter of when and under what circumstances the custom was introduced and became characteristic of the Englishman is not clear. It seems evident, however, that Hickey would not have noticed it, if Englishmen of his time either had originated it or had adopted it in intensive fashion.

From overseas, also, came various accessories to the complete costume. The substitution of the cane or stick for the sword really typified the displacement of the feudal lord by the gentleman. As late as 1700 swords continued to be worn as a customary appendage by men of fashion, though the well-bred gentleman found them an encumbrance. To a well-ordered society they were weapons, rather than adornments, in the hands of the unscrupulous. The first step toward their banishment came in 1701 when footmen were forbidden to disport side-arms.[58] Within thirty years polite young gentlemen had substituted large, heavy sticks for the sword.[59] Within another thirty

years the sword had become quite obsolete and walking sticks were reduced to a useful size. It was quite
evident, however, that the wearer was not yet accustomed to the new complement to costume:

But do not some of us strut about with walking-sticks as long
as leaping-poles, as if we were pioneers to the troop of Hickery-
cutters; or else with a yard of varnished cane, scraped taper,
and bound at one end with wax-thread, and the other tipt with
a neat-turned ivory head, as big as a silver penny, which switch
we hug under our arms so gaily? [60]

Materials for the finest canes came from abroad.
Malacca was the favourite wood, while tips were of
silver, gold, amber, or ivory.[61]

The idea of the umbrella came from the Orient,
whence its protective properties against the sun's op-
pressive heat were adapted to the liquid downpours
of the English climate. It could be used to advantage
in safeguarding woman's new finery from rain and
dampness. As a contemporary rhymester put the
matter:

Let Persian Dames th' Umbrella's Ribs display,
To guard their Beauties from the sunny Ray;
Or sweating Slaves support the shady Load,
When Eastern Monarchs shew their State abroad;
Britain in Winter only knows its Aid,
To guard from chilly Showers the walking Maid.[62]

So common did the umbrella become, that it was used
by the lower classes:

The tuck'd up semstress walks with hasty strides,
While Streams run down her oil'd Umbrella's sides.[63]

For a while this useful invention seems to have been considered too effeminate for men.[64]   It was not until the second half of the century that Jonas Hanway dared face the critical glances and comments of his fellows by appearing in public with an umbrella. Since India-rubber waterproofing was not to be discovered until more than a century later, men, as the less favoured sex, had to put their trust in good broadcloth coats or cloaks.   Not until the close of the century did the plebeian umbrella displace the aristocratic cane in rainy weather, and the gentleman could be protected from the wet without calling a sedan-chair or a coach.[65]

Other articles from overseas when suitably adapted became artful aids to costume.   In the early days of the century, when snuff-taking was endemic, snuff-boxes were highly prized possessions of both sexes. Made in all shapes and sizes, the material might be gold, silver, tortoise-shell, or mother-of-pearl, with sometimes an agate, or a "Moco stone" in the lid.[66] Ivory or tortoise-shell combs were used to adorn the heads of the ladies.[67] Similar materials were employed in assembling the fan, as an aid to social distinction. Expensive watches much adorned also came into fashion in the early part of the century.   A watch of gold or silver set with jewels was the proudest possession of the beau, who carried it on a fob or in a pocket of his breeches.   An outer ornamental case was often made of coloured satin or silk.[68]

In articles for the feminine toilet, lands overseas did indeed contribute votive offerings in greatest abundance:

And now, unveil'd, the toilet stands display'd,
Each silver vase in mystic order laid.
First, robed in white, the nymph intent adores,
With head uncover'd, the cosmetic powers.
A heavenly image in the glass appears,
To that she bends, to that her eyes she rears;
Th' inferior priestess, at her altar's side,
Trembling, begins the sacred rites of pride.
Unnumbered treasures ope at once, and here
The various off'rings of the world appear;
From each she nicely culls with curious toil,
And decks the goddess with the glittering spoil.
This casket India's glowing gems unlocks,
And all Arabia breathes from yonder box.
The tortoise and elephant unite,
Transformed to combs, the speckled and the white.
Here files of pins extend their shining rows,
Puffs, powders, patches, Bibles, billet-doux.
The fair each moment rises in her charms,
Repairs her smiles, awakens every grace,
And calls forth all the wonders of her face:
Sees by degrees a purer blush arise,
And keener lightnings quicken in her eyes.
The busy sylphs surround their darling care;
These set the head, and those divide the hair;
Some fold the sleeve, whilst others plait the gown;
And Betty's prais'd for labours not her own.[69]

Facial adornment in the eighteenth century was an
industry, not an art. Every conceivable dyestuff from
overseas bordering on red or white was employed to
its utmost in an effort to improve on nature. Carmine,
yellow ochre, verdigris, used in lip-salves and face-
pastes, must have been trying, if not actually injurious,
to the complexion.[70] None too gentle male critics

complained that the stuff used in cosmetics was "worse than they daub sign-posts with." [71]   The beau of the time was the "emasculated nothing," who swore pretty oaths, likewise painted himself, "purely to oblige the ladies." [72]   Evidently this practice continued throughout the century, for at its close, similar complaints are found.[73]

Dentifrices of exotic composition showed a lamentable ignorance of the first principles in the care of the teeth, if the following is a fair example:

Take four ounces of coral, reduced to an unpalpable powder, eight ounces of very light Armenian bole, one ounce of Portugal snuff, one ounce of Havannah snuff, one ounce of the ashes of good tobacco, which has been burnt, and one ounce of gum myrrh, which has been well pulverized.   Mix all these well together, and sift them twice.[74]

Instead of throwing the mixture away, the victim was advised to rub it on the teeth with his fingers! The use of wash-balls, in lieu of soap, coloured with injurious dyestuffs, must have added the final irritation to a long-suffering cuticle.[75]   A great many foreign soaps, however, scented with local and overseas odours, came into popularity during the century, and undoubtedly mitigated to some degree these earlier evils.[76]

During this period the ladies and dandies were especially fond of sweet smells, perfumes and scents. Charles Lillie, the prince of perfumers, left a score of recipes behind him, using these ingredients, so many of which were exotics:

Spirit of ambergris, musk, benjamin (benzoin), orange, lemons and citrons, bergamot, lavender; otto (*sic*) of roses and sandal (*sic*), citron, perfumed catchui, essence of jessamine; essence of orange flowers, lavender water. . . . Oil of Rhodium, roses, lavender, rosemary, cloves, cinnamon, marjoram, coriander.[77]

These perfumes, delicate and otherwise, were used to scent handkerchiefs, gloves, and all sorts of linen, as well as the hands, face and hair of their owners. The liberal sums spent for sweet odours raised their compounders to the status of conspicuous personages, as in the case of Lillie. The invigourating effect on the users is thus graphically described:

By their delicious smell, they comfort, revive, and refresh all the senses, natural, vital, and animal, enliven the spirits; cheer the heart, and drive away melancholy; they also perfume rooms, beds, presses, drawers, boxes, etc., making them smell surprisingly fine and odouriferous. They perfume the hands excellently, are an extraordinary scent for the pocket, and in short, are so exceedingly pleasant and delightful, so admirably curious and delicate, and of such general use, that nothing in the world can compare with them.[78]

Advertisements from four newspapers, as reprinted in one issue of the *European Magazine,* testify to the continued popularity of cosmetics at the close of the century.[79] The use of soap, now common, not only for the complexion, but for the family washing, made possible a cleanliness of person not dreamed of a century earlier. Clean underwear and shirts washed daily, no longer considered signs of effeminacy, were symbols of the typical English gentleman, whose cleanliness—enhanced by the daily bath—was admired by foreign visitors.[80]

Lands overseas—in particular the Orient—were likewise responsible for delicate, if not radical, changes in the adornment of homes. The eighteenth century opened with a fashionable passion for chinaware. Addison gives this fact prominence in his description of a typical lady's boudoir:

At the end of the folio were great jars of china placed one above the other in a very noble piece of architecture. The quartos were separated from the octavos by a pile of smaller vessels, which rose in a delightful pyramid. The octavos were bounded by tea-dishes of all shapes, colours, and sizes, which were so disposed on a wooden frame, that they looked like one continued pillar indented with the finest strokes of sculpture and stained with the greatest variety of dyes. That part of the library which was designed for the reception of plays and other loose pamphlets, was enclosed in a kind of square, consisting of one of the prettiest grotesque works that I ever saw, and made up of scaramouches, lions, monkeys, mandarines, trees, shells, and a thousand odd figures in china-ware.[81]

This practice increased with the growing popularity of tea-drinking. Defoe found china piled high on tops of cabinets, secretaries, and chimney-pieces, and on shelves set up to hold it.[82] Horace Walpole was a collector as well as a connoisseur of old china, and gave up this hobby for a new love, that of gardening, only late in life.[83] Mrs. Delany devoted considerable time and expense to collecting odd pieces of china, and sent sets of chinaware, including cups, saucers, basins, sugar-dishes, and plates, to her relatives in the country. In her visit to the Duke of Cumberland's lodge she found cabinets filled with precious articles of china, worth six hundred pounds.[84]   The several varieties of fine china made in England, in imitation of the Oriental, were equally expensive. The cost of Derby-ware, for example, was as high as that of silver and proved prohibitive to many prospective collectors.   As Dr. Johnson stated, in a letter to Mrs. Thrale, "I am not yet so infected with the contagion of china-fancy, as to like anything at that rate which can so easily be broken.[85]

Naturally it was inconceivable that English potters should permit vast sums of good English money to enrich Oriental artisans.   As early as 1698 the brothers Eller are supposed to have produced a fine red china, and to have sold tea-pots of this material in their London shop for from twelve to twenty-five shillings.[86]   From 1720 to 1740 the manufacture of fine china made considerable progress,[87] and in 1744 Heylyn took out a patent for making porcelain and china from a material discovered in Virginia, and by 1748 was turning out a ware "not inferior in beauty and fineness and superior in strength to the ware from the East." [88]   The truth of this statement, however, is questionable, for English manufactures of this product generally were considered inferior to the imported. Worcester-ware tea-pots, and other objects for the tea-table, were considered equal to the Chinese, while other pieces could be used to make up costly sets that were broken; yet

somehow or other, this manufacture has never found its way to the dining-table, except perhaps in sauce-boats, and toys for pickles and hors-d'ouvres; but by communicating this defect to the public, some remedy, perhaps, may be found for it.[89]

Josiah Wedgwood, who had already introduced several improvements into the art, answered these criticisms in a practical way. He had perfected a species of earthenware for the table, covered with a rich and brilliant glaze and capable of bearing sudden alterations of heat and cold, and of being manufactured quickly and cheaply. From this time on, then, articles for the dinner-table and for the tea-table, were manufactured in quantity, as well for exportation as for home consumption.[90]

For interior adornment owners sought picturesque pieces of furniture and lacquered ware from the Orient. As a contemporary remarked: "From the greatest gallants to the meanest cook-maids, nothing was thought so fit . . . for the ornaments of chambers like Indian screens, cabinets, beds, hangings, nor for closets like china and lacquered ware.[91] The mania for Oriental furniture and ornaments came to England with William and Mary. With Sir Christopher Wren in charge of the decoration of Hampton Court Palace, alcoves in the dining-room and even the carved chimney-places were equipped with receding shelves for china.[92] Chimney pieces were even modified to take care of large vases and bowls: "The height of the cornice (of the chimney-pieces) should be raised six feet in order that the vases with which they are ornamented may not be knocked down." [93] During the reign of Anne, the fad for Oriental adornment actually increased.   One over-mantel nearly sixteen feet high was adorned with eleven carved images and 275 cups, vases and bowls arranged symmetrically.   For the most part the decorative designs were of Chinese temples and dragons.[94]

As was the case with ceramics, the fancy prices which imported objects brought, induced English cabinet-makers to manufacture articles of furniture at home.   The importation of satinwood, in particular, enabled artisans to imitate successfully imported articles, and eventually to evolve new and attractive period furniture.   Satinwood was first made up by veneering, then was decorated with medallions, some of marquetry, some of Wedgwood ware, and in other instances painted with miniature scenes.[95]   In general English cabinet-makers bowed to the prevailing taste and imitated Chinese and Japanese work in black furniture, with lac-work panels and rich gilt metal mounts, or ornamented in gold-dust with raised Chinese figures.[96]   The importation of such materials as satinwood, teak- sandal- and Japan-woods, logwood, boxwood, redwood, ebony and ivory made possible many variations.[97]

The generic term for this style—Chinese Chippendale—owes its name to Thomas Chippendale, a successful carver and cabinet-maker of the period. His fashionable vogue came with the publication of his *Gentleman's and Cabinet Maker's Directory* in 1754; the list of subscribers included members of the nobility, gentry, joiners, carpenters, cabinet-makers, carvers and engravers.   As the author indicated in his preface: "If his (the prospective customer) taste runs to the Chinese now in vogue, here is an assortment of frets from which to select." There followed descriptions of various articles either in the pure Chinese manner, or in a combination of Chinese and Gothic: a china case, for example, which "was very proper for a lady's dressing-room may be made of any soft wood and japanned any colour"; or "China shelves," candle stands, fire screens, a "library-case and book-case," a number of "gerandoles" with pier-glass frames, and consol-tables, together with tea-trays, tables, chests of drawers, dressing cases, cabinets, clothes-chests, clock-cases—in short, a complete collection of articles of furniture.[98] Inasmuch as the carving on "Chinese" furniture made it too expensive for all but the wealthy,[99] master artisans like Chippendale, Sheraton, Lock and others, made other types of furniture, using for the most part materials from overseas.[100]

In short, the accumulation and the great diffusion of wealth arising directly from oversea expansion led their recipients to seek not only more comfort and luxury but a greater beauty in their own homes. What the purchasers might have lacked in taste was compensated for by their ability to purchase such attractive articles as have been mentioned above. People now, even those of moderate means, could afford glass windows. Tapestry, too often sombre and unhygienic, tended to give way to the more cleanly and attractive wall-paper, which was now often made in the Chinese manner. Feather hangings with their touch of colour

and of the picturesque must have made their owners
feel that former days were drab indeed:

> The birds put off their every hue,
>   To dress a room for Montagu.
> The peacock sends his heavenly dyes,
>   His rainbows and his starry eyes;
> The pheasant plumes which round infold
>   His mantling neck with downy gold;
> The cock his arched tail's azure show;
>   And river-blanched, the swan his snow.
> All tribes, beside of Indian name,
>   That glossy shine, or vivid flame.[101]

Indoors, then, decorations of a bygone age were,
according to a sarcastic commentator, "flung into the
garret as lumber, to make room for great-bellied Chinese pagodas, red dragons, and the ugliest monsters
that ever, or rather never existed." [102]   In exterior
decoration, the Chinese influence was somewhat more
subtle.   In the time of Queen Anne, a reaction set in
to the formal garden—the "Dutch morass" [103]—of
the preceding reign.   Leaders of the revolt were Pope
and Addison. As the latter remarked: "I would rather
look upon a Tree in all its Luxuriancy and Diffusion
of Boughs and Branches, than when it is thus cut and
trimmed into a Mathematical Figure; and cannot but
fancy that an Orchard in Flower looks infinitely more
delightful than all the little Labyrinths of the most
finished Parterre." [104]

In attempting to make gardens resemble nature,
landscape artists went out of their way to make things
irregular.   Following Kent's maxim, "Nature abhors

a straight line," serpentine walks and lakes were introduced, straight canals were replaced by miniature waterfalls, cascades, or artificial winding streams. One gardener actually cut down beautiful avenues of old trees to do away with straight lines.[105] Attempts were made to adapt landscapes to different moods. A wood was planted for rudeness or grandeur, a grove for beauty, a cave or grotto to strike terror in the hearts of observers.[106]

The new school of gardening was influenced by the Chinese; and the responsibility for the Chinese fad has generally been credited to Sir William Chambers, whose *Dissertation on Oriental Gardening,* written in 1772, became the text-book of landscape architects. The latter comprised a new species of experts; they must be acquainted, among other things, with the principles of optics, mechanics, geometry and trigonometry. As one observer put it: "Since it has been thought necessary to embellish rural scenes with all the varieties of architecture, from single pillars and obelisks, to bridges, ruins, pavilions, and even castles and churches, it is not enough for our professor to be as knowing as Solomon." [107]

While still a young man Chambers had made a voyage to China to study and to make actual measurements of Chinese gardens and buildings. The results of this trip were published in another volume, the purpose of which was intimated in his preface:

It was not my design to publish them, nor would they now appear were it not in compliance with the desire of several lovers of the arts, who thought them worthy of the perusal of the publick, and that they might be of use in putting a stop to the extraordinary fancies that daily appear under the name of Chinese, though most of them are mere inventions, the rest copies from the lame representations found on porcelain and paper hangings.[108]

Through the medium of Sir William Chambers, then, the principles of Chinese architecture were drafted into the English scheme, and were used particularly in the designing of homes and estates for the *nouveaux riches*.[109] While the new ideas had many critics, among them the ever-present Dr. Johnson,[110] other Englishmen were proud of the fact that they were the first of Europeans to adopt Chinese gardens.[111] Likewise, a mid-century critic asserted that "our gardens are already the astonishment of foreigners, and in proportion as they accustom themselves to consider and understand them, will become their admiration." [112]

Oriental landscape gardening was in vogue not only in private estates but in such public resorts as Ranelagh and Vauxhall.[113] Among the typical decorative devices were temples, bridges, summer-houses, cascades and waterfalls, dragon boats and treasure boats "as rich and gay as carving, gilding and japanning can make them," [114] palanquins and pagodas.[115] Contemporaries perhaps considered the crowning achievement of Chambers to be the pagoda which he designed for Kew Gardens.[116] This park, begun in 1760 by the mother of George III, represented rather another fashion enjoyed by a considerable number of Englishmen: experimental farming, which offered a lure far more potent than that of a non-productive Chinese estate. A poet of the late century rhapsodises thus on Kew:

> So sits enthroned, in vegetable pride,
> Imperial Kew by Thames' glittering side;
> Obedient sails from realms unfurrow'd bring
> For her the unnam'd progeny of Spring;
> Attendant Nymphs her dulcet mandates hear,
> And nurse in fostering arms the tender year;
> Plant the young bulb, inhume the living seed,
> Prop the weak stem, the erring tendril lead;
> Or fan in glass-built fanes the stranger flowers,
> With milder gales, and steep with warmer showers.
> Delighted Thames through tropic umbrage glides,
> And flowers antarctic, bending o'er his tides;
> Drinks the new tints, the sweets unknown inhales,
> And calls the sons of Science to his vales.[117]

Both inside the house and out of doors, then, the Chinese influence was prevalent. A critic of the time who was aware of the phenomenon, prophesied that soon the usual cultural trip would be made to China, rather than to Paris, and that the former would succeed to the dictatorship over the empire of taste: "Without doors, from the seats of our dukes, to the shops of our haberdashers, all is Chinese; and in most places within. . . . Raphael and Titian give place to the more pleasing masters of Surat and Japan."[118]

REFERENCES TO CHAPTER IV

[1] *The Fan.* See also the *Spectator* for 27 June, 1711.

[2] For statistics of cotton importations and effect on English industry, see above, Chapter II.

[3] *The Tatler,* 5 Jan., 1709/1710.

[4] Some authorities claim that at the time of the Revolution the French patterned their dress after the simplicity of the English and Americans, whose ideas of liberty and equality they desired to adopt. Lockitt, *The Relations of French and English Society* (1763-1793), pp. 40-42.

[5] Fairholt, *Costume in England,* p. 378.

[6] See below, Ch. VI.

[7] The *Spectator,* July 28, 1711.

[8] The *Female Tatler* (1709), quoted in Hill, *A History of English Dress,* p. 155.

[9] Misson, p. 37.

[10] *Annual Register,* 1761, p. 201.

[11] Even at the beginning of the century, there was a complaint that citizens, country people and servants "appear clothed, for the most part above and beyond their qualities, states or conditions, and far more gay than that sort of people were wont to be in former times." Chamberlayne, *New Present State of Great Britain,* p. 319 (1704).

[12] *European Magazine,* April, 1784, p. 245.

[13] West, *A Trip to Richmond in Surrey* (1787), p. 131.

[14] *Harleian Miscellany,* VIII, p. 36 (1692).

[15] Hill, *op. cit.,* p. 167. See above Chapter II for cotton and the Industrial Revolution.

[16] *The Daily Courant,* 1 Jan., 1712.

[17] *Applebee's Original Weekly Journal,* 13 March, 1736. To reduce the outpourings of bullion in payment for foreign silks, attempts were made to introduce silk-worms into the southern plantations. *Annual Register,* 1760, pp. 132-133.

[18] See above Ch. II.

[19] In *The Post-Boy,* 15 Nov., 1709, the above articles were advertised as lost. The early popularity of cottons is also to be noticed.

[20] *The Spectator,* 2 June, 1711; *The Weekly Register,* 10 July, 1731. See also Mrs. Delany, *op. cit.,* I, pp. 57, 173-174, 213-214, and II, p. 23, for further descriptions of jewels and costumes; also, Malcolm, *Anecdotes,* II, p. 320.

[21] Fairholt, *op. cit.,* pp. 358-359; Malcolm, *op. cit.,* II, p. 320.

[22] *Ibid,* II, p. 336; see also Ashton, I, p. 150.

[23] Malcolm, *op. cit.,* II, pp. 334-335.

[24] *Ibid.*

[25] *Ibid*, II, p. 337.

[26] Hill, p. 142.

[27] Malcolm, II, p. 336; likewise a silk gown made of material from Georgia.

[28] Lord Hervey, quoted by Mrs. Delany, I, p. 79.

[29] See below, pp. 107-110.

[30] Lockitt, *op. cit.*, pp. 40-42.

[31] *European Magazine,* July, 1785.

[32] Roberts, *Memoirs of the Life and Correspondence of Mrs. Hannah More,* I, p. 46. Feathers of the better grades, of course, came from overseas.

[33] Fairholt, pp. 389, 394; Hill, pp. 133, 150.

[34] *Ibid,* p. 73.

[35] Malcolm, II, p. 322.

[36] "Pretty black beaver tuck'd under his arm,
If plac'd on his head, might keep it too warm," in Hill, p. 107.

[37] Craik, II, p. 205.

[38] Oldmixon, I, p. 566.

[39] Anderson, IV, p. 441.

[40] *The Tatler,* 6 April, 1710; *The Spectator,* 19 Mar., 1711.

[41] Malcolm, II, p. 314.

[42] Hill, p. 145.

[43] See above Chapter II.

[44] "A List of the Woollen or Worsted Stuffs that the Callicoes Interfere with," is given in *The Weekly Journal,* 9 Jan., 1720.

[45] Steele, *The Female Manufacturers' Complaint,* p. 347.

[46] Mrs. Delany, II, p. 23.

[47] *Letter to Mrs. Dewes at Bath,* in *Ibid,* II, p. 82.

[48] Anderson, IV, p. 64 ff; Defoe, *Plan for English Commerce,* p. 296.

[49] Ashton, I, p. 155.

[50] Hill, pp. 138, 180.

[51] Gay, *The Beggar's Opera;* Fielding, *On the Late Increase of Robbers,* p. 222.

[52] *The Weekly Journal,* 17 Jan., 1717.

[53] Ashton, I, p. 161.

[54] *Ibid,* I, pp. 148-149.

[55] Malcolm, *Anecdotes,* I, p. 325.

[56] *Ibid,* II, pp. 320-321.

[57] Spencer, *Memoirs of William Hickey* (1749-1775), I, p. 209.

[58] Fairholt, p. 402; Traill, *Social England,* V, p. 497; *The London Gazette,* 1 Jan., 1701.

[59] *The Universal Spectator,* 1730, quoted in Malcolm, *Anecdotes,* II, p. 325; see also below, p. 271.

[60] "The History of the Fashions," in the *London Chronicle,* XI (1762), p. 167.

[61] Gay, *Trivia*, Bk. I.

[62] *Ibid.*

[63] The *Tatler*, 17 Oct., 1710. Cowper complainingly says of the maid:
"Too proud for dairy work or sale of eggs,
Expect her soon with footboy at her heels,
No longer blushing for her awkward load,
Her train and her umbrella all her care." *The Task*, IV, ll.
549-552.

[64] *The Female Tatler*, 12 Dec., 1709.

[65] *Traill*, V, pp. 494-495.

[66] The *Spectator*, 8 Aug., 1711; Ashton, I, pp. 158-159.

[67] The *Tatler*, 13 Aug., 1709, and 3 June, 1710. See also diary of a
lady in *Spectator*, 11 Mar., 1712.

[68] Ashton, I, p. 159.

[69] Pope, *Rape of the Lock*, Canto III.

[70] China supplied materials for face-pastes: a black eyebrow colour,
a red mixture for the cheeks and a pearl powder for the neck, while
India sent the roots for lip-salves. Hill, p. 83.

[71] Johnson, *The Gentleman Cully* (ed. 1702); *The Spectator*, 19
July, 1712.

[72] *The Tatler*, 14 Apr., 1709; *St. James's Park, a Satyr* (1709);
Baker, *Tunbridge Walks*, p. 26.

[73] *European Magazine*, Jan., 1783, p. 13.

[74] *The Wkly. Jl., or Sy's Post*, 21 May, 1720.

[75] Hill, pp. 82-84.

[76] Ashton, I, p. 127; Hill, pp. 171-172.

[77] Ashton, I, p. 126.

[78] Malcolm, *Anecdotes*, I, pp. 240-241.

[79] "Olympian Dew or Grecian Bloom-water, Cypress Hair Powder,
Poudre d'Artois, for finishing the hair, Pomade a la Mareschal Blanc,
Essence of Pearl for the teeth, Pearl Dentifrice, Pomade de Grasse,
for thickening the hair, the Balm of Lillies, Lilly Wash Ball, Liquid
Bloom of Roses, the Superlative Arabian Powder, for changing the
colour of the hair or eye-brows, the Blossom-milk of Circassia."
European Magazine, Jan., 1783.

[80] Grosley, *A Tour to London*, p. 66; *Memoirs of Mrs. Elizabeth
Carter*, I, p. 452; for comparison with French, Huchon, *op. cit.*,
p. 167 ff.

[81] *Spectator*, 12 April, 1711; see *The Lover*, 18 March, 1714, quoted
in Malcolm, I, pp. 242-243, for the popularity of this craze.

[82] Defoe, *Tour*, I, p. 122.

[83] *Letter of Walpole to Sir Horace Mann*, 3 May, 1749.

[84] *Mrs. Delany to Mrs. Dewes*, 25 Jan., 1745; *Ibid*, 11 July, 1747;
Ibid, 22 Sept., 1750; *Mrs. Delany to Bernard Granville*, 22 Sept.,

1750; *to Mrs. Anne Granville,* 1 Apr., 1729; *to Mrs. Dewes,* 9 June, 1757.

[85] Boswell, III, p. 163 and footnote; III, p. 339.

[86] Bradley, *The English Housewife in the Seventeenth and Eighteenth Centuries,* p. 187.

[87] Traill, IV, p. 117 f.

[88] *Ibid,* V, p. 318. Cookworthy was the first to discover the variety of clay from which Chinese porcelain was made in Cornwall, and to use native materials in the manufacture of porcelain. See *A Guide to the English Pottery and Porcelain in the Department of British and Medieval Antiquities* (Brit. Mus.), pp. 97, 115, 117; see also, Arnoux, *Pottery,* in *British Manufacturing Industries* (ed. Bevan), p. 53.

[89] *Ann. Reg.,* 1763, pp. 104-105.

[90] Anderson, IV, pp. 698-699. "To this manufacture the Queen was pleased to give her name and patronage, commanding it to be called 'Queen's Ware.'" *Ibid.*

[91] Pollexfen, *A Discourse of Trade, Coyn and Paper Credit,* p. 99.

[92] Singleton, *The Furniture of our Forefathers,* p. 412.

[93] Daviler, *Cours d'architecture* (1691) quoted in *ibid,* p. 416.

[94] *Ibid,* p. 418.

[95] Pollen, *Furniture and Woodwork,* in *British Manufacturing Industries* (ed. Bevan), p. 150.

[96] Singleton, p. 419.

[97] See above, Chapter II.

[98] Chippendale, *op. cit., passim.*

[99] Singleton, pp. 455-456.

[100] Pollen, *op. cit.,* p. 150.

[101] Cowper, *On Mrs. Montagu's Feather-Hangings.* For the use of other oversea commodities in decoration, see Mrs. Delany, I, p. 160.

[102] *The World,* 27 Mar., 1755.

[103] *Ibid,* 12 Apr., 1753.

[104] *The Spectator,* 25 June, 1712. Pope appealed for natural gardens in *The Guardian,* No. 173.

[105] Cecil, *A History of Gardening in England,* p. 246.

[106] *Ibid,* pp. 246-248.

[107] *The World,* 10 Apr., 1755.

[108] Chambers, *Plans, Elevations and Perspective Views of the Gardens and Buildings at Kew, seat of the Princess Dowager of Wales . . . with 43 plates,* preface. See also Halfpenny, *Rural Architecture in the Chinese taste, being designs for the decoration of gardens, etc.,* (1750), which Chambers included in his list of unauthentic reproductions.

[109] Chambers, *Dissertation.*

[110] Boswell, IV, p. 188, and footnote.

[111] *The World,* 3 Apr., 1755.
[112] *Ibid.*
[113] Boswell, IV, p. 60, V, p. 186; see below, p. 225f.
[114] Mrs. Delany, I, p. 175.
[115] Chambers, *Dissertation;* see also *The World,* 27 Mar., 1755.
[116] Chambers, *Plans, Elevations,* etc.; and Cecil, p. 246. See below, p. 230f.
[117] Darwin, *The Botanic Garden* (1791).
[118] *The World,* 2 Dec., 1756.

CHAPTER V

THE acquisition of an empire overseas, and the reorganization of commerce, agriculture and industry resulting therefrom, tended vitally to change the structure of English society in the eighteenth century. Without doubt the outstanding feature of this period was the rapid increase of wealth, or more exactly, the phenomenal growth of individual fortunes. Simultaneous with it was the rise of the middle class, the membership of which embraced the many thousands who took advantage of opportunities offered in various fields of endeavour.

Naturally the wealth of the Indies was not divided equitably among all Britons. At the same time it is true that every man, woman and child in the new England was to benefit eventually by the material success of their fellow-countrymen. Of chief significance was the fact that this wealth lay, not in owning or tilling land, but in operations in the marts of trade, and later, under the momentum of the Industrial Revolution, in the field of manufacturing. It is true that land had long held forth inducements: stability, the slight chance of depreciation or deterioration, the fixed

116

standing for its owner in the community and in national life, and the possibility of a slow but steady rise in value of the holding.   Its disadvantages were none the less certain.   Seldom, if ever, did the opportunity arise to double or treble one's investment.   Besides, the chance to invest on a large scale in landed property was denied the general public: the unwritten law of tradition, of custom, had constructed an insurmountable wall about the great estates of England, which none but the scions of old families dared scale.   Ownership of land, and social and political prestige, were inseparable; such rewards were not readily to be exchanged for wealth of a value yet to be appreciated.

On the other hand, trade and commerce—and later in the century, manufacturing—offered opportunity limited only by the uncharted resources of lands overseas.   Thus one might be assured of those luxuries which till now only the wealthy had enjoyed: the satisfaction of a desire for gold, silver or precious stones; the stimulation of jaded appetites with tasty and exotic foodstuffs, the appeal to vanity and changing fashion with furs, silks and satins.   By arousing human curiosity and longing for novelty, one might, with little effort, create a market for new commodities from Occident or Orient.

Thus there was endless opportunity for the wholesale merchant who specialized in a certain field; for the shipper, who was content with the more modest profit of the carrying trade; or for the retailer who catered to his expensive, though no longer exclusive, clientèle.   There is no need, perhaps, to make the list exhaustive: the openings were ever present, and men were not slow to seize them.

Those who preferred not to engage in active business found equally profitable channels in promoting or financing stock companies, or in manipulating, scientifically or otherwise, the vagaries of the Stock Exchange. Success in any case meant wealth and all the advantages that popular belief ascribed to wealth: the acquisition of those conveniences and luxuries, at the time enjoyed only by the landed aristocracy; the chance to ape their superiors' exclusive manners and customs; soon, perhaps, a share in making their country's laws and in determining its policy, and eventually admission into the ranks of its élite. Certainly the goal was sufficiently attractive, while there was little to be lost if one fell by the wayside.

Finally, these possibilities were open to all. Nowhere else does one find a democracy approaching that of trade during periods of its rapid expansion. Titles, traditions, membership in ancient and honoured families, counted for little as assets in commercial pursuits. In fact, for the most part, such families either ignored or despised trading and trades-people, and themselves refused to enter the most captivating and profitable pastime and struggle of modern life. Commerce, then, and business in general, offered equal opportunity to all; it attracted especially the ambitious, the adventurous, those discontented with their lot— in the last group, those unfortunate to be born younger sons, otherwise destined to end their days as vicars of country parishes. Capital was an advantage, but not essential; the qualities which elected one to the new aristocracy of business, were daring, coupled with shrewdness, industry combined with imagination, and that mysterious ability to sense one's fellowman— briefly, those same qualities which make up the successful business man of to-day, or of any day. And when later on it becomes necessary to criticize the *nouveaux riches* of the eighteenth century one should remember that they were pioneers in their own fields, that they possessed the defects as well as the virtues of frontiersmen. And it was true in the eighteenth century, as to-day, that the genus profiteer was abhorrent, and despised by the virtuous.

To understand clearly the effects of the increase of wealth on the social structure of the age, it is advisable to consider the more patent means by which fortunes could be made or unmade. The successful merchant was to play an increasingly important rôle in social and political life; his point of view, and the manner in which he amassed his wealth, largely determined the character of his social activities.

While the spectacular fortunes made in the stock markets by speculators, and those made in India by the nabobs, were more or less parasitical in origin, it is necessary to remember that these instances of wealth were numerically few in comparison with fortunes made in the marts of trade; for interwoven with the vast increase of colonial and foreign trade is the rise of hundreds of great merchant princes, and of vast and permanent mercantile and banking houses. Careers and fortunes were made at once honestly, and for the most part without ostentation. The most notable pioneer of this group was Thomas Pitt, whose ability to profit by the India trade placed him in the front rank of merchant princes of his generation. Famous in his own time as the owner of the "Pitt Diamond," he was later remembered as the founder of a house destined to be famous in the commercial and political annals of England. Other careers, while less brilliant, bear witness to the rise of a considerable and an influential middle class. The life of William Miles is merely one of a hundred similar cases. This young man came to Bristol with three half-pence, obtained a job as a porter, and did evening work for a small ship-builder. On the completion of his apprenticeship, by which time he had saved £15, he qualified as ship's carpenter in a Jamaica merchantman. There he bought a cask or two of sugar, which he sold in Bristol at a huge profit. With this money he stocked up with articles in greatest demand in Jamaica, and repeated his former investment. Saving his earnings, which became larger each trip, he settled down in Bristol as a sugar-merchant, in which capacity he amassed a large fortune. In 1793, his son joined him in partnership, not only in the West India trade, but in the largest sugar-refining business in Bristol.[1]

Similarly the necessity for financing oversea trade resulting in the growth of great banking houses, centring chiefly in London. Henry Hoare, for example, who had carried on the banking end of a large oversea business,[2] accumulated a fortune, while a younger son of this house was able to spend no less than £190,000 in the rehabilitation of his country estates in Dorsetshire and Wiltshire.[3] In like manner did David Barclay make his start in American and West Indian commerce.[4] John Baring, too, was a merchant of wealth and eminence, even before he founded the banking-house bearing his name.[5] Francis, who continued the business on a vastly extended scale, became an East Indian proprietor, a holder of bank stock, was made a baronet in 1793, and upon his death, left property worth £1,100,000.[6]

In the growth of Liverpool, however, and in the rise of its merchant princes, is unfolded the drama of oversea expansion. In 1690, a visitor to this city considered it merely a quiet, unostentatious seaport. Returning in 1726, and again in the following year, he remarked that "it was increasing in people, buildings, wealth and business"; [7] for during that time Liverpool had become the chief tobacco centre for England and the continent.[8] During the following decades sugar, rum, and coffee made this city "the greatest and most opulent seaport in the kingdom, next after London and Bristol." [9] The profits of the slave trade and the increased demand for cotton characterized the third phase in the evolution of this metropolis as the representative, and most exclusively commercial, city of Britain.[10]

Liverpool, then, whose very existence was bound up with commerce, can best show the democratic origin of its merchant princes, and the manner in which their success was attained. Here docks and warehouses were thronged with penniless boys, enthusiastic and adventurous pioneers in a new field of romantic endeavour. Edward Norris, the first of that famous house, returned from India (1701), with 87,000 rupees, with which to set himself up as merchant.[11] Thomas Johnson, of yeoman stock and penniless, became the leading tobacco merchant of the early century, and made Liverpool the largest importer of this commodity for England and the continent.[12] Bryan Blundell, who had risen rapidly from apprentice to master of a ship engaged in the West India trade, retired from the sea, purchased several stately ships, and made an honourable place for himself among the prosperous merchants of Liverpool.[13] Foster Cunliffe, who died in 1758, became wealthy in the tobacco trade,[14] while his successors were pioneers in the far more remunerative slave trade.[15] In 1753, there were one hundred merchants engaged in various branches of oversea trade, all of whom were self-made men, or sons of self-made fathers.[16] Unusually fortunate, perhaps, were the careers of Arthur and Benjamin Heywood, who were apprenticed to John Hardman and James Crosby, respectively, oversea merchants. Both married into wealthy business families, and while still young men, took rank with the oldest and richest Liverpool merchants.[17] With them began what was to become Liverpool's greatest bonanza—the importation of American cotton.[18] The Heywoods further increased their prosperity by becoming bankers; it is interesting that eleven of fourteen Heywood descendants to 1815 became either merchants or bankers.[19] Old John Earle, to cite another example, profited

enough from occasional oversea adventures to start
his three sons in the sugar and the slave trade. The
Earles have continued as merchants to the present
time.[20] Among other self-made men, whose fortunes
were gained in oversea trade, mention should be made
of Sir John Gladstone, William Rathbone, James
Cropper, Thomas Leyland, William Ewart and Alexander Brown.[21]

Opportunities for accumulating fortunes were afforded, too, by the manufacture of raw products from
overseas. Mention has been made of the successful
sugar refinery operated by William Miles and his
son,[22] an industry which was followed by twenty other
merchants of Bristol alone.[23] In other cases manufacturers sought to replace imported articles with those
of British make. It was the popularity of chinaware,
and the rare profits which its sale brought, that led
Josiah Wedgwood to found, in 1769, a centre of new
industrial activity.[24] Significantly his partner was
Bentley, a Liverpool merchant engaged in the slave-
trade.[25] Among the manufacturers of Birmingham
John Taylor built up a large establishment principally
in the manufacture of snuff-boxes, and accumulated
for himself a fortune of £200,000. It was said that
his workmen earned 70 shillings a week by painting
snuff-boxes, for one farthing each.[26] Matthew
Boulton gained fame and wealth by his manufacture
of gold and silverware, both solid and plated, and
for his articles of tortoise-shell.[27] Through Boulton's
efforts Birmingham became famed for jewelry and
trinkets.[28] The Soho Mint, established by this genius,

was employed by the East India Company, and by the colonies, to coin money for their use,[29] and in 1797, received a contract to strike off all copper coins for the government.[30] Birmingham, then, may well be considered a new centre of industrial activity, due directly or indirectly to oversea activity. From a town of but 28 streets and a population of 15,000 in 1701, it had grown by 1801 to a metropolis of 250 streets, and a population of 73,670.[31] Among its wealthy, self-made men who had both brought about, and profited by, the city's growth, three were worth more than £100,000, seven worth £50,000, eight worth £30,000, seventeen worth £20,000, eighty worth £10,000, and ninety-four worth £5,000. Of these 209, 103 began life with no more than their natural ability.[32] Elsewhere, and in general, the capitalist manufacturer was a self-made man; and curiously enough, few who entered the trade rich were successful:

The men who did establish themselves were raised by their own efforts, commencing in a very humble way, and pushing their advance by a series of unceasing exertions, having a very limited capital to begin with, or even none at all save that of their own labour.[33]

Undoubtedly, the outstanding figure in this group was the first Sir Robert Peel, who came partly of yeoman, partly of domestic-manufacturing, stock.[34] His fortune was made in calico-printing. Of similar origin were Joshua Fielden and Jebediah Strutt.[35] Others from yeoman stock who made their fortunes in manufacturing were Radcliffe—whose agricultural prospects had been ruined by enclosures—Wilkinson, Durby, Cranshaw and Kennedy, all of whom started life with little or no capital.[36]   Other merchants became wealthy in the iron trade, which would probably have died, had it not been for the introduction of large quantities of American iron, and improvements in the use of coal.[37]   Without the transformation of the iron trade, railways and steamships would have been impossible,· nor even the vast establishment of cotton, woollen and linen factories.   So, also, the prosperity of the younger towns, Manchester, Liverpool, Glasgow, Dundee, Leeds, Bradford, Birmingham, and Sheffield, each the centre of a great and wealthy district, and each the nucleus of a group of merchant princes and of capitalist manufacturers, would have been impossible.   In the coal-mining industry alone did the capitalist class come in part from the old aristocracy, as is evidenced by such mine-owners as Londonderry, Durham, Fitzwilliam, Dudley and the Duke of Portland.[38]   Even here, however, the owners, hitherto of moderate circumstances, of property that possessed coal deposits became immensely wealthy.[39] Furthermore the sudden development of manufacturing industries, especially in Lancashire, created new markets for food supplies, and small self-sufficing farms of the old type were "turned into factories for bread and meat." [40]   In such neighbourhoods the rentals of land increased from 1500% to 3000%, resulting on the one hand in vast profits for the owner,[41] and on the other, a change of occupation and residence for former tenants.[42]

Apart from a purely commercial career, a considerable group of men accumulated fortunes either through office-holding, or by settling in the West Indies as plantation-farmers. The governorship of Jamaica brought its incumbent £5,000 a year, in addition to various perquisites, including a share of prizes of a varying and indeterminate value.[43] The governorship of Barbados, and of the colonies of North America, was valued, too, as a means of recouping lost fortunes. Several oversea posts were eagerly seized by unfortunate victims of the South Sea Bubble.[44] Many lucrative positions were held by people who never saw service, but who sold them to deputies at a stipulated sum per annum. One man, for example, who resided in England, held nine offices, and received £1,500 a year without doing a stroke of work.[45] The secretaryship to Jamaica was alone worth £1,000 a year, which the principal farmed out at from £600 to £800.[46] As this practice continued throughout the century, these absentee officials must have been numerous, and their emoluments, considerable.

The individuals concerned, however, were merely parasites, who fed on the real wealth of the West Indies. Addison truly said that "trade . . . has given us a sort of additional empire; it has multiplied the number of the rich, made our landed estates infinitely more valuable than before, and added to them the accession of other estates more valuable than the lands themselves." [47] It was chiefly the sugar planters who reaped the golden harvest of the West

Indies.   Here, again, it is impossible to estimate their exact number or amount of their fortunes.   It is known that in one of the Jamaica parishes, St. James's, there were 132 landed proprietors in 1754,[48] and in all of Barbados, approximately 4,000.[49]   In Jamaica there were 700 sugar estates in 1772, a remarkable increase over the estates which the island boasted ninety-seven years before.[50]   The continued prosperity of sugar planting is shown by the fact that 83 new estates were started during the last six years of the century.[51]   The average value of these estates was estimated at from £30,000 to £40,000.[52]   With regard to the returns on capital invested, it is stated that

the West Indians are not remarkable for their gigantic opulence, or an ostentatious display of it.   They do not emerge rapidly from poverty and insignificance into conspicuous notice. Some of them who possess fortunes of distinguished magnitude, as some gentlemen of Jamaica are happy to do, are not the creations of a day.[53]

It is necessary to agree with this statement, to the extent that the West India planters were plodders in comparison with their confrères the Anglo-Indian nabobs, that they had to run the risk of storms, of bad years, of taxes, and of the expense and dangers of war-time.[54]   At that it seems clear that the net profit amounted to at least 10% a year.[55]   Undoubtedly the individuals who returned to England and staggered their countrymen by ostentatious display were exceptions.[56]   Still others, as an uncle of Bryan Edwards, and Bryan Edwards himself, returned to England and became members of Parliament.[57] Others again, as the notorious Jenkins, were planters, only as a cloak to their unscrupulous adventures as treasure-hunters along the Spanish main.[58] Although the sugar planters as a whole were prosperous, the owners of indigo and cocoa plantations suffered heavy losses, due in part to taxation, and to the declining demand for their commodities.[59] On the other hand, the coffee planters attained a new and permanent prosperity toward the close of the century.[60] Outside of the owners themselves, work on the plantations was highly profitable, for it was estimated that every white man, woman, or child in the plantations earned an average of £60 annually.[61]

Finally, two other groups, apart from merchants dealing in actual commodities, realized profits from the West Indies. One comprised of the increasing number of absentee landlords who preferred to reside in England and to turn over their affairs to "planting attorneys," either on the basis of a salary or of a percentage of sales.[62] The other was composed, either of honourable merchants who financed estates, or of financial sharks who advanced enough to start an estate, but before it began to pay demanded a return of their money, and appeared at the forced sale as the only bidder.[63] On the other hand, many British merchants who had advanced sums in good faith, were compelled against their wish to become planters themselves.[64]

Of different ilk were the Anglo-Indian profiteers, commonly called "nabobs." It was said, and with more than a grain of truth, that "no man ever went

to the East Indies with good intentions." [65]   The
salaries paid by the Company to its servants in India
were mere pittances,[66] and the latter accordingly were
permitted to eke out a living in the profits of private
trading.   As might be expected, some seized this privilege with such avidity that complaints reached India
House of the luxury and ostentation of its young servants.[67]   By arrangement the Company's goods were
exempt from all taxes and tolls in Bengal, but this
privilege was not intended to cover the private trade
of the Company's servants, or even less that of the
natives.   So,

out of the exemption grew up a vast system of open smuggling,
in which the Company's servants led the way.   Every middle-
man, every native adventurer who could hire a *dastak* or fly a
Company's flag, cheated the revenue in the same fashion.   It
was said that the youngest writer in the Company's service
could make two or three thousand rupees a month by selling
passes to native customers.[68]

While the lesser servants were thus busied in piling
up fortunes, higher officials even more neglected the
Company's business in their endeavours to accumulate
wealth during their short terms of service.   During
the "golden age" of Clive, and afterwards, the Company's profits failed to correspond with the amount
of business actually carried on.   Appeals from the
Court of Directors failed to check this reign of corruption.   In many places officials obtained the monopoly of internal trade for themselves, and by forcing
natives to sell cheap and buy dear, accumulated enormous fortunes.[69]   In 1768, for example, the Com-

pany's servants began to trade illicitly in salt, and within five years, £1,500,000 was thus distributed among them.[70]

With the acquisition of new provinces in India, a correspondingly larger territory was opened up for greed and avarice.   When Clive brought under English control the whole kingdom of Bengal, it was said that

when all expenses are paid, there will be remitted to England nearly a million and a half; we may buy another war with Germany and subsidize two or three electors, for we shall scorn to be the better for this money ourselves;[71]

and that

we have taken Tanjore, and a General Smith has got £150,000 for his share. . . . We have nothing to do but to break a truce, and plunder a city, and we find the pretty metal ready coined, and brilliants ready cut and mounted.[72]

Similarly the chances for rapidly-acquired fortunes were gratified with the acquisition of the province of Oude, with its four million inhabitants and three or four millions of revenue.[73]   Furthermore, by taking part in native intrigues, usually by supporting one candidate against another for a "nabobship," British officials acquired enough for retirement.   In one case, occurring in 1765, presents to the value of £140,000 were distributed among those concerned.[74]   Again, at the installation of Mir Kasim Ali as native ruler, Vansittart was said to have pocketed a present of £50,000, Holwell a gift of £27,000, while two other members of the Council received £25,000 cash, and Col. Caillaud obtained £20,000 for himself.[75]

Although the records naturally do not afford much definite information regarding the exact fortunes secured through the usual underground, but tacitly permitted, channels, several facts are clearly evident: that throughout the eighteenth century, India was the scene of constant plunder; that opportunity for it, in one form or another, was offered to servants, both high and low, of the East India Company, and finally, that ships returning from India brought back hundreds of men who had thus amassed the fortunes which were to open to them the paths of social and political advancement.

Fortunately, it is possible to cite the cases of several highly successful nabobs, other than those mentioned above. The most renowned of this group was Robert Clive, who from a mere clerk in the Company's service at Madras built up the Indian Empire by his own ability, and in so doing amassed great wealth. It was said that he brought back to England, upon his return in 1760,

a million for himself, two diamond drops, worth £12,000 for the Queen, a scimitar, dagger, and other matters, covered with brilliants, for the King and worth £24,000 more. These *baubles* are presents from the deposed and imprisoned Mogul, whose poverty can still afford to give such bribes.[76]

Scarcely less fortunate was George Pigot, owner of a celebrated diamond that sold for 9,500 guineas. His fortune enabled him to purchase an estate for £100,000 upon his return to England. He became, too, the agent for the Nawab in the Carnatic, at an annual salary of 12,000 pagodas. More unique, per-

haps, was the career of Sir Thomas Rumbold,[77] who
from a waiter in White's became Governor of Madras.
During his three years of office he amassed a fortune
of £164,000, and upon his return to England became
a more or less respected member of Parliament.   In
like manner did Francis and Paul Benfield [78] retire
from service, in 1785 and 1786 respectively, with large
fortunes.[79]   Warren Hastings, however, who kept
apparently aloof from the mad scramble for ill-gotten
gains, was considered the poorest of the nabobs.   Yet
his fortune ran, according to estimates, from £80,000
to £130,000.[80]

For centuries, it may be remembered, the Englishman had been content with the moderate and reasonably sure profits from products of the soil.   Business
and trade were fascinating enigmas to the layman.
He knew little of their intricate workings, though their
possibilities were constantly brought to his attention
by the frequent sight of merchants living in dazzling
opulence.   He was reminded of the wealth of lands
overseas by incoming ships unloading their cargoes,
and by the absurdly high prices they brought in the
retail shops.   Seemingly both the supply and the
demand were limitless, though investors of this time
did not heed the inexorable economic law that governed their relation.   Nor was he allowed to forget
that the descendants of early investors in the East
India Company were now rolling in luxury.   In other
enterprises, too, he saw clerks of yesterday become
capitalists of to-day.

The average investor did not realize that those who

succeeded were pitifully few in number, compared with the failures. Equally unappreciative was he of the fact that the majority of successful merchants had learned their lessons in the bitter school of experience, were trained in methods of organization, knew how to scour the distant corners of the earth for articles in demand, or to create a new market for new commodities, or to pare profits to meet keen competition, and yet be able to meet possible losses. In short, the magic of limitless opportunity, which certainly existed, lulled the senses of the layman to the inflexible laws of business economy. The open sesame to wealth was simply to gamble on the 'Change, or to subscribe to some stock company dealing in oversea commodities. Stock in the successful East India Company was high in price and difficult to obtain. Fortunately, though, other ventures, modelled along similar lines, were willing— nay, anxious—to open their books to new subscribers.

While speculation was rife throughout the century, the most spectacular changes in fortunes occurred during the winter of 1720-1721. The occasion was the meteoric rise of South Sea stock.[81] At first this security had sold at £86 a share; in a few months it rose to £1,100—of course a fictitious value, and a proof of the gullibility of the public. Those who had bought stock early realized fortunes over night.[82] Many of the country gentry sold noble estates of £2,000 and more a year, the seats of ancient families.[83] The directors, of course, and their friends gained prodigious sums by the almost hourly rise in the quotations of stock, sometimes at the expense of one another.[84] Members of the nobility gambled successfully: the Duke of Chambos, for example, made a fortune from his investment of £30,000,[85] and the Duchess of Ormond from her outlay of £20,000.[86] People of various walks in life plunged successfully: John Barber, Swift's printer, ran £20,000 to over £100,000; through speculation [87] Walpole rebuilt Houghton, and began his famous collection of pictures; others were Mrs. Howard, Col. Campbell, Sir Robert Sutton, and Sir Matthew Decker.[88] Humble folk, too, made their fortunes, and with them came the rise of a new aristocracy, of lowly origin, but of great wealth. The number of South Sea equipages, orders by the thousands in the hands of tailors for handsomely embroidered coats, and the sudden popularity of gold watches, show as well that thousands of people of the lower walks in life had grown rich in this manner. It was indeed demonstrated that "Fortunes came unaccountably like manna from above. Vast sums are spent for patrimonies by those who never had a foot of land. So many Coaches are set up, that Farmers fear a Dearth of Horses for Ploughing; even the Taylors are become mutinous." [89]

The effect of the South Sea boom on "legitimate" securities was most stimulating: those of the Bank of England soared to the unprecedented height of £405.[90] Naturally the people who bought cheap and sold dear pocketed a satisfactory difference.

Accounts in journals of the time picture the consternation that reigned in that great mart of money—

Exchange Alley—upon the bursting of the South Sea Bubble, and of the thousand and one lesser bubbles.[91] More lasting was the sobering effect on the English people and on business life in particular. Those who were caught in this gigantic instance of charlatanism or in any of the lesser frauds, paid dearly for their experience. There were still lures for the gullible or the adventurous in the vagaries of the stock-market or in ventures outside the usual risks of business enterprise. But, in general, a healthy reaction now set in. Englishmen both business men and others, had learned their lesson at a dear price. The bubbles served a good purpose in turning a money-mad people back into a more sophisticated frame of mind, and to ordinary and time-honoured, if less romantic, methods of earning a living,—a change which the press was largely responsible in bringing about.[92]

On the other hand, those who purchased stock in a legitimate oversea enterprise like the East India Company, for the purpose of investment rather than for speculation, were assured of a moderate and steady profit. In 1773, for example, the number of English proprietors who possessed stock to the amount of £1,000 or more was 487.[93] The total amount of their holdings was £1,018,398.[94] The number of smaller investors who held stock to the amount of £500, but not above £1,000, was 1,246. Their holdings totalled £634,464.[95] The return on their investment may be noted in the following table, which shows the net profits of the Company:

1772-3	£ 567,866	1781-2	£ 275,782
1773-4	1,031,806	1782-3	1,029,622
1774-5	1,625,336	1783-4	1,163,224
1775-6	1,871,021	1784-5	1,128,612
1776-7	1,767,491	1785-6	1,038,987
1777-8	1,200,623	1786-7	1,660,868
1778-9	1,040,437	1787-8	2,232,943
1779-80	377,677	1788-9	2,767,369
1780-1	354,454	1789-90	2,807,444 [96]

Looking at the matter from another angle, it may be said that by 1700 religious and political persecution had ceased to serve as a stimulus to English emigration. Furthermore, by then, the roughest of pioneer work in the colonies had been accomplished; the element of chance had largely disappeared with the establishment of a stable political and economic organization; and success was practically assured the emigrant to the American colonies who possessed moderate capital and ability. The majority of this class went with the distinct hope of receiving greater reward for their industry there than at home. On the other hand the prospective West India sugar-planter had to be equipped with an initial capital of £30,000. This amount was usually furnished by men in trade with the hope of speedy returns.[97] Naturally emigration of this type was selective in character and limited in extent.[98] Its peak was reached in 1729, when of 6,208 emigrants to America but 267 were men of any capital.[99]

The colonies attracted, too, and in considerable numbers, men of the learned professions, especially lawyers, doctors and clergymen; for the first two of these classes could expect ample financial returns and

exceptional opportunity for advancement.   Furthermore, the

British navy and army likewise contribute considerably to the
augmentation of the white inhabitants.   Individuals in both
these professions, either from the inducement of agreeable connections . . . or captivated by the new prospects which open
to their contemplation, very frequently quit the business of
arms, and the dangers of a tempestuous element, and become
peaceful citizens and industrious planters.   Next to these may
be reckoned the mercantile part of the inhabitants, such as factors, storekeepers, bookkeepers, and clerks; who are followed
by tradesmen and artificers of various kinds, such as mill-
wrights, carpenters, masons, coppersmiths, and others; most
of whom, either through accident or necessity, after some years'
residence, become adventurers in the soil.   Then come the husbandmen, or cultivators of the soil, professedly such; who are
commonly distinguished by the appellation of managers, over-
seers, and plantation bookkeepers.[100]

According to an advertisement published in 1720, all
artificers, including carpenters, bricklayers and masons,
farmers and labourers, who agreed to settle themselves
and families in the Bahamas, "shall not only have a
Competency of Ground assigned to them sufficient for
themselves and Families . . . but shall on their Arrival be, on easy Terms, supply'd with all necessary
Conveniences and Materials to enable them effectually
to carry on their said Undertaking." [101]

Beginning in 1723 the Jamaica legislature made
efforts, though in a bungling fashion, to encourage
such emigration, as well as the settlement of husbandmen of moderate means.   In 1736 a bill was passed
which appropriated 15,000 acres for emigrants, families, and slaves.   In the case of poorer emigrants

free land was awarded, an ample supply of food for the first year furnished, and passage and subsistence were to be repaid by the recipient within seven years.[102]   Some families took advantage of this scheme for self-betterment, though the plan as a whole was considered a failure.[103]   A further attempt to introduce a middle class of planters and skilled artisans was made in 1750, when 108 families arrived.   In 1754, however, the parish of St. James, in Jamaica, had but 132 landed proprietors, while Barbados, of the same size, had nearly 4,000.[104]

Opportunity for servants in England to better their condition abroad was afforded by membership in the domestic staff of emigrants of the wealthier type. Maids and valets were highly valued for their efforts to mitigate the rigours of a ruder civilization.[105]   Later in the century arrangements were made to bring over such servants for a term of years, sometimes at a salary of £35 to £40 a year.[106]   There was, too, a considerable class of temporary bondsmen, bound by indentures, and commonly called "Kids," who served out their term in the colonies as house-servants, or in industrial employment.[107]   Afterward they were free to pursue an independent career, and to return to England, if not with a fortune, at least with the experience necessary to attain a higher rank in society.[108]

As in the seventeenth century, the belief that England was overpopulated, coupled with a real and continuous economic distress, proved stimuli to emigration of another type.   The indigent at home were considered a burden and a public misfortune.

It is for this sort that our Foreign Settlements are extremely commodious, and it is certainly of singular Advantage to a Nation, that when its Arts and Manufactures are overstock'd, and its Inhabitants jostle each other in the Ways and Methods of Life, there should be a Retreat provided for the dissatisfied Part of them, that their Industry and Ingenuity may be of Use to themselves abroad, when their Clamours and Discontents can only be dangerous to Society at Home.[109]

Sending such people to the colonies would aid rather than hinder the employment of the poor at home. The possibility of relieving distress in this way led a group of "Noblemen, Gentlemen and Merchants," headed by James Oglethorpe, to petition the king for the grant of lands and to conduct charities, "in carrying over and establishing unfortunate Families in America. . . . The Petitioners undertake without any Benefit to Themselves, all the Toil of soliciting Charities, of Cloathing, Supplying, Arming, Establishing, and Supporting a Colony of such Persons, as they judge to be most proper Objects of Charity." [110]

In the autumn of 1732, Oglethorpe embarked with 114 colonists, who, "through misfortunes and want of employment are reduced to great necessity." [111] As a harbour for the distressed of England, Georgia was of prime importance, and vigourous efforts were made for its speedy population. The idle and useless of English cities, who were considered detrimental to national welfare, made up the first few embarkations. Within three years more than 400 human wrecks found new homes in Georgia.[112] For the next decade the jail and the poorhouse furnished its quota for the wilds of that province. When a vote in the House of

Commons provided for the transportation of paupers[113] the first example in modern times was furnished of state-aided emigration, as a remedy for distress at home. In the following year, Rev. James King wrote that "many families of our own poor have already settled there; and they have been joined by the indigent protestants of other countries." [114]

It had already been discovered, however, that the idle and useless at home could not be transformed overnight into successful farmers in the New World, and for many years Georgia continued to be the weakling of the thirteen colonies.[115] The breaking of ground in the new colony required bold and hardy men, who were supplied, not from the scum of English city life, but from Scotland and the Germanies. From 1741 to 1754 but one-quarter of the grants of land were held by men of English names.[116] From this time on Georgia began to emerge slowly from her early difficulties, even if it was still "but indifferently peopled, though it is now twenty-six years since its first settlement. Not one of our colonies was so slow of growth, though none had so much the attention of the Government or of the people in general." [117]

A type of colonist more suitable to the environment was attracted to the Carolinas during the thirties by various privileges and indulgences granted by the Crown, and by 1735 "many industrious people in different parts (of England) had resolved to take the benefit of His Majesty's bounty." [118] Here, too, the gates were opened to the oppressed of Ireland, Holland and the Germanies.[119]

As the century wore on economic distress continued to be a potent factor in emigration to the New World. This movement had become a common topic of conversation, and was even looked upon with alarm.[120]   Particularly did the high rents caused by the enclosure movement and the high-handed treatment of the smaller farmers turn them indignant towards America, whence they proceeded after selling their stock.[121] Between 1772 and 1792 6,400 of these emigrants sailed in search of better opportunities, taking with them no less than £38,400.[122]   As final evidence of the connection of hard times with emigration, it is known that many of the workmen who were discharged and thrown idle during the commercial panic of 1793 either enlisted in the army or emigrated overseas.[123] Generally speaking, however, it is safe to assume that wholesale emigration was checked by the Industrial Revolution, which offered increased opportunity to workers at home.[124]

To the number of emigrants must be added those who went unwillingly either by the unlawful means of kidnapping, or by the legalized system of transportation.   In the days of Queen Anne kidnapping was a profitable profession, and its members were wont to prowl the streets of London, dressed often in the cast-off suits of the fashionable, to

seduce People, who want Services, and young Fools crost in Love, and under an uneasiness of Mind, to go beyond Seas, getting so much a Head from Masters of Ships, and Merchants who go over, for every Wretch they trapan into this Misery. These young Rakes, and Tetterdemallions you see so lovingly herded, are drawn by their Fair Promises to sell themselves into Slavery, and the Kidnappers are the Rogues that run away with the Money.[125]

Unfortunately conviction of these rascals was difficult, since they testified, in collusion with the merchants concerned, that their victims went willingly.[126] It is impossible to estimate the number who thus made their way across; it is only certain that thousands overcome in moments of drunkenness or taken by force were hurried on board and found themselves exposed for sale for a limited period—as slaves on the plantations.[127]

Of greater import was the practise of transporting convicted criminals to the colonies. By a series of statutes [128] courts were permitted to send felons to New York, New Jersey, Pennsylvania, Delaware, Maryland, Virginia, the Carolinas, and after 1733, to Georgia. The system was popular with the government, which was not only freed from the expense of caring for the criminals, but received £5 a head from the contractors, who in turn disposed of them in colonial markets for at least £10 a head; with the colonists, who thus obtained cheap and sometimes efficient labour; and with the prisoners themselves who, released from jail, could work their way to actual freedom.[129]

Here again one can only approximate the total number of this class of emigrants. At the Old Bailey, for example, during the month of December of the respective years, 27 were sentenced to transportation in 1717; 137 in 1718; 184 in 1719; 173 in 1720; 200 in 1721; 182 in 1722; 219 in 1723; 226 in 1724; 290

in 1725; 234 in 1726; and 187 in 1727.[130] In August, 1718, 106 convicts from Newgate were put aboard ships; in May of the following year, 105 felons were taken from country jails, and transported to Maryland; in May, 1720, 92 from Newgate, and 62 from Marshalsea were sent to Virginia; in February, 1723, 36 from Newgate, to Maryland; in January, 1732, 68 men and 50 women, from Newgate to Virginia; in January, 1736, 140 from Newgate and 18 from Southwark, while in May, 106 were placed aboard ships; in May, 1747, upwards of 1,000 were transported to Virginia and Maryland.[131] From 1749 to 1771 the total from Old Bailey numbered 5,600, of whom 400 had received the sentence of death.[132] Between the years 1750 and 1772, 1,182 convicts on the Norfolk circuit, and 1,057 felons on the Midland circuit, were transported, while in the two years, 1773-1775, 1,179 were shipped to the New World from Newgate alone.[133] Writers agree that between 1750 and 1776, the transportation of criminals, principally to the southern colonies averaged not fewer than 500 annually.[134]

The American Revolution put an end, temporarily, to this system which had flourished for fifty-six years, and for some time the government failed to find a satisfactory outlet for criminals. The project to send them to a West African island was soon abandoned,[135] and in 1776 they were huddled in convict galleys, among them the *Justicia,* in the Thames. The horrors there led to a Parliamentary investigation in 1779,[136] and four years later the Crown was authorized to determine places to which offenders might be transported.[137]   The discoveries of Captain Cook were believed to have opened up "a glorious country for the British merchant now in trouble about declining trade in America." [138]   In 1779, however, Sir Joseph Banks, who had fitted out the *Endeavour* for Cook's expedition, and had himself taken part in the voyage to the Pacific,[139] recommended before a Committee of the House of Commons Botany Bay as fit for a penal colony.[140]   The voyage of seven months, he urged, would make escape difficult while convict labour might well pave the way for later colonization of more satisfactory description.[141]   During the winter of 1787-1788, accordingly, a great penal settlement was founded at Botany Bay under the leadership of Governor Phillip, and to it transported convicts and other unfortunates were sent.   It was better than death, for there one might work his way to salvation:

> What tho the garb of infamy I wear,
>   Though day by day along the echoing beach,
> I cull the wave-worn shells, yet day by day,
>   I earn in honesty my frugal food,
> And lay me down at night to calm repose. . . .
>   On these wild shores Repentance' saviour hand,
> Shall probe my secret soul, shall cleanse its wounds,
>   And fit the faithful penitent for Heaven.[142]

The future of this large number of poor settlers and convicts overseas was of utmost importance.   As for the former class, "they go there poor, and come back rich; there they plant, thrive and increase."[143]   In many cases, then, was the mother country enriched by the return of these self-made men, who would other-

wise have been condemned to a life of helpless poverty
at home. Those who had some money could "bid
themselves in" during the journey, in which case they
were free upon their arrival in America.[144] Others
were sold, and more than often found a stimulus to improve themselves in the New World: [145]

Even your transported felons, sent to Virginia, instead of
Tyburn, thousands of them, if we are not misinformed, have,
by turning their hands to industry and improvement, and which
is best of all, to honesty, become rich, substantial planters and
merchants, settled large families, and been famous in the country; nay, we have seen many of them made magistrates, officers
of militia, captains of good ships, and masters of good estates.[146]

In this way did thousands in England escape the brand
of criminals and attain respectability and higher social
status.

The rise of a heterogeneous middle class, which has
been outlined above, formed the crux of social readjustment in the eighteenth century. To the time of the
discoveries English society had been cast in a more or
less unchanging mould. A species of caste system, sur-
viving so great a crisis as the Black Death, satisfied an
age when social ambition was not a ruling passion in
the lives of men. The serf, the artisan, the petty
tradesman, saw no chance of self-betterment save
within their own occupation and sphere of life; so it
was of little moment that the limits of advancement
were closely prescribed. To the empire-builders of
the Tudor and the Stuart periods, however, accrued
both glory and profit. These rewards continued to

serve as powerful incentives to adventure and ambition;
and the eighteenth century offered opportunities, in
many fields of endeavour at home and abroad, for their
gratification. Socially, business life was truly democratic, drawing as has been seen thousands of recruits
from the lower ranks of life:

> Nothing has wrought such an alteration in this (the lower)
> order of people, as the introduction of trade. This hath in-
> deed given a new face to the whole nation, hath in great meas-
> ure subverted the former state of affairs, and hath almost totally
> changed the manners, customs, and habits of the people, more
> especially of the lower sort. The narrowness of their fortune
> is changed into wealth; the simplicity of their manners into
> craft, their frugality into luxury, their humility into pride, and
> their subjection into equality.[147]

Moreover, while the nobility still affected to disdain commerce many of its younger sons chose trade,
rather than poverty, or a life of sloth.[148] Voltaire
seemed surprised that Lord Townshend's brother was
happy to be a merchant in the city, that Lord Orford's
brother was a factor at Aleppo; and above all marvelled that these careers could be followed with no
prejudice to gentility.[149] Forty-five years later, Grosley made a similar comment about Thomas and Richard Walpole, one a banker, the other a merchant.[150]
If disdain for commerce, then, be dismissed as idle
vapouring, business life was a powerful influence making for the fluidity of society.

So, too, was the influx of wealth from overseas,
which continued without interruption throughout the
century. Nabobs, planters, merchants, manufacturers,

were quietly and continuously accumulating fortunes. To these self-made men a return to their old social status was intolerable, if not impossible. Thus a new aristocracy of wealth was added to the old aristocracy of birth, which in the final reckoning meant a welding of the two. During this change a society that was mobile, rather than rigid in character, came to the fore, and one in which it was possible for the individual to determine or to dominate class distinctions.

The effect of the century's commercial career on the social structure of the nation may be visualized by examining its most spectacular hoax, the South Sea Bubble. As already seen, thousands were raised from poverty or moderate circumstances to wealth. Immediately they sought to satisfy their subconscious desire —emulation of the old aristocracy:

Our South Sea Equipages increase every Day, the City Ladies buy South Sea Jewels, hire South Sea Maids and take new South Sea Houses; the Gentlemen set up South Sea Coaches, and buy South Sea Estates, that they neither examine the Situation, the Nature or Quality of the Soil, or Price of the Purchase; only the Annual Rent, and the Title; for the Rest, they take all by the Lump, and give 40 to 50 Years' Purchase. This has brought so many Estates to the Market to be Sold, that the Number of Land-Jobbers begins to increase to a great Degree, almost equal to the Stock-Jobbers that we had before.[151]

If antiquity of family could not be purchased, money could at least obtain the other perquisites of the socially privileged. Several of the directors of the South Sea Company, too, were awarded the distinction of baronetcies.[152] Many of the West India planters purchased estates upon their return to Eng-

land. After 1718, for example, the population of Barbados was considerably decreased by the removal of
the "most eminent Planters to England, where they
have Purchased Estates, and live in great Affluence
and Splendour.[153] This desire to emulate the landed
aristocracy of England seems to have been universally
followed by the Anglo-Indian nabobs.[154] Clive's estate
was celebrated, or damned, for its splendour and mag-
nificence.[155] Sir Thomas Rumbold purchased an estate
as a preliminary to his election to Parliament.[156] Pigot,
owner of the famous diamond, spent £100,000 for the
purchase of the Patshull estate in Staffordshire.[157] In
like manner Sir Robert Palk acquired Haldon House
in Devonshire, the ancient seat of the Chudleigh family.[158]   Paul Benfield purchased an estate in Durham.[159] In fact so great was the demand for country
seats by nabobs, and so eager the desire for purchase
at any figure, that both helped to raise the price of land
beyond all reason.[160] Similarly, the London merchants
—and those of other large commercial and manufacturing centres—imitated the landed aristocracy by the
purchase of estates in the suburbs. That this exodus
was a general one, is testified by a visitor to Epsom:

By the conversation of those who walk there, you would fancy
yourself to be this Minute on the Exchange, and the next
Minute at St. James's; one while in an East-India factory, or a
West India Plantation, and another with the Army in Flanders,
or on board the Fleet in the Ocean; nor is there any Profession,
Trade, or Calling, that you can miss of here, either for your
Instruction, or for your Diversion. Behind the Houses, are
handsome though not large Gardens.[161]

The admission of these groups to ownership of land, and the social advantages accruing therefrom, removed one more prop from the support of the caste system, and was a decided step in the formation of a new democracy, or more exactly perhaps a new oligarchy.

Not alone by ownership of land, but by admission to Parliament, by the rewards of titles, and by inter-marriage with the aristocracy, could the middle class enter the circle, and obtain the political and social advantages of the élite. Election to the House of Commons was a simple matter of purchase to the wealthy Anglo-Indian or West India planter, many of whom had bought landed property and established county families. Beginning with men like Sir Basil Firebrace, who had become wealthy through connec-tion with the East India Company, and Anglo-Indians like Thomas Pitt, many of the *nouveaux riches* found their way into Parliament. Stratton, on his return, purchased a seat in the House of Commons; [162] Pigot represented in turn Wallingford and Bridgworth; [163] Rumbold was returned for New Shoreham, Yarmouth, and Weymouth,[164] Palk for Ashburton,[165] and Ben-field for the notorious borough of Cricklade.[166] Not only did the nabob purchase a seat for himself, but his wealth could afford him a group of henchmen in Parliament.[167] By the time of the American Revolu-tion, the Anglo-Indians formed a group on the benches below the gangway on the government side of the House.[168]

Successful merchants of London and Liverpool and

other commercial centres found their way to Parliament. Outstanding examples were the descendants of Thomas Pitt, who not only sat in Parliament, but were influential in directing national affairs. The Norrises of Liverpool were represented by three of their family, Thomas (1688), William (1695) and Edward (1701).[169] Thomas Johnson, that city's leading tobacco merchant, sat in the House of Commons from 1701 to 1721.[170] Manufacturers likewise sought at one and the same time to gain social prestige and to protect their business interests. The Foleys, iron manufacturers of Worcester, not only entered the House of Commons but became baronets.[171] Cotton manufacturers did not enter Parliament until the closing years of the century. The first Robert Peel took his seat in 1790, held it for thirty years, and received a baronetcy.[172] John and Samuel Horrocks were the only other manufacturers of this period to sit in the House of Commons.[173]

Many of the newcomers were ambitious for the peerage and invariably supported the administration, in the desire to curry favour for this end.[174] This honour, however, during the early part of the century, was conferred upon but a few. Queen Anne added only five to the peerage, one of whom was her Lord Treasurer.[175] At the accession of George III there were but 174 British peers. In order to destroy the Whig majority and to maintain his influence in the lower House, he created or promoted during the first ten years of his reign forty-two peers, during the administration of Lord North, thirty, and during the first five years of Pitt's leadership, forty-eight, so that by 1801, one hundred and forty new peers had been created.[176]   Peerages were occasionally conferred on bankers and Anglo-Indians, but George III clung closely to his policy that no man engaged only in trade, however large his fortune, should be created a British peer.   All that the most wealthy traders and manufacturers could expect, accordingly, was knighthood or a baronetcy.[177]

In like fashion, the increase of trade made for a more mobile aristocracy.   The younger sons, of course, continued to descend into the ranks of the commoners, unless through an exceptional career preferably in the military or naval service they could again enter the circle of nobility.   Intermarriage, too, of peers and commoners had always been legal, and since the seventeenth century, more frequent.   Sir William Temple, writing in 1685, remarked:

I think I remember within less than fifty years, the first noble families that married into the city for downright money, and thereby introduced by degrees this public grievance which has since ruined so many estates by the necessity of giving good portions to daughters.[178]

The need of a land-poor aristocracy for money, and the tempting marriage portions offered by the *nouveaux riches,* still further bridged the narrowing gap between these two classes.[179]   It also happened that many younger sons, apprenticed to trade, gained through the death of elder brothers the right to their titles.[180]   In particular, though, did those who profited from the South Sea affair arrange advantageous matches for their daughters—matches incidentally of advantage to both parties.[181]

It must not be assumed, however, that every one who engaged in commercial or business life was successful. Reverses were common, and although these cases in large part were not recorded, it is safe to believe that most of the victims dropped down a rung in the social ladder. The collapse of the South Sea Bubble depicts the fate of these failures:

> They who lately rode in great State to that famous Mart of Money (Exchange-Alley) now humbly condescend to walk the Streets on Foot, and instead of adding to their Equipages, have, at once, lost their Estates; and even those of the trading Rank, who talked loudly of retiring into the Country, purchasing Estates there, building fine Houses, and in everything imitating their Betters, are now become Bankrupts, and have shut up their Shops, because they could not keep them open any longer.[182]

In a word, the road back to poverty and oblivion was shorter and easier than the upward path; nor was its course so enlivened by pleasurable publicity.

Events were taking place in rural England which brought about a further regrouping of social classes. The displacement of old landowners by returned nabobs and West India planters has already been noted. Many seats of ancient families, too, were sold for investment in South Sea securities.[183] The holdings of farmers in Hertfordshire were decreasing; for land in the suburbs of London appealed to city merchants for residential purposes. Elsewhere forces were operating to bring about the decay of the small farmer, the country squire and the yeoman.[184] The burden of taxation due to oversea wars, particularly the American Revolution, proved intolerable to these classes.[185] The changes brought about by the Agricultural Revolution, too, made farming on a small scale and without capital unprofitable. By enclosures land was thrown together in large holdings at the expense of the small landowners.[186] By the middle of the century the decline of the small holders was in evidence.[187] This change was hastened by the Industrial Revolution, which ended domestic manufacturing and established industry in great cities. Farms, also, were turned into factories for bread and meat, operated by capital and according to scientific methods, for supplying industrial centres with food. In Lancashire, particularly, where the factory system made greatest headway, were the yeomen and squires forced into other activities and into another social class. Here

The yeomanry, formerly numerous and respectable, have greatly diminished of late, but are not yet extinct; the great wealth, which has, in many instances, been so rapidly acquired by some of their neighbours, and probably heretofore dependents, has offered sufficient temptation to venture their property in trade, in order that they might keep pace with these fortunate adventurers. . . . Not only the yeomanry, but almost all the farmers, who have raised fortunes by agriculture, place their children in the manufacturing line.[188]

Many of the freeholders, then, were able by selling their land, either to increase their income or to start their children in business. The more ambitious of the yeomen went to the cities,[189] while the feebler ones became tenants or labourers, working under conditions which were indescribably miserable. On the other hand, the new type of landholder was a better educated man, commanded more capital, was open to new ideas, and generally more enterprising. Arthur Young commented favourably on this change:

> I have not seen a set more liberal in any part of the kingdom. Industrious, active, enlightened, free from all foolish and expensive show . . . they live comfortably and hospitably as good farmers ought to live; and in my opinion are remarkably void of those rooted prejudices which are sometimes objected to in this race of men.[190]

In 1793 and 1797, years of financial crisis, agriculture became a still more desirable form of investment. This was true, not only because of satisfactory returns, but because of the comparative safety thus attained.[191]

The very fluidity of society, then, was a most potent factor in the levelling of social distinctions; and this equalizing process, as has been observed, was due directly or indirectly to the great expansion of industrial, commercial, and agricultural life, brought about by oversea expansion:

> The influx of foreign riches, has almost levelled every distinction, but that of money, among us. The crest of noble or illustrious ancestry, has sunk before the sudden accumulation of wealth in vulgar hands; but that were little, had not the elegance of manners, had not the dignity of deportment, had no pride of virtue, which used to characterize some of our high-born names, given way to that tide of fortune, which has lifted the low, the illiterate, and the unfeeling, into stations of which they were unworthy.[192]

The story of the nineteenth century, however, must furnish the proof of their worth or failure.

REFERENCES TO CHAPTER V

[1] Fox Bourne, *op. cit.*, II, p. 18; *New Bristol Guide* (1799) ; p. 82.

[2] Died 1725. Fox Bourne, II, p. 26.

[3] Died 1785. Hoare, *Pedigrees and Memoirs of the Families of Hore and Hoare*, pp. 11, 26-30; Forbes, *Memoirs of a Banking-House*, pp. 2-9.

[4] Of the famous banking house of Barclay. Fox Bourne, II, pp. 136-137.

[5] Nolte, *Fifty Years in Both Hemispheres, or Reminiscences of a Merchant's Life*, p. 157; *Public Characters of 1805*, p. 51.

[6] *Gent. Mag.*, lxxx. pt. ii, p.382; Fox Bourne, II, pp. 240-243.

[7] "A Tour through the Whole Island of Great Britain," cited in Anderson, III, p. 143.

[8] Craik, II, p. 153, who stated that "half of the shipping and half the wealth of Liverpool are now engaged in this business."

[9] Anderson, III, p. 325.

[10] In 1716, Liverpool had but one twenty-fourth of the whole kingdom's shipping; in 1792, more than one-sixth. In short, while the nation's commerce increased threefold, that of Liverpool increased twelve-fold. Brooke, *Liverpool as it was during the last quarter of the Eighteenth Century*, p. 234.

[11] *Norris Papers*, p. 30; Fox Bourne, II, pp. 37-38.

[12] *Norris Papers*, pp. 30, 49, 78, 100.

[13] Fox Bourne, pp. 53-55.

[14] Baines, *History of Liverpool*, p. 427.

[15] The Cunliffes had four vessels, with a capacity of 1,120 slaves, which made three or four voyages a year between Guinea and the West Indies, and brought back profit enough to stock a dozen vessels with rum, sugar, etc., for sale in England. Williamson, *Liverpool Memorandum Book*.

[16] Fox Bourne, II, pp. 57-59.

[17] *Ibid*, II, pp. 61-63.

[18] Baines, *op. cit.*, p. 441.

[19] Fox Bourne, II, pp. 78-79.

[20] *Ibid*, pp. 64, 79.

[21] Baines, pp. 538, 658; Fox Bourne, II, pp. 293-297, 300-301.

[22] See above, p. 120.

[23] *New Bristol Guide* (Bristol, 1799), p. 82.

[24] In all fairness to this master artisan, it should be mentioned that the artistic appeal was no less strong than financial gain: "We are every day finding out some ingenious man, or curious piece of workmanship; all of which we endeavor to make subservient to the im-

provement of our taste, or the perfection of our manufacture." *Letter of Wedgwood,* 4 Nov., 1769, in Boardman, *Bentleyana,* p. 10.

[25] Meteyard, *Life of Wedgwood,* I, p. 112.

[26] Smiles, *Lives of Boulton and Watt,* p. 232; Fox Bourne, II, p. 85.

[27] Smiles, *op. cit.,* pp. 168-169.

[28] In 1773 Boulton wrote: "In the town and neighbourhood of Birmingham, within a few years past, workers in gold and silver have become very numerous, together with carvers, charm-engravers, designers, enamellers, jewellers, and other artists in the precious metals, so that these productions have been sold advantageously both at home and abroad." *Memorial relative to Assaying and Marking Wrought Plate at Birmingham.*

[29] Smiles, pp. 390-391.

[30] Fox Bourne, II, p. 114. After the battle of Trafalgar, the Soho Mint struck off medals, and gave copies to all officers and men participating in the victory. Muirhead, *Life of Watt,* p. 174.

[31] Hutton, *History of Birmingham,* 6th ed., pp. 23, 77.

[32] Fox Bourne, II, p. 84.

[33] Gaskell, *The Manufacturing Population of England,* p. 45.

[34] Thursfield, *Peel,* pp. 2-10.

[35] Roscoe, *The English Scene in the Eighteenth Century,* p. 209.

[36] Hammond, *The Town Labourer,* p. 8.

[37] Fairbairn, *Iron, its History, Properties and Processes of Manufacture,* pp. 283-287.

[38] Hammond, *op. cit.,* p. 9.

[39] *Ibid,* p. 10.

[40] Prothero, *op. cit.,* p. 161.

[41] Hammond, pp. 9-10.

[42] See below, p. 153.

[43] Cundall, *Studies in Jamaica History,* p. 54, q. v. for the amounts of prizes and their recipients.

[44] See below, p. 133f., and Chapter VI.

[45] Gardner, pp. 142-143.

[46] Oldmixon, II, p. 357.

[47] *Spectator,* 19 May 1711.

[48] Gardner, p. 160.

[49] *Ibid,* p. 164.

[50] *Ibid,* p. 156.

[51] *Ibid,* p. 321.

[52] *Ibid,* pp. 156-157.

[53] Edwards, III, p. 348.

[54] *Ibid,* III, pp. 77-78.

[55] Gardner, p. 157.

[56] Edwards, III, p. 296.

[57] *Ibid,* I, intro. p. xiii; Cundall, *op. cit.,* p. 63. There were many

instances of men who made fortunes of from £100,000 to £150,000 in Barbados and returned to England. Oldmixon, II, p. 166.

[58] *Gentleman's Magazine,* Jan., 1739, p. 121.

[59] Gardner, p. 159; see also above, Chapters II and III.

[60] Beginning probably about 1780, when the production of coffee reached 735,398 pounds. Gardner, p. 159.

[61] Oldmixon, I, intro. pp. xix-xx.

[62] Gardner, p. 162; Edwards, III, p. 64.

[63] *Ibid,* III, pp. 64-65, 313, 348, 81.

[64] *Ibid,* III, p. 81.

[65] *Letter of Walpole to Geo. Hardinge, Esq.,* 17 May, 1783.

[66] Bengal, Bombay and Madras were each governed by a president and a council of senior merchants. The former received £300 a year, councillors from £40 to £100; senior merchants, £40; junior merchants, £30; factors, £15; and writers only £5 a year. Trotter, *Warren Hastings,* (in *Rulers of India*), p. 13.

[67] *Ibid,* p. 13.

[68] *Ibid,* p. 28.

[69] Willson, *op. cit.,* pp. 168-169.

[70] *Ibid,* p. 220.

[71] *Letter of Walpole to Sir H. Mann,* 20 April, 1766.

[72] *Ibid,* 28 March, 1774.

[73] *Ibid,* 6 Feb., 1780.

[74] Willson, p. 182.

[75] Trotter, *op. cit.,* pp. 21-22. See also instances cited below.

[76] *Letter of Walpole to Sir Horace Mann,* 20 July, 1767. See also, *ibid,* 20 April, 1767, 12 Feb., 1772, and 9 April, 1772, and *to the Earl of Hertford,* 2 Dec., 1763. Also, Malcolm, *Life of Robert, First Lord Clive,* II, p. 187, and Cunningham, *Lives,* V, p. 344.

[77] Willson, p. 167; *Dictionary of National Biography,* XLV, pp. 278-280.

[78] *Ibid,* XLIX, pp. 397-399; Willson, p. 248.

[79] *Ibid,* pp. 307, 312.

[80] Trotter, pp. 38, 202. The pension which was granted him by the Directors alone enabled this distinguished governor to retire to a comfortable country-seat. *Ibid,* p. 210; Willson, p. 311. For correction of abuses, see below, Chapter VI.

[81] See below, Chapter VI.

[82] *The Weekly Journal,* etc., 15 Oct., 1720.

[83] *Applebee's Original Weekly Journal,* 15 Oct., 1720.

[84] *Ibid,* 24 Sept., 1720.

[85] *Portland MSS.,* V. p. 593.

[86] *The Weekly Journal or Saturday's Post,* 15 Oct., 1720.

[87] *Portland MSS.,* VII, p. 282.

[88] *Ibid.*

[89] *The Weekly Journal or Saturday's Post,* 15 Oct., 1720. For corroboration of the humble origin of thousands of South Sea profiteers see Applebee's *Original Wkly. Jl.,* 24 Sept., 1720; *The Wkly. Jl. or Sy.'s Post,* 1 Oct., 1720; Applebee's *Orig. Wkly. Jl.,* 1 Oct., 1720; *ibid,* 8 Oct., 1720; *ibid,* 15 Oct., 1720; *The Wkly. Jl., or Brit. Gaz.,* 2 Nov., 1720, 26 Nov., 1720; also, Wright, *Caricature History of the Georges,* p. 46; Melville, *The South Sea Bubble,* p. 152 f; Swift, *The South Sea Project,* passim.

[90] Entick, II, p. 382.

[91] See *The Wkly. Jl., or Sy's Post,* 1 Oct., 1720, and below, Chapter VI.

[92] See *The Wkly. Jl., or Brit. Gaz.,* 7 Jan., 1720; 13 May, 1721; Mist's *Weekly Jl.,* 20 July, 1728.

[93] Anderson, IV, p. 166.

[94] *Ibid.*

[95] *Ibid.*

[96] Willson, *Ledger and Sword,* pp. 310, 312, 314.

[97] Edwards, III, pp. 64-65.

[98] Jeffery, R. W., *The History of the Thirteen Colonies of North America,* p. 190; also, Egerton, *Origin and Growth of English Colonies,* passim.

[99] Craik, II, p. 204; Anderson, p. 155.

[100] Edwards, II, pp. 203-204; see also Douglass, *A Summary, Historical and Political, of the First Planting, Progressive Improvements, and Present State of the British Settlements in America,* I, pt. i., p. 115.

[101] *The Orig. Wkly. Jl.,* 2 July, 1720.

[102] Gardner, p. 120.

[103] *Ibid,* p. 121.

[104] *Ibid,* pp. 160, 164.

[105] *The Wkly. Jl., or Brit. Gaz.,* 27 May, 1721.

[106] Gardner, p. 160.

[107] Jones, H., *Present State of Virginia,* p. 54.

[108] Whitmore, *The Cavalier Dismounted,* p. 20. Servants of this rank were not submitted to the same hardships or humiliations as the convicts. See below, n. 129.

[109] *The Wkly. Jl., or Brit. Gaz.,* 27 April, 1728.

[110] *Gentleman's Magazine,* Feb., 1731. See also *The Country Journal, or Craftsman,* 5 Feb., 1732, and *The Grub-Street Journal,* 29 Mar., 1732.

[111] Force, *Historical Tracts,* I, p. 160; Whitmore, *op. cit.,* p. 14.

[112] Carroll, *Historical Collections of South Carolina,* I. p. 310.

[113] 29 June, 1742.

[114] Quoted in Whitmore, p. 23.

[115] Boswell, I, p. 128, footnote. Ben Franklin has summed up the situation in his *Memoirs*: "Instead of being made with hardy, in-

dustrious husbandmen, it was with the families of broken shop-keepers, and other insolvent debtors; many of idle habits, taken out of the jails, who being set down in the woods, unqualified for clearing land, and unable to endure the hardships of the new settlement, perished in numbers, leaving many helpless children unprovided for."

[116] White, *Historical Collections of Georgia*, p. 37.

[117] Burke, *An Account of the European Settlements in America*, II, p. 272.

[118] Dr. Hewit's *Historical Account* (1779), quoted in Carroll, *op cit.*, p. 324.

[119] *Ibid;* also, see Whitmore, p. 12.

[120] Boswell, III, p. 231 and V, pp. 27, 212, 236, and 278.

[121] *Ibid*, V, p. 137.

[122] *Ibid*, V, p. 150.

[123] Craik, III, p. 136.

[124] *Eur. Mag.*, July, 1784, p. 20.

[125] Ward, *The London Spy;* see also Gay, *The Beggar's Opera,* and *Polly;* and Ashton, II, pp. 248 ff.

[126] *The Wkly. Jl. or Brit. Gaz.*, 27 May, 1721.

[127] Whitmore, p. 20.

[128] 4 Geo. I, c. ii; 6 Geo. I, c. 23; 16 Geo. II, c. 15; 20 Geo. II, c. 46.

[129] Colquhoun, *Police of the Metropolis*, pp. 436-437; Lecky, II, p. 12. That the ends of humanity and philanthropy were not served in the journey across the Atlantic is pictured with minute detail, if not accuracy, in Defoe's *Moll Flanders*. After sale the convicts worked out the term of their sentence, along with the negro slave, under the lash of the overseer. Whitmore, p. 19.

[130] *Ibid*, pp. 29-30.

[131] *Ibid*, pp. 30-31.

[132] Howard, *State of the Prisons in England and Wales*, p. 482.

[133] *Ibid*, pp. 484-486.

[134] Whitmore, p. 31; Egerton, p. 262. At any rate, the number of criminals so transported was so large as to constitute a menace to those colonies. Wm. Douglas, *op. cit.*, writing in 1749, felt that "Maryland and Virginia have been for many years and continue to be a sink for transported Criminals." I, pt. i, p. 115.

[135] Walpole, *Last Journals*, II, p. 38.

[136] Howard, *op. cit.*, p. 465; Colquhoun, *op. cit.*, pp. 299-309; Egerton, p. 262.

[137] 24 Geo. III, c. 65.

[138] Dalrymple, *A Collection of Voyages to the South Seas*, p. 364.

[139] Maiden, *Sir Joseph Banks.*

[140] Wood, *The Discovery of Australia*, p. 423.

[141] Egerton, p. 263.

[142] Southey, *Elinor,* in *Ann. Reg.,* 1797, p. 133.

[143] Postlethwayt, *Univ. Dict.,* II, p. 319.

[144] Whitmore, p. 19.

[145] Jones, *op. cit.,* p. 54.

[146] Postlethwayt, *op. cit.,* II, p. 319.

[147] Fielding, *An Inquiry into the Causes of the Late Increase of Robbers,* p. 156.

[148] "Trade has been much increased by taking younger Brothers off from their slothful Way of Living, and applying them with Patrimonies to Traffick . . . enabling them to live in Equality with their Elder Brothers, and sometimes with the Proverb of being the best Gentleman." *Mist's Weekly Journal,* 20 July, 1728; also, Brown's *Estimate of the Manners and Principles of the Time,* I, pp. 31-35. Thousands of younger sons were attracted to government positions in the West Indies alone. Oldmixon, II, p. 346.

[149] Voltaire, *Lettres Philosophiques, No. X, Sur le commerce* (1727).

[150] Lockitt, *op. cit.,* p. 37.

[151] *Applebee's Orig. Wkly. Jl.,* 6 Aug., 1720.

[152] *Melville,* p. 61.

[153] Oldmixon, II, p. 126; Edwards III, p. 346; Gardner, p. 162. See also above, p. 127.

[154] *The Lounger,* 28 May, 1785, 8 Oct., 1785, and 30 Dec., 1786.

[155] Boswell, III, pp. 400-401.

[156] *Dict. of Nat. Biog.,* XLIX, p. 397.

[157] *Ibid,* XLV, p. 280.

[158] *Ibid,* XLIII, p. 112.

[159] *Ibid,* IV, p. 221.

[160] *Walpole to Geo. Montagu, Esq.,* 7 Aug., 1767. Actually, however, nabob land-hunger was but one factor in the increased cost of land. See below, p. 153.

[161] Macky, *op. cit.,* p. 76; also Defoe's *Tour,* I, pp. 255-256; see below Ch. VII.

[162] Willson, p. 247.

[163] *Dict. of Nat. Biog.,* XLV, p. 278.

[164] *Ibid,* XLIX, pp. 397-398.

[165] *Ibid,* XLIII, p. 112.

[166] *Ibid,* IV, p. 221.

[167] *Letter of Walpole to Sir Horace Mann,* 2 Feb., 1781.

[168] Porritt, *The Unreformed House of Commons,* I, p. 522. See also below Chapter VII.

[169] Fox-Bourne, II, pp. 37-38.

[170] *Norris Papers,* 30, 49.

[171] Porritt, *op. cit.,* I, p. 523.

[172] *Ibid,* I, p. 523; Fox Bourne, II, pp. 162-163.

[173] Porritt, I, p. 523.

[174] Oldfield, *Representative History of Great Britain and Ireland*, IV, p. 449; Trevelyan, *Life of Fox*, p. 503.

[175] *The Post-Boy*, 3/5 Jan., 1712.

[176] May, *Constitutional History*, I, pp. 232-238.

[177] Porritt, I, p. 524.

[178] Sir Wm. Temple, *Of Popular Discontents*, in Works III, p. 61.

[179] Sir W. Petty, *Political Arithmetic*, p. 118.

[180] *Mist's Weekly Journal*, 20 July, 1728.

[181] *The Wkly. Jl. or Sy.'s Post*, 15 Oct., 1720.

[182] *Ibid*, 24 Sept., 1720.

[183] *Applebee's Orig. Wkly. Jl.*, 15 Oct., 1720.

[184] Farming accordingly gave returns insufficient in comparison with the value of the land. Young, *Hertfordshire*, p. 18.

[185] Watson, *Anecdotes of his own Life*, II, p. 253.

[186] Prothero, p. 291. The average size of English farms was slightly less than 300 acres, and the tendency was still toward concentration. Young, *Northern Tour*, IV, p. 192.

[187] "By the influx of riches and a change in manners, they were nearly annihilated in the year 1750." "Suffolk Gentleman," quoted in Johnson, *The Disappearance of the Small Landowner*, p. 136.

[188] Holt, *General View of the Agriculture of the County of Lancaster*, p. 13. For the condition of the yeomanry in other districts, see Arthur Young's *Norfolk* (1804), p. 17, *Suffolk* (1797), p. 7, and *Essex* (1807), I, pp. 39-40.

[189] See above, p. 125.

[190] Arthur Young, in *Report to Board of Agriculture* (1799).

[191] Prothero, pp. 211-213.

[192] *The Lounger*, No. 100, in *The Works of Henry Mackenzie*, VII, p. 28.

CHAPTER VI

MORALITY IN BUSINESS AND PUBLIC LIFE

It has already been noted that the successful business man was to play an important rôle in the social and political life of the eighteenth century. To a considerable extent his conduct in private life was determined by his attitude toward business and colleagues, by his code of commercial morality. Indeed the psychology of the *nouveaux riches* may be perceived by an understanding of their business ethics. The easiest and quickest way to make money was by speculation in the stock market. The buying and selling of stock, of course, more closely resembled gambling than the exchange of legitimate securities. There were no financial experts to enlighten popular ignorance with accurate knowledge; nor was there a vigilant board of directors to expose shams or legislation to prevent the foisting of fraudulent stock on the public. On the contrary, every means was taken to fascinate the public mind by vague rumours of imaginary advantages. False reports of fabulous profits were seemingly substantiated by dividends which could never be paid from legitimate gains. Particularly in the case of the South Sea hoax, and of the thousand and one lesser bubbles, did the Government share the blame, with the stock-jobbers themselves for the stimulation of human cupidity.[1] Nominally every one was on the same footing, and was inspired by the desire to get something for nothing. Actually, however, "those in the know can buy and sell two or even three Times, till the greatest Part of a Kingdom is got into the Hands of a Few Persons, who will undoubtedly govern all the Rest." [2]

These transactions were not only considered legal according to the moral standards of the day, but by common practice, legitimate. The speculators were pioneers in their field, who matched their wits against all comers and who were successful as the survival of the glibbest. It is not surprising that lamentations were frequent and bitter:

There has lately risen up in our Age, a new-fangled and fantastic Credulity . . . whereby the poor, innocent, industrious and unwary People have been delivered into the ravenous and polluted Jaws of Vultures and Tygers . . . and Thousands, I had almost said Millions, have been sacrificed to satiate the Gluttony of a Few.[3]

In an age when the sole aim of stock-jobbing was speculation for vast gains, rather than investment, it is obvious that not only the general public, but merchants and bankers, should frequently be the victims of their own cupidity. Unfortunately business life of the period came to be fashioned after the same pattern and with equally unfortunate results. As one writer complained, "It hath changed honest Commerce into Bubbling, our Traders into Projectors, our Industry into Tricking, and Applause is earned where the Pillory is deserved." [4]   Little sympathy need be wasted on the losers, whose objectives and methods were as unmoral as those of the winners.

For the new and universal business of stock-jobbing, the coffee-house, or the machinery of the Stock Exchange, served admirably.   The latter was by no means a new institution, for the Royal Exchange had been restored after the great fire of 1666, at a cost of £80,000.[5]   Here merchants and those with whom they dealt met every afternoon; "and for the more regular and readier dispatch of business, they dispose themselves in separate walks." [6]

To furnish the cost of repairing and the expensive up-keep of the building, a gallery was built over the four sides of the Royal Exchange, which housed some two hundred shops, let out at a rental of from £20 to £60 a year.   For some years a considerable trade was carried on here.   Then the centre of fashionable retail trade took another turn.   By 1766 the shops were deserted and the galleries let out to the "Royal Exchange Assurance office, the merchants' Seamen's office; the marine society, and to auctioneers, etc." [7]   In short, the entire building became devoted to enterprises connected with the great commercial activities of the nation.   Here gathered every afternoon foreign and domestic traders,

although those of the better sort meet in Exchange Alley, at three celebrated coffee-houses, called Garraway's, Robin's, and Jonathan's.   In the first, the people of quality who have business in the City, and the considerable and wealthy citizens frequent. In the second, the Foreign Banquers, and often even Foreign Ministers . . . and in the third, the buyers and sellers of stock.[8]

In this setting there came to pass possibly the most dramatic, and in its effect the most far-reaching, tragedy in the financial history of the eighteenth century. Strangely enough the enterprise concerned had a legitimate excuse for existence, and if honestly promoted, might have proved a paying venture. To the surprise of the nation, it was discovered in 1711 that England had been plunged into a debt of some £9,000,000, that this obligation was constantly increasing, and that no plans had been formed looking toward its reduction. In this connection it is interesting to note that to establish a fund for the payment of the annual interest, all the duties on tobacco, India goods, and wrought silk (among other commodities) were rendered permanent.[9]

Schemes, accordingly, for the reduction of the national debt and the restoration of public credit looked toward possibilities overseas. In order to allure government creditors with the hope of advantages from a new commerce, the monopoly of a trade to the South Seas (*i.e.*, the coast of Spanish America), was granted to a company composed of the holders of the debt. An Act of Parliament, considered by its panegyrists a masterpiece, by its opponents anathema, incorporated the subscribers under the name of the "governor and company of merchants of Great Britain trading to the South Seas and other parts of America."[10]

The popularity of the procedure was bound to be certain. Since the days of Elizabeth and her glorious adventurers the profits of this commerce had been greatly exaggerated. It was reported, for example, that the trade of France in the South Seas had been so successful as to repay that country's war debts.[11] Furthermore a rumour, industriously circulated, that four ports on the coasts of Peru and Chile were to be ceded by Spain, inflamed the general ardour.[12] Here at last was the chance for all Englishmen to share in a bonanza, to grow rich overnight without a stroke of work. After all, was not the prospect of exchanging gold, silver and valuable drugs for the manufactures of England, a plausible allurement for a commercial nation?

The scheme in fact rested on a false foundation, though it is doubtful whether the founders fully realized this at the time. Instead of admitting the English to freedom of trade, Philip V of Spain granted the Company only the Asiento contract (1713),[13] the terms of which were modified three years later. This included the privilege of supplying Spanish America with negro slaves for a period of thirty years, and of sending a ship annually to Porto Bello.[14]

Unfortunately the Company failed to take advantage even of these limited opportunities. Not until 1717 was the first voyage made, and in the following year the trade was suppressed by a rupture with Spain.[15] Its factories, merchandise and representatives were seized and detained. It was evident that the Company had failed as far as trading went, and that prospects for the future were dubious. Fearing lest this plan for reducing the national debt should fail, the ministry now adopted the visionary schemes of its promoters, and "gave to the Company the power of fascinating the minds of the public, and spreading an infatuation similar to that which had recently involved France in a national bankruptcy." [16] This privilege of hoaxing the public the Company obtained for the enormous sum of £7,567,500.[17]

During the winter of 1720-1721 the meteoric rise of South Sea stock reached its climax. And the same could be said of the gullibility of the public, which was clamouring for stock now at the fictitious value of £1,100 a share.[18] To keep the public mind in this state of intoxication, imaginary advantages were held forth; vague rumours as to hidden treasures and valuable commercial privileges were circulated in 'Change Alley,— rumours which neither the government nor the press sought to deny. False reports of fabulous profits were substantiated by dividends of ten, thirty, and even fifty per cent., voted by the directors—dividends which could never be paid from legitimate gains.[19] Plainly enough,

> While some build castles in the air,
>   Directors build them in the seas;
> Subscribers plainly see them there,
>   For fools will see as wise men please.[20]

To these mysterious hints, another ballad of the day bears witness:

What need have we of Indian wealth;
  Or commerce with our neighbours?
Our constitution is in health,
  And riches crown our labours.
Our South Sea Ships have golden shrouds,
  They bring us wealth, 'tis granted,
But lodge their Treasure in the clouds,
  To hide it till it's wanted.[21]

Nor was this cupidity confined to the South Sea scheme. The whole nation turned stock-jobber and promoter, with every day bringing forth new proposals basking in the opulence of the South Sea. Naturally its success served only to inflate still further the paper value of the stock and to increase the mania for speculation. Sharpers, alias promoters, hitherto covering their schemes with some semblance of reasonableness, in view of the public frenzy now offered for popular subscription stock issues unexcelled in audacity. In fact the *Weekly Journal* [22] complained that these individuals "are infinitely too numerous for the Bubbles; since the Stocks they have proposed to raise Amount to £28,000,000, above twice as much as the current Coin of the Nation." Sir Josiah Child was but one of the many, who by circulating false rumours and causing the rise or fall of stocks accumulated a fortune for himself and laid the foundations of an opulent family.[23]

On their face most of these schemes were obvious frauds; a few culled at random show the low level which public sanity had reached: "For raising the growth of raw silk, £1,000,000" (an enterprise utterly

unsuited to the climate or traditions of England);
"For carrying on the undertaking business, for furnish-
ing funerals, £1,200,000,"—to be sold appropriately
enough, at the Fleece-tavern, Cornhill—and a scheme
surely with no chance of success, save in the event of
a national catastrophe.[24]   One group of "projectors"
attempted to raise the sum of £2,000,000 to carry
coals from Newcastle to London, while the sum of
£1,500,000 for a Greenland fishery was so quickly
raised that a second subscription was offered to those
disappointed gentlemen "who were not timely apprised
of the same." [25]   Nor can one help but admire the
audacity of the promoter who advertised:

> This day, the 8th inst., at Sam's Coffee House, behind the
> Royal Exchange, at three in the afternoon, a Book will be
> opened for entering into a Joint Company Partnership for
> carrying on a Thing that will turn to the Advantage of All
> concerned.[26]

And equal admiration may be expressed for the promoter who expected to raise £1,000,000 for "a perpetual motion by means of a wheel, moving by force
of its own weight." [27]   Attractive baits there were of
mysterious wealth overseas in the subscription offered
at Mulford's:

> to establish Colonies, and settle a Trade in New Brittania, and
> other Parts, where Gold and Silver do abound in Great Plenty
> (more than in Mexico or Peru), well known unto great Num-
> bers of Persons in this Kingdom (as well as the Undertaker
> hereof) although the Value is unknown to the Inhabitants
> there.[28]

Another group proposed to raise £2,000,000 for

"importing the walnut tree from Virginia." [29]   Again,
the unwary might invest in a scheme for the "development of the Golden Islands off the Coast of Carolina"
by the Pennsylvania Company: [30]

> Come all ye Saints that wou'd for little buy,
> Great Tracts of Land, and care not where they lie,
> Deal with your Quaking-Friends, they're Men of Light,
> The Spirit hates, and scorns to Bite. [31]

Or still again, in the Bahama Islands:

> Rare fruitful Isles, where not an Ass can find
> A verdant Tuft, or Thistle, to his Mind.
> How, then, must those poor silly Asses fare,
> That leave their Native Land to settle there. [32]

The popularity of this mania for speculation is
evidenced by advertisements in the contemporary press.
In one number of the *Daily Post*,[33] selected at random,
eighteen of twenty-four advertisements are given over
to "blue-sky" proposals.   It is impossible to state
even approximately the amounts that exchanged
hands; probably, however, the estimate of £110,000,-
000 is somewhat exaggerated.[34]   With the inevitable
crash in South Sea stock, which came in the early part
of September, 1720,[35] there followed the bursting of
the thousand and one parasitic bubbles, making good
the prophecy of the contemporary doggerel:

> Five hundred millions notes and bonds,
>   Our stocks are worth in value;
> But neither lie in goods or lands,
>   Or money, let me tell you;

Yet, though our foreign trade is lost,
  Of mighty wealth we vapour,
When all the riches that we boast,
  Consist in scraps of paper.[36]

It may not be irrelevant to note here, that even
had stock-jobbing been non-existent, man's inherent
desire to gain something for nothing could not be kept
in the background. In stimulating this passion the
government had to share responsibility with the stock
market. A typical eighteenth century institution, the
lottery, was used by Parliament in 1709 to raise a fund
of £1,500,000 to be put out at interest with annual
prizes.[37] Such was the eager response that the entire
sum was subscribed, in £10 shares, in six weeks.[38]

Lotteries were at their full vigour in the reign of
Queen Anne. The Greenwich Hospital Adventure,
certainly in the aid of a worthy cause and one closely
connected with oversea activity,[39] was sanctioned by
Act of Parliament. Similarly, Westminster Bridge,
the need of which was occasioned by the growth of
trade, was built for the most part from funds raised
by lotteries (beginning 1736).[40] And in 1753, the
profits from lotteries procured the Harleian Manuscripts and the Sloane Collection for the British Museum.[41] The government lottery, then, was a popular
way of raising money and was not suspended until
1823. With this encouragement by the government,
the rage for lotteries continued uncontrolled. The
newspapers of the day teem with proposals issued by
every adventurer who could collect a few articles. In
self-defense, shop-keepers converted goods ordinarily

for sale into prizes. It is interesting that many of the prizes were articles of oversea origin,[42] such as fans, snuff-boxes, silks, furs, and plate, as well as other "little goes," which proffered anything and everything, from a shave or a slice of roast-beef, to sixty guineas.[43] In spite of efforts to check this evil, little could be accomplished, while the government, by its own proposals, kept alive the spirit of gambling.[44] This baneful influence of the Stock Exchange was felt well into the following century, and with little change, save that "the State Lottery begins drawing 13 Oct., 1806, containing more Capital prizes, and 5,000 less Tickets, than the last Lottery." [45]

It took a calamity, nation-wide in extent—namely, the bursting of the bubbles—to remedy the worst abuses of stock-jobbing, and to raise, or more exactly to determine, the standards of the financial world. Singularly enough, it was the press, rather than the business world itself, which turned a money-mad people to one more sophisticated, and which brought back ordinary and time-honoured, if less romantic, methods of earning a living. The newspapers were influential in counselling thousands who were sore at heart and empty of pocket, advising them "to turn our thoughts from Stock-Jobbing to Industry and frugal Methods of life. . . . We have made a Jest of Honesty and public Spirit and cancell'd all Respect for whatever our Religion or Laws reputed sacred." [46] Above all, the catastrophe of the South Sea Bubble left business in the hands of men who proposed to make of it a life career, eager to study its intricacies,

and to take into consideration its risks. True, the
passion for making large fortunes was undiminished,
but men were now wary enough to pass by the purely
speculative. A salutary effect, also, resulted from the
moral indignation aroused by the guilty practises of the
South Sea directors and their hirelings.

> Go on, vile Traters, glory in your Sins,
> And grow profusely Rich, by wicked Means . . .
> Impoverish Thousands by some publick Fraud,
> And worship Int'rest as your only God;
> Though you may gain in Time, a South Sea Coach,
> And ride through London, loaded with Reproach,
> Become a proud Director, and at last;
> Be bound to render what you got so fast;
> Perhaps be punish'd when your All is lost;
> With Gallows, Pillory, or Whipping-Post,
> Or if you have your Gold, be doom'd to float,
> To H—ll, in this infernal Ferry-boat.[47]

It should not be inferred, however, that the stock
market was forever purged of dishonesty and unscru-
pulousness. Jobbers still continued to make money
from buying or selling stock. The profiteers in the
latter half of the century, moreover, were for the most
part members of the House of Commons and their
friends. Charles Townshend, among others, was
accused of using his political information to amass
a fortune for himself in East India stock. Walpole
complains that

in truth it is a very South Sea year, for at least one-third of the
House of Commons is engaged in this traffic; and stock-jobbing
now makes patriots, as everything else has done. From the
Alley to the House, it is like a path of ants.[48]

In 1769, speculation in East India stock, which continued to be mixed up with Parliamentary politics, was again reminiscent of the operations connected with the South Sea Bubble:

> The East India Company is all faction and gambling. Such fortunes are made and lost every day as are past belief. Our history will appear a gigantic lie hereafter, when we are shrunk to our little island. People trudge to the other end of the town to vote who shall govern empires at the other end of the world. Panchaud, a banker from Paris, broke yesterday for £70,000 by buying and selling stock; and Sir Laurence Dundas paid in £140,000 for what he had bought. The Company have more and greater places to give away than the First Lord of the Treasury.[49]

The American Revolution offered further opportunities for the speculators. Again, lies were spread on every hand; on this occasion, not only stock-jobbers, but moneyed citizens, and even newspapers were "the vehicles of lies, blunders and scandals."[50] Fortunately, the general public had learned its lesson and left the market largely to professional brokers. For the most part it now fulfilled only its legitimate functions. Even the financial crises of 1793 and 1797 were due to over-expansion, and ignorance of the operation of credits, rather than to untoward speculation.

The spirit of speculation gave an impulse to the institution of insurance, which became in this century an established factor in business life. Insurance, with its wide social and economic significance, grew largely out of the need for the protection of English merchant ships, and speculation which infected all business of the time was its first *modus operandi*. Strictly speaking, the beginnings of the insurance movement belong to the late seventeenth century.   In coffee-houses, more particularly at Lloyd's, men of capital met ship-owners and merchants at fixed hours.   After consider-able haggling over condition of ship, crew and cargo, and length of voyage, contracts were drawn up.   Fire insurance had its inception about 1680, while the first mutual plan for life insurance was incorporated in the Friendly Society (1684).   As late as 1720, marine insurance was still considered a gamble:

> In vain are all Assurances, for still
> The raging Winds must answer Heav'n's Will.[51]

Underwriters, however, profited by their earlier specu-lations, and began to evolve a scientific approach to their problems.   Aside from economic considerations, insurance eventually made for the elimination of undue risks from business enterprises.   The man who insured his property and his life had accomplished two things: he had substituted foresight for hazard, and had elimi-nated chance of total loss as far as possible from busi-ness.   In short, by his own conduct, he had done more than repressive legislation to destroy the gambling spirit.   Finally, in sharing the burden of risk with his colleagues, he accomplished far more for humanity, than by occasional acts of charity.

On a par with the monarchs of the Stock Exchange were the servants and officials of the East India Com-pany, whose conduct has already been considered. Complaints of their unconscionable greed, and of their disregard for the lives and property of natives, began to be aired as early as 1732.[52] It became a matter of common knowledge, that for the greater part of the century the East Indies were the scenes of untold tyranny, plunder and corruption.[53] "We are Spaniards in our lust for gold, and Dutch in our delicacy in obtaining it," [54] wrote Walpole. Here, as in the stock market, the sole object was to acquire the maximum fortune in the shortest time.

Ruthless plunder in the Indies, however, could not be done without reproach, without incurring the condemnation of fellow-countrymen. Walpole expressed the sentiments of self-respecting Englishmen when he wrote further:

They (the nabobs) starved millions in India by monopolies and plunder, and almost raised a famine at home by the luxury occasioned by their opulence, and by that opulence, raising the price of everything, till the poor could not afford to purchase bread. Conquest, usurpation, wealth, luxury, famine. . . . If you like it better in Scripture phrase, here it is: Lord Chatham begat the East India Company; the East India Company begat Lord Clive; Lord Clive begat the Maccaronis, and they begat poverty; all the race is still living.[55]

Abuses in the East India Company had become, therefore, not so much a question of profits, as of English honour.[56] Unfortunately the efforts made by Parliament in the middle of the century were based on the assumption that the Company was enormously wealthy, and nothing of constructive value was accomplished.[57] The attempts of Clive to check the corruption and extortion by which he himself had gained an enormous fortune were perhaps the first serious efforts

to remove the source of the evil.[58] Soon again, however, the "golden age" which Clive had promised
proved only the source of more plunder for Company
officials.[59] With the Company itself facing bankruptcy came the conviction that the time had passed
for the government of so vast a region to be carried
on by a commercial organization. In 1773, accordingly, the charter was completely changed, and the government of India passed in large part into the hands
of the ministers of the Crown.[60] Even after the reorganization of government and the readjustment of salaries in India conditions remained intolerable. Fox
complained that "inhumanity, false policy, peculation
and brutality were to be discovered in almost every
step," [61] so that it could justly be said, "the very name
of Englishman is detested, even to a proverb, through
all Asia, and the national character is become degraded
and dishonoured." [62]

The administration of Warren Hastings, tyrannical
as it was, restored some semblance of order, although
it was felt that his place should be filled by a person
of independent fortune, "who had not for an object
the repairing of his estate in India, that had long been
the nursery of ruined and decayed fortunes." [63] Pitt's
India Bill (1784) restored public confidence in the
Company, and provided for public trial of those who
were suspected of extortion.[64] Although abuses in
India by no means ceased, the trial of Warren Hastings
had a chastening effect, and the fear of losing ill-
gotten gains, coupled with the possibility of a prison
sentence, proved to prospective fortune-hunters the

necessity of their respecting in some measure the rights of others. The West India planters belonged to another category; for the most part, they were plodders, and accumulated their fortunes by hard work. The employment of slave labour could hardly condemn them, for not until towards the close of the century did it begin to be placed beyond the pale of business ethics.[65]

Smuggling, too, was universal,[66] and people felt no prejudice toward it, except for political reasons. Merchants, as a rule, resented Walpole's practice of saddling the burden of taxation on manufactured and imported goods, and felt that any means to dodge the levies were justifiable.[67] Even Thomas Johnson, otherwise the most scrupulous of Liverpool merchants, continually entered tobacco on the sly, and claimed remission of duty on the ground that the goods were damaged and unmarketable.[68] Nothing taxed or prohibited was exempt from the activities of smugglers.[69] Brandy, coffee, playing cards and tea were the favourite articles concerned. Dealers in tea actually appealed to Parliament to prevent its clandestine running, "so prejudicial to the Fair Trader, and the general Interest of the Nation."[70]

In spite of strenuous and persistent efforts of legislators, the evil continued.[71] Pitt complained that of thirteen million pounds of tea imported annually into the United Kingdom less than half paid duty.[72] Indian calicoes, too, continued to be imported, after their use had been forbidden, to such an extent that the Spitalfields weavers revolted.[73] So extensive was smuggling throughout the century, that statistics for the importation of all dutiable goods give only approximate quantities.[74]   Other practices, like piracy and the adulteration of foodstuffs, continued from earlier times, but were without the pale of public sanction.[75]

On the whole the bitter and expensive lesson taught by the South Sea Bubble was not forgotten.   True, risks remained and there were always chances to be taken; but speculation for its own sake and as a means for accumulating fortunes became less frequent.   By a thorough study of their problems, capitalists learned to discriminate between "good" and "bad" risks.   As the century waned, the keen competition of capital in its search for opportunity finally determined the survival of the fittest.   The crowded docks and warehouses of London and Liverpool, and the busy factories of Manchester and Birmingham, were built up by those traders and manufacturers who gained, and maintained, a reputation for scrupulous dealing. Customer and merchant were in even closer contact than to-day; continued prosperity for the latter depended largely on honest price and quality.   The successful business man, too, wished his good name and that of his firm to continue as an asset for future generations.   A further cause and effect of this changed conception of business was the gradual admission of the class associated with it to the privileges, and sometimes to the social and political position, of the landed aristocracy.   Honesty in business, then, and the development of a code of commercial ethics, are evidenced by the silence of those who would be most eager to criticize abuses, by the efforts of business men themselves to reform the worst evils in their sphere, and finally by their new standing in the community. It is well to remember, also, that the British Empire has been held together, partly by good fortune, partly by the weakness of rivals, partly by the strength of a powerful fleet, but principally by the integrity of the British trader, merchant and banker.

The upward climb to respectability found support in the press. As one periodical put it: "Industry is the first principle of a Citizen, is an infallible Specifick to keep the Spirits awake, and prevent that Stagnation and Corruption of Humours which make our fine Gentlemen such horrible torments to one another and to themselves." [76] According to a more radical editor, men should be esteemed according to the wealth they bring their country, and "trade is accounted of all professions the most honourable." [77]

The code of political ethics in the early eighteenth century closely approximated the standard of business morals. As a versifier of the time expressed it:

> When you censure the Age,
>   Be cautious and sage,
> Lest the Courtiers offended should be;
>   If you mention Vice or Bribe,
>   'Tis pat to all the Tribe,
>   Each cries, that was levell'd at me. [78]

Although Parliamentary corruption dates back to the reign of Charles II, [79] flagrant dishonesty came to the fore during the administration of Walpole. At least there was nothing hypocritical in this corruption. Bribery was frankly the normal process of Parliamentary government, and the public knew it; there was no pretense at deception.[80] The low tone of public life was due chiefly to the fact that the moneyed classes, now so powerful an element in the state, did not as yet have representation in Parliament sufficient, according to their lights, for the protection and promotion of their vast interests.

The prime object of Walpole was to serve the interests of his supporters, who belonged to this group, and to build up a substantial material prosperity. In his attempts to maintain a Parliamentary majority, he resorted to methods which would not be tolerated to-day.[81] Few prominent statesmen retired to private life without having accumulated fortunes during their stay in office. Walpole himself made enough to settle in comfort in the country. His own son was never thought honest till he was out of power.[82] Lord Somers barely escaped conviction for having made grants to Captain Kidd.[83] James Craggs, secretary of state, was relieved by death of punishment for holding fictitious South Sea stock.[84] Godolphin and Bolingbroke, however, retired from the ministry poor men, and no suspicion was cast at Pulteney, Windham, Onslow, Carteret, Barnard or Pitt.[85] This meager list shows most clearly the deplorable state of office-holding during the reign of Anne and the first two Georges. Curiously enough those men who indulged in corrupt practices rose on occasion to great heights in the furtherance of their country's interests.

The purchase of seats in the House of Commons was a new phase of corruption, peculiar to the eighteenth century, and was due to the insatiable demand of the commercial classes for representation. Their ambition was further curtailed by the Landed Property Qualification Act of 1712. Its passage, an act of self-defense on the part of the landed aristocracy, showed that "power, which, according to an old maxim, was used to follow land, had now gone over to money." [86] Even the keen jealousy of the country gentry could not prevent the admission to political power of the men of business—if not legally, then by the very force of their money. In 1701 the elections turned principally upon the contention between the Old and the New East India Companies. [87] For the first time, complaints were made of the purchase of elections:

When the House met, reports were brought to them of elections that had been scandalously purchased by some who were concerned in the new East India Company. Instead of drinking and entertainments, by which elections were formerly managed, now a most scandalous practise was brought in of buying votes, with so little decency, that the electors engaged themselves by subscription to choose a blank person before they were trusted with the name of their candidate. [88]

The country gentry were "vexed, put to great expenses, and even baffled," by these newcomers at elections, and many members of Parliament were felt to be directly or indirectly under their influence. [89] Not only did persons endeavour to purchase elections in counties where they were unknown, but brokers appeared on the Stock Exchange, to sell seats at stated prices. The Earl of Dorset complained that "a great number of persons have no other livelihood, than by being employed in bribing corporations." [90] So great was this evil that bitter complaints were heard in Parliament of the growing cost of elections.[91]

Frantic efforts were made by the landed aristocracy to check corruption, especially the species by which members of the commercial class entered Parliament. The purchase of seats was diminished by legislation in 1743,[92] and by Beckford's Bribery Bill of 1769.[93] During the reign of George III, however, the masters of wealth outgrew the bonds of existing legislation. Merchants who had made their wealth in London, or those who had acquired it in enterprises of the East India Company, had bought landed property, and established county families.[94] Above all, a flood of nabobs was returning to England, laden with the spoils of India and eager to enter Parliament. As Chatham phrased it:

The riches of Asia have been poured in upon us, and have brought with them not only Asiatic luxury, but, I fear, Asiatic principles of government. Without connections, without any natural interest in the soil, the importers of foreign gold have forced their way into Parliament by such a torrent of private corruption as no private hereditary fortune could resist.[95]

With competition so keen the price of seats and the cost of elections advanced sharply. In the time of George I, a fair price for a seat was £1,400 or £1,500.[96]

At the first general election in the reign of George III, a nomination could be purchased for £2,000.[97]   Within a short time the price had advanced to £4,000,[98] while Chesterfield complained that the election at Northampton cost the contending parties £30,000 a side, and that one borough had sold for £9,000.[99]   In attempting to purchase an election for his son Chesterfield had to face competition with the wealth of nabobs.   His offer of five and twenty hundred pounds was contemptuously refused by a borough jobber, who said

that there was no such thing as a borough to be had now, for the rich East and West Indians had secured them all, at the rate of three thousand pounds at the least; but many at four thousand, and two or three that he knew at five thousand.[100]

The rotten borough system, now at its worst—as in the case of old Sarum, Sudbury, and Cricklade—could result only in open sale of seats, and in flagrant bribery at the polls.   In the smaller household boroughs, where nabobs were wont to try their fortunes, bribery was so open and profuse that often a candidate was actually taken into custody by the sergeant-at-arms.[101] Walpole was convinced that expenses never ran so high, and implored his fellow-citizens to "think of two hundred men *of the most consummate virtue,* setting themselves to sale for three weeks!"[102]   Nine members of Parliament were believed to have been retained in the interest of the nabob of Arcot alone.[103]   Dr. Johnson deplored the decay of respect for men of family and permanence, and the willingness to sell political power for gold.[104]   Walpole in particular has left a most graphic picture of political corruption and of popular resentment towards its flagrancy:

Whatever mysteries or clouds there are, will probably develop themselves as soon as the elections are over, and the Parliament fixed, which now engrosses all conversation and all purses; for the expense is incredible. West Indians, conquerors, nabobs and admirals attack every borough; and there were no fewer than nine candidates at Andover. The change in the Parliament used to be computed at sixty or seventy, now it is believed there will be a hundred and fifty members. Corruption now stands upon its own legs—no money is issued from the treasury; there are no parties, no pretence of grievances, and yet venality is grosser than ever! The borough of Sudbury has gone so far as to advertise for a chapman! We have been as victorious as the Romans and are as corrupt; I don't know how soon a praetorian militia will set the empire to sale. Sir Nathaniel Curzon has struck a very novel stroke, advertising that the king intended to make him a peer; and therefore, recommending his brother to the county of Derby, for the same independent principles with himself. He takes the peerage to prove his independence, and recommends his brother to the Opposition to prove his gratitude.[105]

It was that group which formed a nucleus of corrupt interests at home to support corrupt government abroad,[106] a combination which was "ubiquitous, persistent, rich, powerfully handled, a direct menace to the state." [107]

Fortunately, as a corrective to this element, public opinion brought, in the election of 1780, a better type of individual into politics.[108] William Pitt was a young man of stainless morals, the finest type of patriot, as were Fox, Shelburne, and Sheridan. The notorious borough of Cricklade was disfranchised, "on account of its enormous corruption." [109] So, too, an army of revenue officers—estimated at from 40,000 to 60,000 [110]—was disbanded. More than forty employments were abolished and the pension-list was reduced to £90,000.[111] Burke was responsible for regulating his own position of paymaster-general, which was the most lucrative of government posts. Shelburne's bill provided that government appointees to posts in the colonies must reside there.[112] It was this group, moreover, which brought about the first constructive reforms of abuses in India.[113] Pitt and other members of the new generation of statesmen governed without those instruments of bribery that were formerly the chief assets of Parliamentary leaders.[114] Swept into power on a popular wave of enthusiasm, these honest, patriotic young men completely terminated direct Parliamentary corruption, checked the careers of those who were fattening on the spoils of empire, satisfied the awakening conscience of the nation, first by mitigating the evils of the Middle Passage,[115] then by abolition of the Slave Trade, and finally set an example for later legislators by instituting an era of clean constructive political life. Unable, in the face of powerful interests, to abolish the evils of the rotten borough system, they were at least prophets of the great crusading spirit which expressed itself in the Reform Bill of 1832.

REFERENCES TO CHAPTER VI

[1] See above Chapter V.

[2] *The Country Journal or Craftsman,* 8 Jan., 1732.

[3] *Ibid,* 8 Jan., 1732. Defoe exposes in graphic manner the vagaries of the stock-market, in his *Anatomy of Exchange Alley,* p. 16.

[4] *Ibid.*

[5] Entick, *A New and Accurate History and Survey of London, Westminster, Southwark and other Places adjacent,* IV, p. 99.

[6] *Ibid,* IV, p. 103.

[7] *Ibid,* IV, p. 103.

[8] Macky, *Journey through England,* I, p. 190; Entick, *op. cit.,* IV, p. 111. See also under coffee-house, pp. 208-212.

[9] Coxe, *Memoirs of Sir Robert Walpole,* I, p. 219.

[10] Posthlethwayt, *Historical State of the South Sea Company;* Anderson, III, p. 43; 9 Anne, c. 21.

[11] *Mist's Weekly Journal,* 13 Jan., 1728.

[12] Stanhope, *History of England,* II, p. 3; Coxe, *op. cit.,* p. 219.

[13] Melville, p. 14 f.

[14] Anderson, III, p. 55.

[15] Melville, p. 26.

[16] The Mississippi Bubble. Coxe, I, pp. 130, 221; Stanhope, *op. cit.,* II, p. 3.

[17] Melville, p. 52.

[18] *The Wkly. Jl.,* etc., 15 Oct., 1720; *Applebee's Orig. Wkly. Jl.,* 15 Oct., 1720. See also above, p. 162.

[19] Coxe, I, p. 232; Anderson, III, p. 96; Melville, p. 62.

[20] Swift, *The South Sea Project.*

[21] Boyer, *Political State of Great Britain,* XX, p. 178.

[22] 24 Sept., 1720.

[23] Defoe, *Anatomy of Exchange Alley,* pp. 14-15.

[24] All of the above schemes are listed in Malcolm, *Anecdotes,* I, pp. 111-117, which see for the complete list.

[25] *The Daily Post,* 23 Feb., 1720.

[26] Malcolm, *op. cit.,* I, p. 113.

[27] *Ibid.*

[28] *The Daily Post,* 21 April, 1720.

[29] Malcolm, I, p. 111.

[30] *The Post-Boy,* 17, 20 Sept., 1720.

[31] *The Weekly Journal or Brit. Gaz.,* 26 Nov., 1720.

[32] *Ibid.*

[33] 20 April, 1720.

[34] Malcolm, I, p. 117.

[35] Briscoe, *The Economic Policy of Robert Walpole*, p. 47.

[36] Quoted in Malcolm, I, p. 127; for effects of the South Sea Bubble on social morality, see below, Ch. IX.

[37] *Post-Boy*, 27 Dec., 1709.

[38] *Ibid*, 3 Feb., 1710.

[39] See below, Chapter XI.

[40] Lecky, I, p. 52.

[41] *Ibid*, I, p. 523.

[42] Macpherson, *Annals*, III, p. 23.

[43] *Ann. Reg.*, 1777, pp. 206-7; *The Times* (London), 22 July, 1795.

[44] See below Chaptter IX for gambling.

[45] Malcolm, II, p. 4.

[46] *The Wkly. Jl. or Brit. Gaz.*, 7 Jan., 1720.

[47] *Ibid*, 13 May, 1721.

[48] *Walpole to Sir Horace Mann*, 19 Mar., 1767.

[49] *Letter of Walpole to Sir Horace Mann*, 19 July, 1769.

[50] *Ibid*, 17 Sept., 1778; see also *ibid*, 24 Aug., 1780.

[51] *The Wkly. Jl. or Brit. Gaz.*, 26 Nov., 1720.

[52] *The Country Jl. or Craftsman*, 25 Mar., 1732; see above Chapter V.

[53] *Letter of Walpole to Geo. Hardinge*, 17 May, 1783.

[54] *Ibid to Sir Horace Mann*, 12 Feb., 1772. See also, Boswell, *Life of Johnson*, III, p. 20.

[55] Letter of Walpole to Sir Horace Mann, 9 April, 1772. The fortunes acquired during the early part of the century were insignificant compared with those of later times. Boswell, *op. cit.*, III, p. 30.

[56] Chesterfield, *Letters to his Son*, 30 October, 1767.

[57] Macpherson, *Annals*, III, pp. 463-466.

[58] Willson, *Ledger and Sword*, p. 196; *Letter of Walpole to Sir Horace Mann*, 20 July, 1767; Malcolm, *Clive*, II, pp. 335-338.

[59] Chatham *Correspondence*, III, pp. 61, 199, 200, 216, 269; IV, pp. 276-277; Burke's *Correspondence*, I, pp. 210-211, 389-390; Walpole, *Last Journals*, I, pp. 169, 207, 210, 242-246.

[60] Mill, *History of British India*, IV, ch. ix.

[61] Fox, *Speeches*, II, p. 203.

[62] *Ibid*, II, pp. 238-240.

[63] *Parliamentary History*, XXIII, p. 757; see also, Boswell, IV, p. 213, footnote.

[64] "A Review of the Proceedings of the Parliament of 1784," in *Works of Henry Mackenzie*, VII, p. 208.

[65] See below Ch. XII.

[66] Lecky estimated that 40,000 were engaged in this lucrative practice, and that the whole population was willing to share its benefits. V, p. 29.

[67] Pitt believed that smuggling was due to excessive duties. Lecky, V, p. 53.

[68] *Norris Papers*, p. 81.

[69] Boswell, III, p. 188, n. 5.

[70] Read's *Weekly Journal or Brit. Gaz.*, 14 Feb., 1736; Hanway, *Letters*, II, p. 179. For effects of smuggling on legitimate business, see *The Wkly. Jl.*, or *Sy.'s Post*, 19 Aug., 1721.

[71] Read's *Weekly Journal*, etc., 2 Oct., 1736.

[72] Macpherson, *op. cit.*, IV, pp. 49-50.

[73] Hill, *op. cit.*, p. 194.

[74] See above, pp. 31-45.

[75] Hanway, *Letters*, II, p. 264. For earlier activities of pirates and buccaneers who infested the West Indies, see *The London Journal*, 3 Aug., 1723, and Traill, *op. cit.*, V, p. 23.

[76] "Bruyere" in the *London Journal* (1727), quoted in Malcolm, *Anecdotes*, II, p. 283.

[77] *Mist's Wkly. Jl.*, 20 July, 1728.

[78] Gay, *The Beggar's Opera;* see also *Mist's Wkly. Jl.*, 23 Mar., 1728.

[79] Lecky, I, p. 366.

[80] *The Wkly. Jl.*, or *Sy.'s Post*, 17 Mar., 1722. "Never was treating, buying of voices, freedoms, and freeholds, and all the corrupt practices in the world, so open and barefaced." Willson, *Life of Defoe*, II, p. 362. And again: "It is not an impossible thing to debauch this nation into a choice of thieves, knaves, devils, anything comparatively speaking, by the power of various intoxications." *Ibid*, III, pp. 23-24.

[81] Coxe, *Walpole*, II, pp. 492-493; *ibid, Marlborough,* ch. xcvii; *Marchmont Papers*, II, pp. 205, 245, 248; *Chatham Correspondence*, I, pp. 167-168.

[82] Walpole, *Memoirs of George II*, I, p. 236.

[83] Cunningham, G. E., *History of England in the Lives of Englishmen*, IV, pp. 74-75.

[84] *Ibid*, IV, p. 94.

[85] Lecky, I, p. 373.

[86] Swift, *Examiner*, No. 13.

[87] Burnet, *Own Time*, II, pp. 258-259.

[88] *Ibid*, II, p. 209; see also, Craik, II, pp. 136-137.

[89] Bolingbroke, *Letter to Windham,* quoted in Lecky, I, pp. 201-202.

[90] *Parlt. Hist.*, VII, p. 297. According to D'Avenant, in his *Balance of Power,* most of these individuals were connected with stockholders in the Bank of England and the East India Company.

[91] *Parlt. Hist.*, VII, p. 335.

[92] Lecky, III, p. 171.

[93] The chief supporters of the later bill were "country gentlemen

who can ill afford to combat with great lords, nabobs, commissaries, and West Indians." Walpole, *Memoirs of the Reign of Geo. III*, p. 159. See also, Boswell, II, p. 339, footnote.

[94] Porritt, *op. cit.*, I, p. 521.

[95] Chatham, *Correspondence*, III, p. 405. See also, Trevelyan, *Life of Fox*, p. 143; Massey, *History of England in the Reign of George III*, I, pp. 336-337.

[96] Porritt, I, p. 357.

[97] *Ibid;* see also Walpole, *Letters*, III, p. 397.

[98] Porritt, I, p. 521.

[99] Chesterfield's *Letter to his Son*, 12 April, 1768. The expenses of Wilberforce's election to Parliament amounted to £9,000. *Life of Wilberforce*, p. 19. See also, Reid, *Memoirs of the Public Life of John Horne Tooke*, p. 55.

[100] *Chesterfield's Letter to his Son*, 19 Sept., 1767.

[101] Porritt, I, p. 521. *Letter of Walpole to Sir Horace Mann*, 26 June, 1747.

[102] *Ibid*, 24 Dec., 1744.

[103] *Ibid*, 28 Jan., 1781.

[104] Boswell, V, p. 106; II, p. 153.

[105] *Letter of Walpole to Sir Horace Mann*, 3 Mar., 1761. Armed violence was used and murder committed at elections for Westminster in 1784, 1788, and 1790. Reid, *Memoirs*, etc., p. 45.

[106] See *Dictionary of Nat. Biog.*, XLV, and *Official List*, I, pp. 317-318, for instances of corruption and violence at the polls.

[107] Hammond, *Charles James Fox*, p. 222. See also, Fox, *Speeches*, II, p. 203, and pp. 238-240.

[108] By 1794 there were several societies for Parliamentary Reform. Reid, *op. cit.*, p. 56.

[109] *Parl. Hist.*, XXII, p. 1345.

[110] *Ibid*, XXII, p. 1337.

[111] Lecky, IV, pp. 2-8; 22 Geo. III, c. 82.

[112] Lecky, IV, p. 220.

[113] Hammond, *Fox, passim;* see above, p. 117f.

[114] Hammond, *op. cit.*, p. 76.

[115] See below, p. 337.

CHAPTER VII

THE DEVELOPMENT OF METROPOLITAN STANDARDS

THE active spirit of industry and commerce which permeated the eighteenth century led directly to the rise of several towns, formerly of scant importance, to great cities. Thus Bristol, Hull, Liverpool, Manchester, Birmingham, Sheffield and Leeds, the scenes of change and of bustling human activities, became metropolitan centres.[1] London, the heart of the commercial and financial system, at once the warehouse and the clearing-house of business life, remained even more significantly the metropolis of England. Statistics of the growth of population, based on inexact data, give but scant idea of the growing importance of the city in the life of the nation. In 1739 Maitland estimated the population of London at 725,903, while Sir Wm. Petty guessed it to be a million, and Defoe, in his usual optimistic mood, credited the city with a million and a half souls.[2] More illuminating are changes in topography, and graphic contemporary accounts of the city's teeming life and activity. Cheapside was no longer the great public market, but was now "well-built and inhabited by capital tradesmen."[3] Cornhill, which as the name signifies had once been a corn-market, was now occupied by substantial shops and dwellings of reputable merchants.[4]   So rapid was the expansion of London that seven new parishes were erected between the opening of the century and the accession of George II.[5]   Defoe commented on the "prodigious increase of building." [6]   Walpole, writing in 1776, marvelled at the growth of London during the three preceding decades:

Rows of houses shoot out of every way like a polypus; and so great is the rage of building everywhere, that if I stay here a fortnight, without going to town, I look about to see if no new house is built since I went last.   America and France must tell us how long this exuberance of opulence is to last!   The East Indies, I believe, will not contribute to it much longer.[7]

Old cow pastures had now become populous residential districts, and congested traffic made progress slow and difficult.[8]

Final evidence that London was not alone a city but a metropolis, is shown by the increased number of the villas of merchants in the suburbs, removed from the heat and dust of London's streets.[9]   For the most part these structures were "elegant mansions, showing opulence and good taste." [10]   As an observer noted: "Their houses are generally built in a row, to resemble as much as is possible the streets in London. Those edifices which stand single, and at a distance from the road, have always a summer-house at the end of a small garden," [11] and sometimes fountains, statues and temples—in fact, all the usual adornments of the prevalent fad.[12]

Such a place was Greenwich, with its royal park

nearby, "open for the recreation of all that behave with decency and good manners," or Blackheath, "celebrated for its good and wholesome air, which has occasioned the building of many good houses." [13]   The neighbouring towns of Hackney and Clapton "cover more ground, and contain more houses and wealthy inhabitants than many cities."   Islington, also, was celebrated for "the sweetness of the air, which brings many citizens to lodge in it, for their health, and contributes chiefly to the increase of new buildings upon that spot."   In the same class was Chelsea.[14] Defoe refers in particular to Cashalton, "the most agreeable spot this side of London, as is abundantly testified by its being crowded, as it were, with fine houses of the citizens of London; some of which are built with such a Profusion of Expence, that they look rather like Seats of the Nobility, than the Country-Houses of Citizens and Merchants." [15]

Doubtless, then, the commuting class of earlier days owed its origin, not only to the craving for fresh air, but to the equally strong desire to emulate the nobility, the landed gentry of England.[16]   That this migration was a general one and confined largely to wealthy merchants, is shown by the visitor to Epsom.[17] Naturally those who had accumulated sufficient fortunes to retire purchased estates in the country, and were able to emulate the country gentry.[18]

Along with the growth of suburbs one reads of seats of the nobility in the outskirts of London refitted by "projectors," as houses for pleasure and entertainment.   The former estate of the Earl of Chesterfield served, not only as a rendezvous for card-players and dancers, but as a place where ladies and gentlemen of the town were entertained with tea and coffee every Sunday for sixpence each.[19]   In like manner was the old mansion of the Earl of Ranelagh turned into a breakfasting-house and "dedicated to that luxury (*i.e.*, the fashion of dining out) which overspreads the face of the Nation." [20]

So self-sufficient had the Londoner become in his social life, so varied the order of his amusements— further signs of the growth of a metropolitan *credo*— that he was no longer anxious to risk the discomforts and dangers of travel by stage-coach.   Except for the cultural "Grand Tour" on the Continent, the Londoner was properly labelled as a stay-at-home.   As one critic observed: "A rich citizen of London has perhaps some very valuable relatives or friends in the West; he thinks no more of visiting them than of travelling the deserts of Nubia, which might well be in the moon, or in Limbo Patrum, considering them as a sort of separate being." [21]

Clearly, the metropolis itself had outgrown its mediæval cocoon.   Its narrow, dirty streets, its susceptibility to disease, and its haphazard methods of policing and lighting were incompatible with commercial progress.   The enterprising merchant realized that such conditions were not conducive to continued prosperity.   Better business demanded a thorough house-cleaning: the city must be made safe and attractive for visitors and local citizens.   In achieving this better business unconsciously awoke and developed a new community—more exactly, a new metropolitan-spirit.

The wretched condition of the streets was a constant menace to health and safety. Veritable quagmires when it rained, a shower meant that they would bring inevitable tragedy to all but satirists like Swift:

> Careful Observers may fortel the Hour
> (By sure Prognostics) when to dread a Show'r. . . .
> If you be wise, then go not far to dine,
> You'll spend in Coach-hire more than save in Wine. . . .
>
> Now in contiguous Drops the Flood comes down,
> Threat'ning with Deluge this devoted Town.
> To shop in Crowds the draggled Females fly,
> Pretend to cheapen Goods, but nothing buy.
> The Templer spruce, while ev'ry Spout's a-broach,
> Stays till it is fair, yet seems to call a Coach.
> The tuck'd-up Sempstress walks with hasty Strides,
> While Streams run down her oil'd Umbrella's Sides.
> Her various Kinds by various Fortunes led,
> Commence Acquaintance underneath a Shed.
> Triumphant Tories, and desponding Whigs,
> Forget their Feuds, and join to save their wigs.[22]

Even with normal business and social life so upset by this deluge—an occurrence by no means infrequent—passage through the streets was unpleasant even in fair weather. Filth abounded at all times.[23] Householders invariably failed to sweep the road in front of their homes, and even threw ashes and refuse from their windows.[24] A lesser evil was the encroachment of bay-windows on the narrow passage-ways, put out by the shop-keepers, eager to attract the prospective customer. The falling of flower-pots and drenching by projecting spouts added to the discomfort or injury of the passerby.[25] It is safe to assume that few pedestrians would shop for the sheer joy of it.

The city's progressive element laboured incessantly to overcome inertia and to improve these conditions. In 1722 residents were required, under penalty of £20, to convey water from the tops of houses and balconies "into channels or kennels, by pipes in the front or the sides of the houses."[26] Later ordinances required holders to clean twice a week the steps leading to their houses, and to pile up dirt and refuse within the yards.[27] Scavengers were appointed to cart away the accumulated "soil, ashes, rubbish, dirt and filth."[28]

In 1762 a committee of the Court of Common Council ordered the removal of obnoxious signs and the placing of street names on every corner.[29] The paving of streets was begun in earnest with the adoption of Aberdeen granite for that purpose and the letting of contracts for the paving of Piccadilly and St. James's Street.[30] By 1800 practically all the important business and residential streets had been completed.[31]

The free circulation of pure air through the streets and the conversion of open squares, breeding grounds of germs and pestilence, into beautiful gardens made for a healthier London. In the seventeenth century the metropolis, suffering from chronic attacks of the plague, was a veritable charnel-house.[32] Not a single instance of this menace was reported during the following century. Deaths from colic and dysentery diminished, while the death rate for contagious dis-

eases declined during each successive decade.[33]   This
change was due in large part to improvements in cleanliness and ventilation of the city.[34]   As a contemporary stated:

Many of the streets have been paved with easy descents
to carry off the water; besides wells in most public yards, and
pipes for conveying plenty of fresh water to keep them clean
and sweet, many late stately edifices, large clean courts, lofty
rooms, large sash-lights, etc., and many excellent conveniences
both by land and water, for supplying the city with provisions
at moderate prices . . . must contribute not a little to make
the city more healthy.[35]

To these achievements of the progressive business
men of the metropolis should be added the scientific
study of medicinal plants, promoted by Sir Hans
Sloane, and the extended use of Peruvian bark and
other drugs from overseas, to ward off the ills of congested city life.[36]

Safety and the æsthetic sense alike demanded proper
illumination of the shopping and residential districts.
At the opening of the century street-lighting depended
largely on the thoughtfulness of those residents who
placed a lantern in their windows, although the city
provided lanterns for sewer openings, or particularly
dangerous holes in the pavement.[37]   The reign of
Queen Anne also marked the introduction of street
lamps, made of thick convex glass, "which illuminate
the Path for People that go on Foot, tolerably
well." [38]   These street lamps were not lighted till six
o'clock in the evening, and only on nights when the
moonlight was not bright.[39]   The streets, therefore,

were still dangerously dark, and there was little inducement to fare forth during the long and foggy nights
of London's winter.   In 1736 an Act of Parliament
for "better enlightening the streets of London," was
put into execution.[40]   Fourteen thousand houses were
assessed, according to the rates, for lights to be placed
twenty-five yards apart in closely settled streets, and
thirty-five yards elsewhere.   In this work

the shop-keepers of London are of infinite service to the rest
of the inhabitants by their liberal use of the Patent Lamp, to
shew their Commodities during the long evenings of winter.[41]

Closely allied with this movement for a safer and
more beautiful London, was the improvement in shop-
windows.   Although the London shops were large and
well-furnished, by comparison with those of lesser
towns, many of them encroached dangerously on the
too narrow streets.[42]   Goods, also, were too frequently exposed, and the conduct of the shop-keeper
towards the innocent passer-by often approached physical violence.[43]   Within a century even the small shop-
keeper prided himself on such neatness as fogs and
smoke permitted; the portico and the pilasters and
cornices were of imitation marble and the owner's name
and business, in gilt letters on the large-paned windows.[44]   Most attractive of all were the shops of
drapers dealing in new muslins and calicoes.[45]   Probably the inspiration for this gorgeousness was furnished by the noble fronts of great banking houses and
insurance-offices with their emblematic statues over
the doors.[46]   Most resplendent were the windows of
goldsmiths, jewellers and pawnbrokers, who

indulge the public with the view of diamonds, pearls, rubies, emeralds, gold and silver, in most fascinating quantities; but the Watchmakers and Glassmen eclipse all competitors in the display of fanciful clocks set in alabaster, ormolu, gold and silver, and the richest cut glass lighted by patent lamps at night.[47]

But one fly remained in the ointment: the fact that amateur roysterers and professional pickpockets and footpads were making the lives of pedestrians miserable and unprofitable.   Extremely troublesome were the bands of young rowdies known as "Mohocks" [48] who indulged in frequent outbreaks during the time of Queen Anne.   Their favourite evening sport was to "roast" porters, knock down watchmen, break windows and remove door-knobs.[49]   Sometimes their escapades were far less innocent, when they clubbed innocent passers-by with sticks, slit their noses, and slashed their faces with knives:

They likewise rowled a Woman in a Tub down Snow Hill, that was going to Market, set other Women on their Heads, misusing them in a barbarous Manner. . . . They have short Clubs or Batts that have Lead at the End, which will overset a Coach, or turn over a Chair, and Tucks (swords) in their Canes, ready for Mischief.[50]

While this particular group was finally disbanded, other scandalous "clubs" were formed, such as the "Bold Bucks" and the "Hell-Fires" composed of criminals who showed an utter contempt for peace and order and were ordered suppressed by proclamation of the king in 1721.[51] Other instances, chosen at random, show that disorder in the streets was a common occurrence.   In 1725 several prosecutions were instituted to prevent the storming of hearses,[52] and a few years later, to prevent the common practice of breaking windows.[53]   In 1733 the introduction of the Excise Bill furnished an excuse for popular outbreaks. Angry mobs paraded through the streets on several occasions during the next three years crying, "No Gin, no King!" [54]   Beginning in 1768, disturbances arose in connection with the Industrial Revolution, when weavers sought to revenge the injuries believed to have been inflicted upon them by the power-loom.[55]

This list of outrages, while incomplete, shows that London had outgrown its antiquated system, or lack of system, of preserving order.   Little wonder that crime and violence were rampant, when the watchmen who served in lieu of police,

were chosen out of those poor decrepit people, who are, from want of bodily strength, rendered incapable of getting a livelihood by work.   These men, armed only with a pole, which some of them are hardly able to lift, are to secure the persons and houses of His Majesty's subjects from the attacks of young, bold, desperate, and well-armed villains.[56]

Furthermore, the chief methods of capturing malefactors was by offering large rewards for information concerning their whereabouts.[57]   Bishop Benson, writing in 1755, stated that "there is not only no safety of living in this town, but scarcely any in the country now, robber and murther are grown so frequent. Our people are now become what they never were before, cruel and inhuman." [58]   Though this condition was due in part to the severity of the penal code,[59] the need for reform was imperative, and the progressive citizens of London added their efforts to those of the constituted authorities.

Toward the close of the seventeenth century there had been formed a "Society for the Reformation of Manners," a body composed of eminent lawyers, members of Parliament, justices of the peace and prominent London citizens, including merchants and tradesmen, whose object was to remedy the imperfect and lax enforcement of laws, by ferreting out criminals and bringing them to justice.   Expenses were met by voluntary contributions.[60]

From its very inception, the inspiration of the movement was linked with zeal for better business, and many of its members were related spiritually to Cromwell's "Ironsides."   It accounts in part for the energy and spirit in which the work was undertaken, as well as for the type of arrests which were made.   This voluntary society divided itself into several groups, not only for the discovery of houses of ill-fame and of robbers and murderers, but for the prosecution of blasphemers, drunkards and Sabbath-breakers.   That such work had the support of the Crown is evidenced by Queen Anne's proclamation against vice and debauchery (1703).   The puritanical Jury of Middlesex also renewed its presentments against the stage and Bartholemew Fair.[61]   The result was that every "kennel of debauchery is quite dismantled by this proclamation; and the beaux who sit at home on Sundays, and play at piquet and backgammon, are under dreadful apprehension of a thundering prohibition of stage-playing." [62]

That this Society was responsible for a considerable, if albeit temporary, moral purging of the metropolis is shown by the amazing total of 99,380 prosecutions during thirty-four years of endeavour.[63]

About the middle of the century a new and greater crime-wave reached London. This was attributed to the rapidly increasing evil of gin-drinking.[64] Sir John Fielding, into whose hands was placed the creation and organization of a permanent city police force, referred to the "new kind of drunkenness, unknown to our ancestors . . . the principal sustenance (if it may so be called) of more than 100,000 people in the metropolis," as responsible for the increase of crime.[65] Under the guidance of Fielding a serious attempt was now made to remove the seeds and sources of crime. Picked constables under Bow Street magistrates achieved considerable success in rounding up a gang of robbers which had alarmed all of London for an entire year (1753).[66] A similar band met a similar fate just four years later. In short, so well did Fielding's police force work, that "the reigning evil of street robberies has been almost wholly suppressed." [67]

With the safety of city streets and the pursuit of business assured, the metropolitan spirit demanded a more rigid discipline than could be secured by ordinary police enforcement. A new Society for the Suppression of Vice was founded at the opening of the nineteenth century, which proved highly successful. As a writer of the time stated:

For this essential service rendered to the Community, they deserve every Praise; and however the public may be divided in opinion as to their method of proceeding, and the propriety of some of their operations, all will agree that vending obscene little-goes, and cruelty to animals, ought to be finally prevented.[68]

The work of such reformers received invaluable aid from the press. Beginning with Addison and Steele, writers in the newspapers and the magazines mercilessly exposed to ridicule the vices and follies of the day. Furthermore they showed the baneful effects of crime in an age when the romance of crime reached its height. Throughout the century the press, an institution conceived by and for the commercial classes, conducted a vigourous and inspiring campaign, not only for the empire, but for the material and spiritual benefits which empire brought: property itself, and its protection, together with high ideals in business and private life. It was admitted that many abuses remained, and for these a study of history showed there could be no specific cure. One enthusiastic contemporary went so far as to assert, in 1761, that

there never was a period since the creation of man when crimes and vices were less atrocious and shocking than in the present age. Manners, now polished and softened, have improved morals. Self-interest was always the ruling passion of all mankind; the old way of gratifying it was by murdering and poisoning; the new fashion by deceit.[69]

Many people, on the other hand, felt that reformers had overshot the mark, and even had interfered with the traditional liberties of Englishmen. Advice, accordingly, was given in turn to "those inferior repairers of wrongs, reformers of abuses, who throng coffee-houses":

Let them begin at home, examine their own hearts, and root out from thence, if they can, the passions of self-love, pride, envy, hatred and malice, the true and secret motives of their censure; and when they have brought that about, they will see things in a very different light, take the world as it is, and drink their wine, their coffee, their punch or their ale, with infinitely more comfort, than they do at present.[70]

REFERENCES TO CHAPTER VII

[1] See above, Ch. V. "Nor is there any complaint of depopulation from the country; Bath shoots out into new crescents, circuses, and squares every year; Birmingham, Manchester, Hull, and Liverpool, would serve any king in Europe for a capital." *Walpole to the Misses Berry*, 8 June, 1791.

[2] Maitland, *History of London*, II, p. 744; Defoe, *Tour*, II, pp. 99, 100.

[3] Entick, *Survey of London*, IV, p. 43.

[4] *Ibid*, IV, p. 98. For other changes see Macky, *Journey through England*, pp. 117-122.

[5] Craik, *History of British Commerce*, II, pp. 214-215.

[6] Defoe, *Tour*, II, pp. 104-108.

[7] *Letter of Horace Walpole to Sir Horace Mann*, 18 July, 1776.

[8] *Ibid, to Miss Berry*, 18 April, 1791.

[9] See below, Chapter VIII.

[10] *The Connoisseur*, 12 Sept., 1754.

[11] *Ibid*.

[12] See above, Chapter VI.

[13] Entick, IV, p. 443.

[14] *Ibid*, IV, pp. 444-445.

[15] Defoe, *Tour*, I, pp. 255-256. Among these homes was the residence of Sir John Fellowes, sub-governor of the South Sea Company in the fatal year, 1720. *Ibid*, I, p. 256.

[16] See above, Chapter V.

[17] Macky, p. 76; see above, p. 148.

[18] *The British Journal*, 21 Sept., 1723.

[19] Defoe, *Tour*, II, pp. 157-158.

[20] *Ibid*, II, p. 164.

[21] *Gentleman's Magazine*, XXII, p. 553; see also above, Chapter V.

[22] *The Tatler*, 17 Oct., 1710.

[23] *The Spectator*, 18 Dec., 1711.

[24] *Ibid*.

[25] Malcolm, *Anecdotes*, II, p. 392.

[26] Entick, *op. cit.*, II, p. 395.

[27] *Ibid*, III, p. 54.

[28] *Ibid*, III, p. 55.

[29] London *Chronicle*, 17 June, 1762.

[30] *Ibid*, 15 Aug., 1765.

[31] Malcolm, *op. cit.*, II, pp. 398, 400.

[32] Short, *Comparative History of the Increase and Decrease of Mankind in England and Abroad* (1767), p. 22.

[33] Lecky, I, pp. 572-573.

[34] Similar results followed the cleaning-up of other large centres. Heberden, *Observations on the Increase and Decrease of Different Diseases* (1801), p. 35.

[35] Short, *op. cit.,* p. 20; Macpherson, *Annals,* III, p. 321; see above p. 192.

[36] Pulteney, *Progress of Botany in England,* II, pp. 85, 99-103; Voltaire, *Lettres sur les Anglais,* No. 11; Nichols, *Literary Anecdotes of the Eighteenth Century,* IV, p. 625; *Gentleman's Magazine,* XXVII, p. 409.

[37] Thoresby, *Diary,* 15 June, 1712.

[38] Misson, *op. cit.,* p. 223.

[39] London *Gazette,* 30 Dec./2 Jan., 1706/1707; *The Tatler,* 19/22 Nov., 1709.

[40] Malcolm, I, p. 381.

[41] *Ibid,* I, p. 383. Further provision was made by regulations of 1750 and later. Entick, *op. cit.,* III, pp. 52, 57.

[42] See above, p. 195, and Chamberlayne, *Present State of England,* p. 347.

[43] Ward, *The London Spy.*

[44] Malcolm, II, p. 402.

[45] *Ibid.*

[46] Incidentally, the fire insurance companies contributed to the new metropolitan spirit in providing porters and watermen, "to attend all the fires, and to assist in putting out the fires, and saving of goods; and they are distinguished by the livery and badge of the society." Entick, *op. cit.,* III, p. 348.

[47] Malcolm, *Anecdotes,* II, p. 403.

[48] This was the popular term of the day for North American Indians, of whom little but their savagery was then known. The usually reliable *Spectator* made the curious mistake of confusing this tribe of Indians with supposed cannibals of India. See *The Spectator,* 12 Mar., 1712.

[49] *The Tatler,* 6 Oct., 1709.

[50] *The Spectator,* 12 Mar., 1712; see also *Ibid,* 8 Apr., 1712.

[51] Malcolm, *Anecdotes,* I, pp. 264-270.

[52] *Ibid,* II, p. 45.

[53] *Ibid,* II, p. 46.

[54] *Ibid,* II, pp. 46-49.

[55] *Ibid,* II, pp. 69-70.

[56] Fielding, *Amelia,* bk. I, ch. 2.

[57] Lecky, I, p. 483; see also, Gay, *The Beggar's Opera.*

[58] Fraser, *Life of Berkeley,* p. 332.

[59] See below, Chapter XI.

[60] Chamberlayne, pp. 333-334.

[61] *The Observator,* No. 92.

[62] *Ibid.*

[63] Malcolm, *Anecdotes,* I, p. 141.   Crime was prevalent during this period all over England, for complaints were common that the prisons were more crowded than they had ever been before.   Applebee's *Orig. Wkly. Jl.,* 3 Mar., 1722.   Whether this was due to a stricter enforcement of law, or to a sudden disposition of the populace to crime, is a matter of opinion.

[64] See below, p. 250f.

[65] Fielding, *On the Late Increase of Robbers,* 1751.

[66] Fielding, *On the Police,* 1753; see also Andrews, *Eighteenth Century* p. 235.

[67] Browne's *Estimate,* I, p. 219; for statistics of robberies from 1766 to 1770, see Malcolm, *Anecdotes,* I, pp. 189-190.

[68] *Ibid,* I, pp. 214-215.

[69] *Annual Register,* 1761, p. 199.

[70] *Ibid,* p. 200.   For an account of the newspaper, and its connection with oversea endeavors, see Chapter VIII.

CHAPTER VIII

CHANGES IN POPULAR DIVERSIONS AND AMUSEMENTS

AN index to the quality of a nation's civilization is the variety of opportunity offered for social and business intercourse. In the opinion of the writer, no people have risen to true greatness who have failed to develop the social graces or the art of beautiful living. Material prosperity itself must suffer when business is the sole aim and end of effort. Even the standardized business life of the present age makes concessions to the social amenities, to the gregarious instinct of man. If this opinion be accepted, the development of characteristics regarded as typically Anglo-Saxon found generous and continued encouragement in the eighteenth century. Help in that direction came from an institution established in the seventeenth century and adopted in the years to follow as a vital necessity by all manner of men. The coffee-house, depending on a product from overseas for its name, and on oversea business for its continued existence, was possibly the greatest single factor in transforming English business and social life.

The institution reached the zenith of its popularity about the time of Queen Anne. Almost, if not quite, from the outset it took on a personal character as shown by the names of the more popular places: "Tom's," "Will's," "John's," evidently founded and operated by several waiters of an earlier period who had contrived to save a little money. As time went on many of the coffee-houses began to assume an individuality. "Garraways" and "Jonathan's," for example, became the rendezvous for sellers of stocks and for foreign bankers. An auction room on the first floor, conveniently near the bar, facilitated the mingling of business with pleasure. Incidentally, much of the gambling connected with the South Sea Bubble of 1720 was conducted here. In like manner, "Lloyd's" and the "Jerusalem," situated nearby, soon became identified with the shipping interests. Here gambling on the safe transport of cargoes developed into the scientific business of insurance.[1]

During the early years of the eighteenth century coffee-houses were used as salesrooms and as marts of trade for a wide variety of merchandise. The following advertisements show that many of the goods offered were of oversea origin:

For Sale
The Japan Co. will expose to sale to-morrow, the 23d, inst., at the Marine Coffee-House in Birchin-lane, Tea-Tables and various Sorts of Lackered ware, with Cabinets, Scrutores, and Desks, one in a Lot. . . . with China, Japan, and Earthenware.[2]
At Baker's Coffee-House in Exchange Alley to be sold fresh parcels of Fans, also Caps, Sashes and Quilted Petticoats, at low rates, they really being Goods of Persons that fail'd.[3]
The volatile Spirit of Bohee-tea is sold only at Batson's Coffee-House near Royal-Exchange.[4]

A choice Parcel of preserv'd Nutmegs, lately arrived from East India, whether Wholesale or Retale, and a Parcel of neat Baskets, at Cowper's Coffee-House.[5]

Naturally these activities ceased for the most part with the growth of permanent establishments having their own offices.[6]

In other resorts professional men were wont to assemble, to discuss mutual topics of interest, and to enjoy other intellectual diversions. "Child's" on Paternoster Row, rejoiced in dispelling the cares of a clergyman's duties; at "Dick's" and the "Grecian" legal lights and shadows shed the brilliance of argumentative wit; while Dryden gave to "Will's" the reputation of being the "Humourist Coffee-House." At the "Smyrna," one might "in the noble Sciences of Music, Poetry, and Politics, be instructed Gratis, with elaborate ESSAYS by word of Mouth. . . . The disciples are to prepare their Bodies with three Dishes of Bohea, and purge their Brains with two Pinches of Snuff." [7] Steele tells of his visit to the establishment of "Don Saltero's" a former servant of Sir Hans Sloane: "When I came into the Coffee-house, I had not time to salute the Company, before my eye was diverted by them upon ten thousand gimcracks round the room and on the ceiling." [8] So famed for its odds and ends did this place become, that in 1729 it published a catalogue.

Other coffee-houses gained a decidedly political complexion. Admission was usually denied prospective customers of opposing political faiths. "St. James's," which later became London's most exclusive social club, served not only as headquarters for Steele and Garrick, but as a rendezvous where leading Whigs might discuss political strategy. At "Ozinda's," or at the "Cocoa Tree," on the other hand, one met the High Tories. Here those who were discontented with the Hanoverians might drink a furtive toast to the Pretender. "White's," on the hand, served as a meeting place for the most fashionable exquisites in town and court. Its patrons, both men and women, indulged in the follies of the day, especially in the prevalent fad for gambling. Their conduct, however, was always distinguished by unusual decorum, and by manners refined and elegant. A new standard was thus set for social intercourse, which frequenters of less fashionable resorts sought to emulate.

The place which the coffee-house as an institution occupied in the life of eighteenth century England is summarized by a well-known visitor to London:

If you would know our manner of living, it is thus: we rise by nine, and those that frequent great men's levees find entertainment at them till eleven, or as in Holland, go to tea-tables. About twelve the beau monde assembles in several chocolate and coffee-houses. . . .

If it be fine weather, we take a turn in the Park till two, when we go to dinner; and if it be dirty, you are entertained at Picket or Basset at White's, or you may talk politics at the Smyrna and St. James's. I must not forget to tell you, that the parties have their different places, where, however, a stranger is always received, but a Whig will no more go to the Cocoa-tree or Ozinda's, than a Tory will be seen at the coffee-house of St. James's.

The Scots generally go to the British, and a mixture of all sorts to the Smyrna. There are other little coffee-houses much frequented in this neighbourhood, Young-man's for officers, Old-man's for stock-jobbers, pay-masters, and courtiers, and Little-man's for sharpers.   I never was so confounded in my life, as when I entered into this last: I saw two or three tables full at Faro, heard the box and dice rattling in the room above-stairs, and was surrounded by a set of sharp-faces, that I was afraid would have drowned me with their eyes.   I was glad to drop two or three half-crowns at Faro, to get off with a clear skin.[9]

The *Spectator* classified the coffee-house patron according to the time of his arrival, and marvelled at the levelling influence of the rendezvous.[10]   Certainly, in a country where, till now, rigid distinctions of caste had prescribed man's mental horizon it must have been a novelty to mingle on a basis of equality with fellow-creatures in other walks of life.   What vast stores of information and ideas to exchange; what inspiration and what shocks must these mortals have experienced!   And how fortunate for England was the existence of such a melting-pot during the adolescence of her imperial career!

The very element of democracy in the coffee-house tended, during the century, to bring about several changes in its character.   Oft-times the privilege of universal welcome was abused; for example, smiths would come in dressed in aprons, and after drinking heavily would become unduly boisterous.   The more respectable customers would thereupon transfer their patronage to more exclusive places.   As a result, the plebeian coffee-houses which admitted all-comers gradually became taverns, where coffee was seldom, if ever, served.   In other cases this sort of coffee-house became a restaurant with none of the sociable traditions of the early days. Professor Silliman, an American visitor to London in 1805, deplored the fact that while the host and waiters of his favourite coffee-house knew him, none of the guests did.[11] In consequence, he added, "a man may appear and disappear, like an apparition rising from the ground and then sinking into it again, and with as little knowledge on the part of the observer, and with much less of interest as to his origin or destination."[12]

Other factors were at work in the transformation of the institution. Life was becoming more complex and more systematically organized. No longer did merchants use the coffee-house as an office or place of exchange, or the lawyers and other professional men, to seek clients. Efficiency, competition and a more highly specialized business life, too, began to deprive men of their opportunity for leisure during business hours. No longer did the fashionable lounger drop in to gossip or otherwise to pass away the hours. At the same time it was only natural that friends of the old coffee-house days, who were still united by a conformity of tastes, schemes of life and ways of thinking should wish to continue their companionship in a more formal manner. From these changes came the modern club-house.

As applied to social groups meeting in taverns, the word "club" appears to have been first used about the time of the introduction into England of coffee-drinking. The practice helped to convert what had been an occasional into a more permanent association. As the clubs had become quite common and their number tended to increase from the early eighteenth century onward, their place of gathering in coffee-houses suggested the desirability of having quarters less public. The club-house was the outcome. In some cases members of new organizations still held meetings at the coffee-house, but at fixed days and hours. Other gatherings, according to a visitor to London in 1765,

were kept at the houses of persons of fortune; they meet in turn at the apartments of the several members, if they are bachelors, and even if they are married, in case their wives do not object to it. He at whose house the meeting is held, supplies the members with refreshments.[13]

Clubs were naturally of different types, according to the preference of their members. Several organizations were formed for discussion of serious subjects, either of political, literary or artistic nature:

Public affairs generally furnish the subject of conversation; every Englishman gives as much attention to these matters, as if he were the Prime Minister. . . . Pleasurable and gay conversation is unknown to these societies. The English find no relief from reflection except in reflection itself.[14]

Nor was dinner an item to be neglected. In groups thus mindful may be included the Royal Society Club (founded in 1731) which numbered Dr. Halley among its members. This society met frequently at "Child's" for dinner, where their members set the limit at half a crown a meal.[15] Equally distinguished was the Sublime Society of Beefsteaks, which assembled weekly for the consumption of steak and port. This group included among its members Hogarth, Hayman, Churchill and Garrick, and in 1785 admitted to its circle the Prince of Wales.[16]

Of a similar character was the Dilettante Society, founded in 1734, which introduced the novel idea of taxing its members on accessions of wealth "by inheritance, legacy, marriage, or preferment." [17]   Most exclusive, and at the same time most brilliant of all these convivial groups, was the Literary Society, where such men of distinction as Sir Joshua Reynolds, Dr. Johnson and Goldsmith met to enjoy brilliant repartee, as well as the satisfaction of physical needs.[18]   Of chief importance is the fact that the early intimacy of the coffee-house was maintained, and was simply transferred to a time and place where its benefits could be most highly developed.[19]

A remarkable outgrowth of the club movement was the formation of women's clubs, at which members were free to discuss affairs in the political and artistic world.[20]   It is perhaps unnecessary to dwell on such exclusive institutions as "White's" and "St. James's," which have lasted on to the present time.   A most interesting feature was the club for the bakers, masons, carpenters and other members of the lower orders. They were admitted for 6d. each; the admission charges included a pint of beer.[21]   At their meetings, which lasted three hours, each member was permitted to speak for five minutes.   "Public affairs and religious topics," wrote Grosley, "equally claim the attention and the speculations of the meeting. . . . Sometimes they make some very shrewd speeches." [22]

In at least one other direction the coffee-house contributed to the moulding of the English bent of mind, and to the development of the increasing proportion of the world's population which could read and write. For amid the fumes of tobacco and coffee the germ of the daily newspaper came into being, and was fostered by such master artisans as Addison and Steele. The demand of coffee-house patrons for shipping-news, and for foreign and domestic political items, as well as the craving for fare more purely intellectual, made inevitable the growth of the periodical essay and of a daily press. Defoe's *Review* was probably the first publication which could be dignified by the name of newspaper, while the *Daily Courant,* published in 1702, was the first daily paper, followed soon afterwards by the *Post Boy*.[23] By 1724, three daily newspapers, five weekly papers and nine published triweekly were in existence. Within seven years, according to the initial number of the *Gentleman's Magazine,* their numbers were so multiplied, "as to render it impossible, unless a man makes it his business, to consult them all." [24] According to the same authority, "no less than two hundred half-sheets per month are thrown from the press, only in London, and about as many printed elsewhere in the three kingdoms; so that they are become the chief channels of amusement and intelligence." [25] By 1776, there were fifty-three newspapers published in London alone.[26]

A refreshing defence of this new institution and its connection with the press was made by an early admirer:

Coffee-Houses! the Schools of Politicks, of Wit, of polite Learning . . . I have always thought that voracious Appetite my Countrymen have after News, to be a particular Blessing to them.

Were it not for Newspapers! What would become of Herds of fine People, whose Transition from Amusement is constantly to Vice? . . . By their Assistance we are preserv'd from degenerating into Brutality, we are soften'd, civiliz'd, nay, humaniz'd. If a Lady or Gentleman lose their dear Spouses, the whole Nation is taught to grieve for in Concert with them. . . . Fires, Executions, Casualties, Deaths, Promotions, etc., are constantly soliciting our Affections of Pity and Joy. . . . If then, any Lady has a bad Husband, and any Parent an undutiful Child, my Advice is to send them to the Coffee-House; the Concern they will learn for the Affairs of the Universe will naturally lead them to a close Attention to their own Peculiar; and he who is taught to have Compassion for whole Nations and Provinces, will be tender of his Family; for it is impossible that he who is become a good Citizen of the World, should not be a provident, good natur'd Member of a private House. . . .

If we take the Number of Coffee-Men, Mercuries, Pamphlet-Shop Men, and Hawkers, we shall find above five Thousand People by this Article.[27]

The place of the press in national life became more and more important with the growth of the century. Political caricatures came in with the South Sea Bubble.[28] The newspapers were powerful factors in exposing the evils of speculation, and after the crash, in turning national life back to normality.[29] The power of the press over the public made its authority in a sense as binding as that of Parliament. As one writer expressed it:

The stuff which our weekly newspapers are filled with is

received with greater reverence than Acts of Parliament, and the sentiments of one of these scribblers have more weight with the multitude than the opinion of the best politician in the kingdom.[30]

Throughout the century the most influential political discussion was published in periodicals or in newspapers.[31]   The letters of Junius resulted directly in the founding of three newspapers, which played an important rôle in the Reform Bill of 1832: *Morning Chronicle* (1770) the *Post* (1772), and the *Herald* (1780).[32] Finally, the publication of the proceedings of the House of Commons was of immeasurable value in acquainting the public of the activities of its representatives, and of keeping alive public interest in political affairs.[33]

Naturally, the very power of the press tempted its abuse.   It was written for "common people" who will "believe anything they hear." [34]   For this reason the responsibility of the editor was all the greater.   As one journal phrased it:

The Pen shoots Poison, though not Bullets, and stabs to the Heart without a Sword. . . . So the War of the Press is carry'd on by a subtil and irresistable Force; here one Man speaks to the Whole Nation; if he has any malicious ill natur'd Thing to be said, he can at once spread it all over the Kingdom.[35]

This complaint was heard again, when Walpole asserted that newspapers were "vehicles of lies, blunders and scandals." [36]

The periodical essay and magazine were even more important in setting a higher standard of intellectual and social life.   It was the ambition of Addison to bring "philosophy out of closets and libraries, schools and colleges, to dwell in clubs and assemblies, at tea-tables, and coffee-houses." [37]   With the public demand for a higher type of reading, the *Gentleman's Magazine* (1731) and its rival, the *London Magazine,* came into being, followed shortly by Dr. Johnson's *Rambler* and *Idler,* and others of like nature.   Their object was to popularize knowledge by essays fit for the capacity of the average reader.   To the growth of popular magazines may be attributed a widening of the circle of intelligence, a marked desire for letter-writing, and a noticeable improvement in taste.[38]

Apart from the coffee-house and its derivatives, with all they may suggest of social life within doors, changes were effected in popular avocations which had to do with out of doors.   In the case of these diversions influences emanating from overseas operated in a subtle though certain manner.   The growth of commercial London accentuated the problem of breathing-spaces in expanding residential or business districts. Fortunately the love of the great outdoors inherent in all Englishmen of leisure preserved several spacious areas from the onrush of business.   Following the days of the Restoration, Hyde Park and St. James's Park vied with each other as the rendezvous of fashion. Promenade hours were fixed by fashion between noon and two o'clock, after the cup of chocolate and the elaborate toilet of the forenoon.   Here took place, also, amusements of a surprising and varied nature: wrestling matches between servants backed by their masters, hopping-matches against time and distance, races between fat cooks and lean footmen, military displays, and fireworks and illuminations on royal birthdays and other anniversaries. It was not long, moreover, before the parks attracted the business men of London and their families. These newcomers, with their clothes and equipages of latest design, but with manners which smacked of the counter, [39] fashion tried vainly to exclude.[40] In these democratic concourses aristocrat, merchant and tradesman indulged the wholesome and universal habit of walking:

No frost, snow, nor East Wind, can hinder a large set of people from going to the Park in February; no dust nor heat in June. And this is come to such an intrepid regularity that those agreeable creatures that would shriek at a hired wheel in a deep gutter are not afraid in their proper sphere, of the disorder and danger of several rings.[41]

Hindered by lack of space, the frequenter of London parks could not enjoy the vigour of the chase as practised by his hardier cousins in the country, which he affected to consider coarse and indelicate.[42] He perforce resorted to the morning saunter in Hyde Park where, like a "puny and starved Exotic," he clung to the shelter of a south wall.[43] Curiously, the sexes seemed to have changed places. The tired business man was content to caper about "on Hobbys of thirteen Hands," while the women were satisfied only with fiery chargers.[44] The vogue of the Mall evidently was over by 1785, when fashion left its shade to "the middle classes, the city ladies, and the country cousins." [45]

Aside from walking and horseback riding, the average Londoner was incapacitated from personal participation in sport by lack of space, time and energy. These factors, coupled with the natural love for competition and combat, marked the beginning of a new era of commercialized sport.[46]   Perhaps the man of business, fatigued by his own struggles, enjoyed all the more the rôle of spectator at the competition of others.   Most satisfying was the newly discovered passion for horse-racing, which found its highest expression at the course at Newmarket.   Here the wealthy merchant, on horseback, or in gay equipage, could meet on an equal basis the aristocrat.[47]   Undoubtedly it was a shock to many, as to Defoe, that here the person of distinction put himself on a level with grooms or riding-boys.[48]   Apart from the excitement of the contest itself, moreover, the race-course offered a supreme opportunity for the gambling passion of the age.[49]   Here the wagers and bets of the business world were duplicated, and too often, dishonestly.   So greatly did rank villainy seem to predominate, that a bill was passed in the reign of George II to regulate race-track evils.[50]   Unfortunately, the suggestion that race-meetings be turned into useful exhibitions of horse-breeding found expression only in the county fairs of the late century.

In some respects, however, the growth of a commercial London failed to raise the tone of sporting tastes.   While the countryman exercised vehemently at football, stool-ball, cricket, pins-on-base, wrestling, or cudgel-playing,[51] there was fiercer and more blood-stirring excitement for the Londoner. Particularly at Hockley-in-the-Hole, one could find bear-baiting, bull-baiting and cock-fighting to his heart's content.[52] Old hand-bills and news-sheets teem with advertisements that testify to the popularity of this resort during the first thirty years of the century, and to the fact that many of its patrons were gentlemen, often young bloods from "White's" and the "Cocoa-Tree." [53] Occasionally a rare treat was afforded, with an animal from distant lands as the victim. In the language of one such advertisement, it appeared as follows: "At the desire of several persons of quality, a leopard 12 feet in length, to be baited to death, and gentlemen who choose to risk their dogs are allowed to assist;" [54] or again, when "an African Tyger on a stage four feet high," was "to be worried to death by six bull and bear dogs for £100." [55] In spite of sermons by the clergy and countless presentments by grand jury, this resort met its overthrow only by the inevitable growth of London, when its sporting-centres were transferred to more distant parts.[56] The sports themselves remained lawful amusements until many years later.[57]

Moreover, by the middle of the century the loyalty of the sporting public had been largely transferred to a new amusement, pugilism. As early as 1681, there is recorded "a match of boxing . . . before his Grace the Duke of Albemarle between the Duke's footman and a butcher." [58] Gradually the taste for this kind of sport was developed and, under the leadership of the celebrated Mr. Figg and the patronage of the great, pugilism attained a sound commercial basis. Editors and essayists waxed enthusiastic over its virtues: the encouragement of fair play, the fostering of British spirit, its superiority over fencing.

Under the rules laid down by one John Broughton, however, and the founding of an "Academy," boxing became more of a "science" than a bruising-match. As a contemporary notes it:

Mr. Broughton proposes with proper assistance to open an Academy at his house in the Haymarket for the instruction of those who are willing to be initiated in the mystery of boxing, where the whole theory and practise of that truly British art, with all the various blows, stops, cross buttocks, etc., incidental to the combatants will be fully taught and explained; and that persons of quality and distinction may not be debarred from entering into a course of these lectures, they will be given with the utmost tenderness and regard to the delicacy of the frame and constitution of the pupil, for which reason mufflers (boxing gloves) will be provided that will effectually secure them from the inconveniency of black eyes, broken jaws, and bloody noses.[69]

With the advent of boxing gloves, then, the young bloods began to develop a taste for physical exercise, even to the extent of forsaking the card-room. This change was probably made easier by the disappearance of the laced ruffle, the powdered wig, and the embroidered waistcoat.   It was considered the correct thing to "put on the gloves with a professor at proper intervals," and thus "if you got into a street row, or were hustled at Vauxhall, it was thought just as well to be able to take your part with your fists, swords at that time being rarely worn." [60]

The advent of such permanent diversions meant of course the passing of the great fairs.   For years the puritanical element, composed largely of business men, objected to a number of features in these gatherings, the especial objects of their dislike being the gin-stalls, gaming-booths, and above all, theatrical entertainments, which were nurseries for the modern theatre. At them, also, one could view a variety of natural curiosities from overseas:

A little Black Man lately brought from the West Indies. . . . Likewise 2 Wood Monsters from the East Indies, Male and Female, being the Admirablest Creatures that ever was seen in this Kingdom. . . . Also a little Marmoset from the East Indies, which by a great deal of Pains is now brought to that Perfection, that no Creature of his Kind ever perform'd the like. . . . Likewise a Noble Civet Cat from Guiny which is admired for his Beauty, and that incomparable Scent which Perfumes the whole Place.   Vivat Regina! [61]

By 1700, the Mayfair in particular had become disorderly, and in that year the Grand Jury of Middlesex tried to restore its old character as a mart of trade. Steele, in the *Tatler*,[62] stated that the Mayfair was "utterly abolished," and in a later issue, that its natural curiosities could be purchased for a song: "A tiger will sell almost as cheap as an ox; and I am credibly informed, a man may purchase a cat with three legs for very nearly the value of one with four." [63]   However, not until 1720 did the grand jury succeed in bringing about its final downfall.[64]   The palmy days of Bartholemew, the greatest fair of all, began to fade about 1750, when the wealthy withdrew their patronage,[65] and lesser folk soon followed.

The great outdoor gardens, too, as distinct from the parks, afforded the Londoner a chance to relax from the fatigue of the day's business, and to escape from the fumes of the coffee-house. The existence of Vauxhall was significant of his conscious effort to support life *al fresco*. Just far enough removed from London proper to exclude the rabble, this resort represents the zenith of the "tea-garden movement." Founded in the reign of Charles II, Vauxhall reached the peak of its popularity during the next century. Addison puffs "the fragrancy of the Walks and Bowers, with the Choirs of Birds that sing upon the Trees." [66] Newspapers, which freely advertised its pleasures, tell of swarms of happy people in evening dress promenading along devious walks in groves or arbours, whose darkness was lighted up "with above 1,000 lamps so disposed that they all took fire together with such a sudden blaze as was perfectly surprising," with the simultaneous crash of music from the orchestra.[67] Watermills, tin cascades, fireworks, artificial caves and grottoes, offered amusement to those who cared little for music.[68] With this brilliance—for Vauxhall seems to have been the first place where artificial light was elaborately employed—the visitor could not help but contrast the dullness and gloom of London streets. Here, too, for the first time in England, one found food renowned for its daintiness: the chickens for their savour, the slices of ham for their unbelievable thinness, with a carver famed for his ability to "cover the whole twelve acres of the premises with slices from a single joint." [69]

Incidentally, another innocent form of amusement followed the importation of gunpowder from China: spectacular fireworks. The ordinary variety of vertical wheels, suns, stars and globes served for usual nightly exhibitions at Vauxhall and Ranelagh. Unusual occasions, however, such as the observance of royal birthdays, brought forth such glories as the "eruption of Mount Aetna.[70]

At Vauxhall was one place in England where proud society could unbend in public, and where the lesser citizen enjoyed occasional contact with the truly great. Above all, the amusement venture was supported largely, not by the nobility nor yet by the common folk whom the admission charge of a shilling excluded, but by the substantial and growing class of merchants and tradesmen.[71]

Other pleasure-resorts open to the public were the beautiful gardens and large amphitheatre at Ranelagh and the Pantheon. According to a visitor at the latter place: "Here the entertainment consists of a fine band of music with an organ, and some of the best voices; and the regale is tea and coffee included in the money paid for entrance." [72] In offering simple amusements, and cool evenings out-of-doors, these amusement places raised considerably public standards of morals. Even so caustic a critic as Dr. Johnson exclaimed: "I am a great friend to public amusements; for they keep people from vice." [73]

The custom of annual summer vacations led the tired business man and his entourage to one of the fashionable watering-places. Bath, which was the most cosmopolitan resort of England, is representative of the levelling of social classes due to the vast increase of wealth.[74] The social range of its visitors ran from people of quality to the city merchants and to the country-folk. Bath was a favourite watering-place of those who made their fortunes in South Sea stock; whereas, after the collapse of the Bubble, it was so deserted that one might, in the height of the season, obtain accommodation at winter rates.[75] The most graphic description of the place at the summit of its popularity, is furnished by Smollett:

Every upstart of fortune, harnessed in the trappings of the mode, presents himself at Bath, as in the very focus of observation. Clerks and factors from the East Indies, loaded with the spoil of plundered provinces; planters, negro-drivers, and hucksters, from our American plantations, enriched they know not how; agents, commissaries, and contractors, who had fattened, in two successive wars, on the blood of the nation; usurers, brokers, and jobbers, have found themselves suddenly translated into a state of affluence, unknown to former ages; and no wonder that their brains should be intoxicated with pride, vanity, and presumption. Knowing no other criterion of greatness but the ostentation of wealth, they discharge their affluence without taste or conduct through every channel of the most absurd extravagance; and all of them hurry to Bath, because here, without any further qualification, they can mingle with the princes and nobles of the land. . . . Such is the composition of what is called the fashionable company at Bath, where a very inconsiderable proportion of genteel persons are lost in a mob of impudent plebeians, who have neither understanding or judgment, nor the least idea of propriety or

decorum, and seem to enjoy nothing so much as an opportunity
of insulting their betters.[76]

Here, then, politicians could become better
acquainted with the needs of men of business, while
country squires came under the mellowing influence
of wits from town.[77] One and all enjoyed the instruction of that master of social graces, Beau Nash. To
his work at this great melting-pot, belongs the credit
for a decided improvement in morals and manners.
Before his arrival, Bath presented a sorry spectacle
when

smoking in the rooms was permitted; gentlemen and ladies
appeared in a disrespectful manner at public entertainments in
aprons and boots. With an eagerness common to those whose
pleasures come but seldom, they generally continued them too
long; and thus they were rendered disgusting by too free an
enjoyment.[78]

Worse, it was famed as "a sink of Iniquity; nor is
there any Intrigues or Debauch Acted in London, but
is Mimick'd here." [79] Its transformation followed
the coming of the inimitable Beau Nash. Now the
balls began at six and ended at eleven, and were performed in impeccable order, men and women gracing
the scene with perfect decorum. He was as strict with
dress. Abhorring the white apron, he excluded those
wearing them, and by using the weapon of ridicule,
persuaded the gentlemen to give up the wearing of
the sword.[80]

The languishing, sentimental heroine of *Humphrey
Clinker* gives an attractive picture of the resort under
the new régime:

All is gaiety, good humour, and diversion. . . . We have music in the pump-room every morning, cotillions every fore-noon in the room, balls twice a week, and concerts every other night, besides private assemblies and parties without number. . . . At eight in the morning, we go in déshabille to the pump-room, which is crowded like a Welch fair; and there you see the highest quality and the lowest tradesfolk jostling each other, without ceremony, hail-fellow well met. . . . For my part, I content myself with drinking about half a pint of the water every morning.

Hard by the pump-room is a coffee-house for the ladies; but my aunt says young girls are not admitted, inasmuch as the conversation turns upon politics, scandal, philosophy, and other subjects above our capacity; but we are allowed to accompany them to the booksellers' shops, where we read novels, plays, pamphlets, and newspapers, for so small a subscription as a crown a quarter. . . . There is, moreover, another place of entertainment on the other side of the river . . . called the Spring Gardens; a sweet retreat, laid out in walks and ponds, and parterres of flowers; and there is a long room for break-fasting and dancing. . . .

After all, the great scenes of entertainment at Bath are the two public-rooms, where the company meet alternately every evening. They are spacious, lofty, and when lighted up, appear very striking. They are generally crowded with well-dressed people, who drink tea in separated parties, play at cards, walk, or sit or chat together, just as they are disposed. Twice a week there is a ball, the expense of which is defrayed by a voluntary subscription among the gentlemen and every subscriber has three tickets.[81]

Next to Bath as a fashionable resort came Tun-bridge Wells, a "Place dedicated to Freedom, no Dis-tinction, either of Quality or Estate, but that ev'ry Man that appears well Converses with the Best." [82] It is interesting to note that people went largely to

drink the waters, not to bathe in them. Epsom Wells
was decidedly lower in tone, for it was within too easy
access of London, and welcomed some "very questionable characters." [83] At both these places, gambling
vied with concerts and the waters for popularity. Other
spas basked in the reflected brilliance and success of
Bath. Hampstead and Richmond Wells, Acton
Waters and Dulwich, Defoe regrets "too often afford
Opportunities for Intrigues and Amours, which give
the Heart-Ach to Parents and Husbands." [84] On the
whole, however, the watering-places favourably served
their purpose to divert and to amuse, while the contact of the *nouveaux riches* and of the country squires
with the élite tended on the whole to raise the standard
of manners, if not of morals.

The same love of outdoor activities was mirrored
in the milder pursuit of gardening, which reached its
height in the first half of the century. The efforts of
Kent, who laid out Kensington Gardens, and Sir William Chambers, who was responsible for certain features of Kew Gardens,[85] attempted to give scope to
the irregular and wild beauties of nature.[86] Unfortunately, however, the results were as artificial as the
formal symmetry which they replaced.[87] The impetus
for a personal interest in gardening was furnished in
part by the botanical exploration of the West Indies
by Sir Hans Sloane, and of the continental American
colonies by other investigators; [88] and "the same
commerce that assembles men of all nations upon the
Royal Exchange in London, stocks the English gardens
with trees of all climates." [89] Kew was undoubtedly

the largest and finest of all scientific gardens. As a distinguished visitor remarked:

In these (hot) houses we wandered among shrubs, flowers and plants, which although natives of tropical countries, were here made to flourish in the forbidding climate of England. . . .

We saw in these gardens among an innumerable host of exotics, the bread fruit tree, the gum guiacum tree, the camphor tree, the cedar of Lebanon, the cork tree, and a great grove of very beautiful orange, lemon, and lime trees.[90]

It is little wonder that the century witnessed the introduction and development of countless new sorts of plants from overseas. In 1700 there were fewer than 1,000 species of exotics, whereas a hundred years later there were more than 5,000.[91] For example, Virginian and Chilian strawberries were introduced early in the century, and crossed with native varieties; in 1731 the first specimens of orchids arrived from the Bahamas; [92] in 1789 the dahlia was first introduced from Mexico; [93] while in 1793 the botanical garden maintained at Calcutta by the East India Company began to send an endless variety of plants to adorn English greenhouses.[94]

The passion for gardening, however, was by no means confined to scientists. Experimental farming became the fashion for men of all ranks. In this manner Addison, Pope and Horace Walpole were enthusiastic gardeners—an example which was followed alike by residents of the suburbs and owners of large estates.[95] Still others, under the spell of the growing love of out-of-doors, loved not only their gardens, but their greenhouses too:

There blooms exotic beauty, warm and snug,
. . . . The golden boast
Of Portugal and western India there,
The ruddier orange and the paler lime,
Peep through their polished foliage at the storm,
And seem to smile at what they need not fear. . . .
All plants, of every leaf that can endure
The winter's frown if screened from his shrewd bite
Live there and prosper. Those Ausonia claims,
Levantine regions these; the Azores send
Their jessamine, her jessamine remote
Caffraria; foreigners from many lands.[96]

Specimens of stuffed animals brought back from far-
off lands were constant reminders that the mysteries
of overseas were now laid bare to western knowledge.
Particularly complete and impressive was the collection in the Museum at Leicester House. On the stair-
case was the "large, docile, amphibious animal, inhab-
iting rivers of Africa and South America." Among
the beasts were a large Greenland bear, royal tyger,
leopard, Persian cat, Persian lynx, Mexican hog,
beaver, otter, badger, oppossum." In another room
the "hippopotamus and young African rhinoceros, two
animals, remarkable when full grown, for bulk and
strength, as well as form; . . . the Armadillo, flying-
squirrel from the East Indies, porcupine, tailless mau-
can, petril-nosed bat, the great ant-eater from South
America."

In the monkey-room there was a fine collection
of various species, conspicuous for "their disgusting
and distorted resemblance to the human form."

Among the birds were found the African and Jamaican flamingo, humming bird, king bird of paradise, silver pheasant from China, the cormorant, large cockatoo, nondescript hawk, the demoiselle of Numidia, zebra bird, curasso, "with a bird, newly inserted, called the angus pheasant, from Pekin in China, very remarkable for the beauty of its plumage, and the elegance and majesty of its form"; the cassowary from the Malay Archipelago, albatross from Cape of Good Hope, crowned African crane, the ugrus crane from Bengal, the golden pheasant, the ring pheasant, and the mandarin duck, all from China, and from America, the scarlet curlew, golden eagle, and Indian pigeon. In the ostrich room, curiously enough, were exhibited musical instruments and tobacco pipes from China, and the East Indies, together with specimens of shells, woods and birds' eggs, while an ostrich seven feet high, in the same case with a pair of hummingbirds for contrast, was the chief feature. In another room, the visitor found dresses of various nations, women's shoes from China, slippers, ornaments, idols and domestic utensils of people in newly discovered lands, "which to an active imagination convey a forcible idea of them and their manners." Finally, there were rooms for warlike weapons of savage folk in America, and for curious Indian dresses, idols, ornaments, bows, etc., from the Sandwich Islands.[97]

Obviously, the sight of the beautiful plumage and sparkling colours of birds and the ferocious stare of animals gave a conviction of reality to things formerly held visionary. Let the visitor tell his story as he proceeds:

The objects before him make his active fancy travel from pole to pole through torrid and through frigid zones. He beholds the manners of men in the forms of their habits; he sees the Indian rejoiced at, and dancing to the monotonous pound of his tom-tom; he sighs to recollect the prevalent power of fear and superstition over the human mind, when he views the rude deformity of an idol carved with a flint, by a hand incapable of imitating the outline of nature. . . . In short, he looks at the vast volumes of actual information, that everywhere surrounds him, and is undeterminate where to begin, or on which to fix his attention most. . . . A duty which gratitude owes to the public-spirited proprietor, who has thus given his countrymen an opportunity of surveying the works of nature, and contemplating the various beings that inhabit the earth.[98]

The eighteenth century witnessed a period of remarkable expansion in the British Museum. In 1753 an Act was passed for the purchase of the Sloane library and museum and of the Harley collection of charters and manuscripts.[99] In 1764 and 1765 a collection of birds, insects and other objects which had been exhibited at Spring Gardens was absorbed.[100] Another valuable acquisition was the natural history collection of Sir Joseph Banks,[101] who like Sloane had spent many years in scientific investigation abroad. So popular, indeed, had such collections become that a museum of curiosities was thought an attraction in a London coffee-house—that of "Don Salteros." Its printed catalogue enjoyed about fifty editions, until the attractions were finally sold off in 1799.[102] Another popular display was found in Adams' Museum, although its exhibits were for the most part unauthentic.[103]

Finally, mention should be made of the Leverian Museum.[104] One room, which was devoted to the memory of Captain Cook, contained a collection of arms, costumes, utensils and idols, which he made in his last voyage.[105] A second room held "a grand collection of birds in fine preservation," while in a third hall, "there is an apartment very gravely devoted to the monkeys. Not satisfied with what the Creator has done, in making these animals so very ludicrous in their appearance and manners . . . the artist has exhibited them as busied about various human activities." [106]

Still more real must have been the effect of gazing upon live specimens brought from overseas. The century's progress in this respect is evident, when one recalls that in Queen Anne's reign the sight of foreign birds and animals was infrequent. For example, at the White Horse Inn, upon payment of a shilling, could be seen a black hairy pigmy, a hyena, a murino, a bird of paradise, a tiger and a monkey [107]—surely a collection that could hardly stimulate a true conception of the variety of the wonders from lands overseas. By the mid-century there were amazing collections of birds and animals from overseas, both in public menageries and in those of private individuals.[108]

The Tower Collection was now well under way, and

its lions, panthers, tigers and ostriches formed a centre of attraction to visitors to London.[109]   Equally
popular were the Zoölogical Gardens in Regents Park,
at least according to one visitor: "Equally suited to
the young and the old, the solitary and the gregarious,
the cheerful and the melancholy, the ignorant and the
learned, all are here sure of enjoyment at least, and
it will be strange indeed if instruction in some shape
or other, does not follow." [110]   Strange animals continued to find their way into one or the other of these
groups.   One East Indiaman returned in 1795 with an
elephant, a curious monkey, some Java sparrows, an elk
and several sheep from the Cape of Good Hope.[111]
Buffaloes from India, monkeys from Africa, and kanga-
roos from Botany Bay offered additional bait to curi-
osity-seekers.[112]

Public appreciation of rarities of the animal kingdom is shown by their increased adoption as pets.
Dean Swift satirically inquires: "Which is it you
love—my page from Genoa, my monkey from the
East Indies, and my lap-dog from Vigo?"   Jack Free-
love, too, found his lady deeply enamoured of her
monkey which was chained in one of the windows.[113]
Marmoset monkeys, "no bigger than a squirrel," were
frequently advertised for sale in the shops.[114]   Likewise, there were "Canary birds, of several Colours,
both cocks and hens, at reasonable rates, also parrots,
which both talk and sing," [115] as well as little East
India hens.[116]   In fact, the woman of fashion had an
almost endless choice in her selection of a pet.   The
parrot at least has retained his popularity to now:

In painted plumes superbly drest,
A native of the gorgeous East,
    By many a billow tost;
Poll gains at length the British shore,
Part of the Captain's store,
A present to his Toast.

*   *   *

Belinda and her bird! 'tis rare
To meet with such a well-matched pair,
    The language and the tone,
Each character in every part,
Sustained with so much grace and art,
    And both in unison.[117]

Aside from "cannibals," who were on exhibition at the fairs, and from negro and East Indian servants, American Indians were the objects of considerable interest. In 1710 the good folk of London were treated to the unusual spectacle of four live Indian chiefs, who pledged the Queen their support against her enemies. They were treated as guests of the nation, and created a furore of excitement on their appearance in public.[118] Ten years later the attitude of two visiting chieftains towards London social life was closely observed. They were surprised to see a chimney sweeper dressed in black velvet dancing with a fine lady in crimson "à la Chinese." "And so in Disgust," remarked one editor, "they think it best to go back and enjoy the native Felicity of Nakedness and Sloth in their own Country." [119] Later in the century Boswell was immensely pleased with his ability to converse in the sign language with a group of visiting Esquimaux.[120] Equally significant were those who

posed as foreigners from overseas, profiting by the
interest which the real visitors had aroused. The most
interesting was one George Psalmanazer who, pre-
tending to be a Formosan, actually invented a new language and grammar.[121]

By the opening of the nineteenth century the appearance in England of East Indians no longer was a novelty, and served to arouse the curiosity of foreign visitors only. The Yale professor, visiting London in
1805, though unable himself to distinguish between
negroes and East Indians, marvelled alike at the social
position which the latter attained, and at the presence
of Eurasians:

You will occasionally meet in the streets of London genteel
young ladies, born in England, walking with their half-
brothers, or more commonly with their nephews, born in India,
who possess in a very strong degree, the black hair, small features, delicate form and brown complexion of the native Hindus.

These young men are received into society, and take the rank
of their fathers. I confess the fact struck me rather un-
pleasantly. It would seem that the prejudice against colour is
less strong in England than in America; for the first negroes
found in this country are in a condition much superior to that
of their countrymen anywhere else. A black footman is considered a great acquisition, and consequent negro servants are
sought for and caressed.

An ill-dressed or starving negro is never seen in England,
and in some instances even alliances are formed between them
and white girls of the lower orders of society.

A few days since, I met in Oxford Street a well-dressed
white girl, who was of a ruddy complexion, and even handsome, walking arm-in-arm, and conversing very sociably with
a negro man, who was as well dressed as she.[122]

REFERENCES TO CHAPTER VIII

[1] These coffee-houses are described in *The Tatler*, 7 Nov., 1710, and *The Spectator*, 23 April, 1711.

[2] *The Daily Courant*, 22 Dec., 1707.

[3] *The Post-Boy*, 1/3 Jan., 1702.

[4] *Ibid*, 29 Dec./1 Jan., 1712.

[5] *The Daily Courant*, 24 Dec., 1712.

[6] For the rôle played by the coffee-house in stock-jobbing, see above p. 164, and insurance, p. 175.

[7] *The Tatler*, 8 Oct., 1709.

[8] *Ibid*, 29 June, 1709.

[9] Macky, *Journey through England* (1727), I, p. 190.

[10] *The Spectator*, 26 April, 1711.

[11] Silliman, *A Journey of Travels in England, Holland and Scotland* (1805-1806), III, p. 103.

[12] *Ibid*, p. 104.

[13] Grosley, *Tour to London*, I, p. 147.

[14] *Ibid*, I, pp. 148-149.

[15] Boulton, *Amusements of Old London*, II, p. 181.

[16] *Ibid*, II, pp. 184-185.

[17] *Ibid*, II, pp. 182-183.

[18] *Ibid*, II, pp. 187-188.

[19] The coffee-house of the early nineteenth century was but a shadow of its former self; see above, p. 213.

[20] Grosley, *op. cit.*, I, p. 150.

[21] *Ibid*, I, pp. 151-152.

[22] *Ibid*, I, p. 150.

[23] Grant, *The Newspaper Press*, I, p. 84.

[24] Advertisement to first number of the *Gentleman's Magazine*, 1731.

[25] *Ibid*.

[26] Fox-Bourne, *English Newspapers*, I, pp. 56, 58.

[27] *The Wkly. Jl. or Sy.'s Post*, 24 June, 1721.

[28] Andrews, *History of British Journalism*, I, p. 129.

[29] See *The Weekly Journal, or Brit. Gaz.*, 7 Jan., 1720, 13 May, 1721; *Mist's Weekly Journal*, 20 July, 1720.

[30] Wm. Danvers, *Parliamentary History*, X, p. 448 (1738).

[31] Miller, *Retrospect of the Eighteenth Century*, III, p. 93.

[32] Andrews, *op. cit.*, I, p. 193.

[33] Lecky, III, pp. 257-262.

[34] *The Humours of a Coffee-House*, 9 July, 1707.

[35] *Applebee's Weekly Journal*, 1 July, 1721.

[36] *Letter of Walpole to Sir Horace Mann,* 17 Sept., 1778; *ibid,* 24 Aug., 1780.

[37] *The Spectator,* 1 March, 1711.

[38] Mrs. Delany, I, p. 551.

[39] *The British Journal,* 21 Sept., 1723.

[40] Anon, *A Trip Through London,* 1727, p. 50.

[41] *The Tatler,* 1 May, 1711.

[42] Brown's *Estimate,* I, p. 49.

[43] *Ibid,* II, p. 78.

[44] *Ibid,* II, p. 79.

[45] Boulton, II, p. 155.

[46] Maitland, *Hist. of Lond.,* II, p. 327.

[47] Hanway's *Journal,* pp. 127-128.

[48] Defoe, *Tour,* I, p. 86.

[49] See below, Chapter IX.

[50] "Jockey and thief are, in the eyes of some people, synonymous terms." Hanway's *Journal,* p. 128.

[51] Chamberlayne, *op. cit.,* p. 51.

[52] *Harl. MSS,* 5931, 46: *A Looking-glass for Swearers,* etc., 1708.

[53] *The Spectator,* 21 July, 1712.

[54] *Orig. Wkly. Jl.,* 7 May, 1716.

[55] *The Daily Post,* 17 May, 1717.

[56] Boulton, I, pp. 31-32.

[57] *Ibid,* I, p. 34.

[58] *Protestant Mercury,* 12 Jan., 1681.

[59] (London) *Advertiser,* 16 Feb., 1747.

[60] Boulton, *op. cit.,* II, pp. 97-98.

[61] *The Post-Man,* 22 June, 1704.

[62] *The Tatler,* 19 Apr., 1709.

[63] *Ibid,* 28 May, 1709.

[64] Boulton, II, p. 50.

[65] *Ibid.*

[66] *The Spectator,* 20 May, 1712.

[67] Boulton, II, p. 31.

[68] *Ibid.*

[69] *Ibid.*

[70] Malcolm, *Anecdotes,* II, p. 276.

[71] Knight, *Popular History of England,* V, p. 96.

[72] Entick, IV, p. 446.

[73] Boswell, II, pp. 168-170.

[74] See above, Chapter V.

[75] *Jane Pitt* (wife of Diamond Pitt, Governor of Madras) *to Hon. Mrs. Pitt,* 2 Oct., 1720, in *Fortescue MSS.*

[76] Smollett, *Humphrey Clinker* (ed. 1811), p. 37.

[77] Goldsmith, *Life of Nash,* p. 60.

[78] *Ibid*, pp. 48 and 60.

[79] *The Spectator*, 27 Aug., 1711.

[80] Goldsmith, *op. cit.*, p. 60.

[81] Smollett, *op. cit.*, p. 50.

[82] Baker, *Tunbridge Walks* (ed. 1703), p. 21.

[83] Shadwell, *Epsom Wells*, p. 33.

[84] Defoe, *Tour*, I, pp. 253-254.

[85] See above, p. 109.

[86] Loudon, *Encyclopædia of Gardening*, pp. 269-277; Miller, *Dictionary of Gardening*, passim.

[87] Evelyn, p. 248.

[88] Lecky, I, p. 525; Angeloni, *Letters on the English Nation*, II, pp. 266-274; Gardner, p. 205. Sloane was, for a time, a resident of Jamaica.

[89] Le Blanc, *Letters on English and French Nations*, I, p. 321.

[90] Silliman, III, p. 73.

[91] *Loudon, op. cit.*, pp. 276-277.

[92] Catesby, *Natural History of Carolina, Florida and the Bahama Islands*.

[93] Evelyn, p. 269.

[94] *Ibid*, p. 279.

[95] Walpole, *Modern Gardening;* Defoe, *Tour*, passim.

[96] Cowper, *The Task*, III, lines 566-585.

[97] *European Magazine*, Jan., 1782, pp. 18-21.

[98] *Ibid*, p. 21.

[99] 26 Geo. II, c. 22.

[100] Murray, *Museums: Their History and Use*, I, pp. 137-139.

[101] *Ibid*, I, p. 140.

[102] *Ibid*, I, pp. 170-172.

[103] *Ibid*, I, p. 174.

[104] Mac Ritchie, *Narrative of the Journey of an Irish Gentleman through England in 1752*, p. 109.

[105] Silliman, I, p. 256.

[106] *Ibid*.

[107] *The Daily Courant*, 15 Sept., 1712; see also *ibid*, 22 Sept., 1712.

[108] *Letter to Mrs. Dewes*, 20 Nov., 1753, in Mrs. Delany, I, p. 435; see also *ibid*, I, p. 38.

[109] Mac Ritchie, *Diary of a Tour through England in 1795*, p. 109 f.

[110] Knight, *The Land We Live In*, IV, p. 85.

[111] Mac Ritchie, *Diary of a Tour*, p. 86.

[112] *Ibid*, p. 93.

[113] *The Spectator*, 3 April, 1712.

[114] *The Post-Man*, 25/27 Mar., 1703.

[115] *Ibid*.

[116] *Ibid*, 13/15 April, 1703.

[117] Cowper, *The Parrot.*
[118] *The Tatler,* 13 May, 1710.
[119] *The Weekly Journal or Sy.'s Post,* 2 April, 1720.
[120] Boswell, II, p. 247.
[121] Ashton, II, p. 63.
[122] Silliman, I, pp. 271-272.

CHAPTER IX

EXCESSES IN SOCIAL LIFE

EXAMINATION of the manners and morals of the eighteenth century must assume that human nature, then as now, was susceptible to outside influence. Never before had the English people been subjected to phenomena of so diverse a nature, or those affecting so intimately and so constantly the character of the individual. New foods, new clothes, new thoughts from overseas and the vast increase of wealth, which have been considered in earlier chapters, had a patent effect on the everyday life of the Englishman. The eighteenth century is commonly considered an age of brutality and coarseness. This feeling possibly is due in large part to the fact that vices and virtues were so subtly and graphically portrayed for the eyes of contemporaries by essayists of the school of Addison and Steele. Their enthusiasm in exposing the follies of the day should not lead solely to a condemnation of the period. Their strictures, rather, were healthy signs of the awakening of a public and of an individual conscience, guide-posts to a higher standard of manners and morals.

To be sure, the acquisition of wealth and the admission of a considerable number of newcomers to the full joys of living had detrimental as well as beneficial results. Prosperity, it was felt, brought avarice, luxury, or effeminacy. At the same time, it supplied necessities, eradicated insularity and prejudice, and spread the spirit of humanity. A state of general plenty, indeed, "diffused general Happiness" and made possible the renaissance of arts and sciences.[1]

One clear result of the speculative nature of business was the universal and respectable practice of gambling as a social diversion. The fevered gains of the stock-market, and the possibilities offered in government lotteries,[2] found their counterpart in private passion for chance. Newspapers teemed with advertisements of proposals by every ravenous adventurer who could collect a few articles. "Goods of every description were converted into prizes, even neck-cloths, snuffboxes, tooth-pick cases, linen, muslin and plate."[3] True enough, an act was passed in 1712 against illicit lotteries, which was followed by a second one to prevent "excessive and deceitful gaming."[4] Evidently these measures proved unavailing, for private lotteries were again proscribed during the reign of George I, under penalty of £500.[5]

Efforts of Parliaments and of city magistrates failed to curb either this mania, or the activities of extralegal operators. A writer of the latter part of the century tells of "an ingenious Sett of lottery merchants," made up of magazine proprietors, tailors, stay-makers, glovers, hat-makers, snuff and tobacco merchants and barbers in shops, "where a man, for being shaved and paying threepence, may stand a chance of getting ten pounds;" and "Lottery eating-houses . . . where if you call for six-penny worth of roast or boiled beef, you receive a note of hand with number which, should it turn out to be fortunate, may entitle the eater of the beef to sixty guineas." [6]   At the close of the century the press complained of private lotteries, called "little goes," seemingly popular and altogether dishonest.[7]

As one views more intimately the private life of the time, it is increasingly evident that the madness for speculation stimulated individual efforts in gambling at home and at the club. Gaiety and pleasure at "White's," for example, centred largely in gambling and gossip[8]—a reputation shared by the "Cocoa Tree" and "Almack's." [9]   Here men succeeded in losing at cards what they had won in the world of business. George Harley Drummond, of the famous banking house of Charing Cross, dropped £20,000 at whist, and was forced to resign his partnership in the firm; while Sir John Malcolm, after losing his fortune acquired in India, remarked nonchalantly, "Another sitting of this kind will oblige me to return again to India." [10]

The vogue of the semi-public gambling house led gullible young men in search of their fortunes in the metropolis to lose "their Money and Reputation." [11] Nor was this vice confined to the sterner sex, for gambling became equally a delight for women. One reads of women who were so covetous of wealth that they played consistently, and were forced to borrow and play again to recoup losses:

Her Jewels are carry'd privately into Lombard Street, and Fortune is to be tempted the next Night with another Sum, borrowed of my Lady's Goldsmith at the Extortion of a Pawnbroker; and if that fails, then she sells off her Wardrobe, to the great grief of her Maids; stretches her Credit amongst those she deals with, or makes her Waiting Woman delve into the Bottom of her Trunk, and lug her green Net Purse full of old Jacobuses, in Hopes to recover her Losses by a Turn of Fortune, that she may conceal her Bad Luck from the Knowledge of her Husband.[12]

Writers of the time implied that women did not always escape with mere loss of money:

> This Itch for Play has, likewise, fatal been,
> And more than Cupid, drawn the Ladies in.
> A thousand guineas for Basset prevails,
> A bait, when Cash runs low, that seldom fails,
> And, when the Fair One can't the Debt defray,
> In Sterling Coin, does Sterling Beauty pay.[13]

Not only, then, did gambling make for immorality among women, but it caused serious physical ills. As one writer phrased it:

> Play, when followed by Assiduity, engrosses the whole Woman. She quickly grows uneasie in her own Family, takes but little Pleasure in all the domestick, innocent Endearments of Life. . . . Hollow Eyes, haggard Looks, and pale Complexions are the natural Indications of a Female Gamester.[14]

Efforts, more or less serious, were made to check this evil during the first half of the century. In the reign of George II an Act was passed, imposing a fine of £200 upon the proprietors of gaming houses, and a fine of £50 upon players therein,[15] while a later measure provided that members of the peerage were not to be exempt from punishment.[16]   Magistrates, too, including Fielding, directed their activities, though with only partial success, toward the suppression of the vice.[17]   In spite of their industry and vigilance, warnings to the public were still considered necessary:

> The artifices and stratagems of the profligate and wicked part of the inhabitants of this great metropolis in order to defraud and impose upon the weak and unwary, being multiplied to an incredible degree, Mr. Fielding has taken pains to lay before the public a detail of such of them as have fallen under his own immediate observation as a Magistrate: in the recital of which, he has mark'd the progress of deceit from the lowest pickpocket to the most accomplished gambler. That none may be in Ignorance of these Snares that are continually laid for them, this history of Gambling is inserted.[18]

In spite of all efforts at reform gambling, especially play for high stakes, continued to be prevalent during the second half of the century.   At Bath and other watering resorts the fever was at its height.[19]   Here, however, there were few complaints of dishonesty, due largely to the example of scrupulousness set by Beau Nash.[20]   In London play for large sums was rife, and the instance of the West Side lady who lost 3,000 guineas at one sitting was by no means exceptional.[21] According to Walpole, there was more deep play at the clubs than ever before.   At "Almack's" young men frequently lost from 5,000 to 15,000 guineas.   Here, at the tender age of 21, Fox shone with the same brilliance he displayed at the House of Commons.[22]   Lord Pigot managed to lose in this way part of his nabob wealth, while at the "Cocoa Tree," [23] one cast at hazard awarded the victor no less than £140,000.[24]   At the same time women of fashion opened their houses to gambling; in particular, Lady Buckinghamshire and Lady Archer. After frequent criticisms in the press had won for these resorts an undesirable notoriety, they were finally forced to close their doors.[25] Faro-banks, however, continued at fashionable gambling houses to the very close of the century.[26]

The effects of speculation on 'Change and in business life in general offered opportunities other than gambling at cards or dice, for betting became widely prevalent during this century. In the reign of Queen Anne gentlemen perpetrated many queer wagers. One adventurous coffee-house youth, "has five Guineas upon Questions in Geography, two that the Isle of Wight is a Peninsula, and three Guineas to one that the World is round," while "there are several of this sort of Fellows in Town who wager themselves into Statesmen . . . and every other Art." [27] The increased interest of Englishmen in world affairs afforded limitless opportunity for the laying of wagers. In the words of a contemporary:

I am told that while wagers were allowed to be made on the taking of towns, and gaining of battles, during the last war, this Exchange Alley was the sharpest Place in the World . . . Some men have got good estates; for trickery is not here reckoned so despicable a quality as abroad, when it is cleanly done; therefore, my friend, when you come here, play not in England, nor venture to lay wagers, except you know your company very well, or are sure of your fact. The fatal South Sea scheme, and the wicked execution of it, proves what I foretold you to be true.[28]

The introduction and amazing progress of betting at

Lloyd's coffee-house was considered a melancholy and powerful proof of the degeneracy of the times. Such bets as on John Wilkes's remaining alive for one year (provided he were kept in prison during that time), and on the declaration of war with France and Spain within a year, were considered innocent enough. But when,

policies came to be opened on two of the first Peers in Britain losing their heads within a year at 10/6 per cent., and on the dissolution of the present Parliament within one year at 5 guineas per cent. . . . it is surely time for Administration to interfere.[29]

During the reign of George III, that most seductive form of all betting—gambling on horse-racing— became popular and firmly established. As might be expected, the lower classes imitated the example of the wealthy, and lost money which could hardly have been spared.[30]

Without condemning the milder forms of play for chance, it is clear that the excessive gambling of the eighteenth century created an unhealthy attitude toward wealth and life itself. The prime objective of the age was to "get money," rather than to "make money." The acquisition of a fortune, preferably without expenditure of creative effort, the absence of fair play in its pursuits, and the failure to regard wealth as a sacred trust to be used primarily for the betterment of one's self and of men in general were all symptoms of a new immorality based on a false philosophy, or perhaps lack of philosophy. The craving for artificial excitement dulled men's fondness for the natural pleasures of the home and the great outdoors.

There resulted a looseness of conduct in public and in relations between the sexes. The real signs of hope lay in the crusades of men who realized these evils, and in the ultimate ability of human nature to right itself, when seemingly approaching a moral cataclysm.

Intemperance in gambling was accompanied by excessive use of spirituous liquors. At the opening of the eighteenth century hard drinking among the upper classes was usual. Oxford was said to have appeared intoxicated before the Queen, while Bolingbroke often resorted to a wet towel on his head after an all-night bout.[31] Addison tells us that "in this thirsty age, the honour falls upon him who carries off the greatest quantity of liquor, and knocks down the rest of the company." [32] During these years, however, ale and beer, together with cheap imported wines,[33] remained the chief drinks of the populace. With the importation of distilled spirits, however, and their manufacture in Great Britain,[34] the passion for gin and rum became epidemic among the masses.[35] Gin-shops sprang up from nowhere; tobacconists and inferior tradesmen dispensed the deadly concoction, offering to make the passer-by drunk for a penny, and dead-drunk for twopence.[36] The puritanical Jury of Middlesex classed gin-shops as public nuisances, and "to be ranked amongst the most disorderly houses," as harbouring the vilest of both sexes, and being responsible for the commission of the worst villainies.[37]

Eminent physicians attributed the increase of patients in the hospitals to "the melancholy consequences of gin-drinking principally." [38] Naturally the hard-headed business men of London, who supported the charities of their city, objected to this added burden, as well as to the increased difficulty in making London a safe city for business purposes. True to their Cromwellian tradition, they discoursed on the harmful effects of drinking on the individual:

> It deprives them of time, money, health, and understanding, weakens and enfeebles them to the last degree . . . raises the most violent and outrageous passions, renders them incapable of hard labour, as well as indisposes them to it, ruins their health, and destroys their lives; besides the fatal effects it has on their morals and religion.[39]

Worst of all was the fatal mistake of giving gin even to the youngest children. While husband and wife spent their money on drink, the children were left starved and naked at home, and "either become a burden to their parishes or . . . are forced to beg while they are children, and learn to grow up to pilfer and steal." [40]

The objections of mercantilists in general, and of business men in particular, were crystallized when the evils of gin-drinking on the national welfare became evident. Drunkenness produced an invincible aversion to work and labour, with the result that "we are deprived of great numbers of useful hands, which would otherwise be employed to the advantage of the publick." [41] Even those who merely tippled lost considerable time thereby, while "the spending of their money in this way, must very much cramp and straiten them, and so far diminish their trade, and the profit which would accrue from thence to the public, as well as to themselves." [42]

With existing evils so detrimental to the welfare of the nation's commerce and industry, a Parliament famed for its unreforming nature, was finally forced to action. In 1736 an Act was passed to restrain excessive drinking by licensing retailers and by imposing a tax of 20s. the gallon on gin. People were forbidden to give this beverage to servants, and workmen's wages were not to be paid in whole or part in it.[43] Violent riots followed this unpopular act, and to the evils of drunkenness were added the subversive tendencies of smuggling and illicit dealing.[44]

The latter half of the century witnessed a reformation of these abuses. The stigma of disapproval came to be placed on those who knowingly purchased smuggled goods, by grouping them in the same class with smugglers.[45] Illicit traffic was diminished by the Act of 1743, which reduced the excessive duty and imposed a heavy penalty on smugglers.[46] Legislative action was, however, but a partial cure. Patriots decried the consumption of liquor in wartime, while England was in the throes of a life and death struggle for empire.[47] The urge to victory inspired men to their best efforts and made work the universal contribution. Herein lay a logical corrective for idleness and dissipation. In the language of a writer of the time:

The Husbandman and Manufacturer must feed and clothe the soldier and the sailor. Pay them for it and they will do it cheerfully, and in the issue as cheerfully contribute their extraordinary labour to the extraordinary charge of supporting war.

What may not be done by the force of industry, where there is a fruitful soil to cultivate and materials to manufacture? . . . The Peasant may grumble, and so may the Lord, but has not the soldier the most difficult part to act?[48]

Finally, satisfactory substitutes for hard liquors were being found in tea and coffee. The former beverage replaced to a considerable extent alcoholic stimulants at Ranelagh and Vauxhall, at the lesser tea-gardens, and at fashionable gatherings in Bath and London. The substitution made for decorum by rendering public drunkenness unfashionable. As Tate, poet laureate to Queen Anne, rhapsodized:

> Whilst Tea, our sorrows safely to beguile,
> Sobriety, and mirth does reconcile;
> For to this nectar we the blessing owe,
> To grow more wise, as we more cheerful grow.[49]

At first restricted because of its cost to people of fashion, this beverage gradually came into common use, following the reduction of duties and the increased importations. It became, in the closing years of the century, a necessity in the daily menu of the farmer, and of the great populations of the new industrial centres.[50] With the ensuing decline in drunkenness, it was now possible for the reformer to devote his zeal to the excessive consumption of tea.[51]

Coffee, too, had a sobering influence. While it is a question whether coffee or stronger beverages may furnish more nourishment, it is at least true that "a man is never tempted to get drunk upon coffee, to lower himself below the level of brutes."[52] And while the coffee-house may hardly be said to have been "the nursery of temperance," [53] "it is certain, whatever else may be doubtful, that the establishment of coffee-shops has worked some change in the prevailing usages of the London working-classes in respect to beverages." [54]

It must not be forgotten, also, that the eighteenth century was an age of the *nouveaux riches,* tinctured with the manners and tastes of those who have acquired wealth too easily and too rapidly. Defoe deprecated the common extravagance of his age:

Such is the expensive humour of the times, that not a family, no, hardly of the meanest, but treat their friends with punch or fine ale, or have their parlours set off with the tea-table and the chocolate pot; treats and liquors, all exotic, foreign and new among tradesmen, and terrible articles in their modern expenses.[55]

Writing at the opening of the following century, Austin remarked:

Nothing has afforded us more amusement than the exhibitions of a certain class of Englishman . . . composed of those who have unexpectedly come to wealth, some few of those who are earnestly in pursuit of fortune, and whose affairs are flourishing, but principally of those who have spent their fortunes, and yet are resolved to support appearances.[56]

According to critics, then, the majority of people were corrupted by wealth, and too likely to be "puffed up by prosperity." [57] Ostentation and extravagance were two unmistakable symptoms of this age. Never were these characteristics more evident than during the boom period of the South Sea Bubble:

Our South-Sea Equipages increase every day; the City-ladies buy South-Sea Jewels; hire South-Sea Maids; and take new country South-Sea Houses; the Gentlemen set up South-Sea Coaches, and buy South-Sea Estates that they neither examine the Situation, the Nature or Quality of the Soil, or Price of the Purchase.[58]

The new "bubble-kings," then, sought to outdo quality in their new foppery, so that "we cannot distinguish at present, who is Quality, and who is not, till we get a few Sumptuary Laws to mortify them." A story is told of one of the new family of upstarts, who taking a friend for a coach-ride, put him in, closed the door and forgot to enter himself.[59] In many cases, too, did a lax morality follow a sudden rise in wealth.[60]

To many, the destruction of the Bubbles came as a heavy blow. Thousands of poor wretches rode to their ruin and filled London with their groans. Those who once drove to 'Change Alley in great state now condescended to walk the streets on foot;

And even those of the trading rank who talked loudly of retiring into the country, purchasing estates, then building fine houses, and in everything imitating their betters, are now become bankrupts, and have by necessity shut up their shops, because they could not keep them open any longer.[61]

The sobering effect of this calamity was of temporary duration. Writers continued to bemoan what they felt to be extravagant display. The chief sources of criticism were the frequent changes in fashion, and the seemingly exorbitant sums spent on clothes. Said one of the critics:

Is it not true, Madam, that hardly a Chambermaid now thinks her condition supportable, unless she cuts more silk to pieces, to adorn her gown, than would be sufficient to make one?

And for what is all this? Methinks you all appear like women of shreds; instead of ornaments, your garments look as if they were in rags. Is this extravagance most melancholy to think of, or most ridiculous to behold?[62]

The same author laments the excessive amount of gold and silver used at home, suggesting as a remedy that these articles be heavily taxed, or melted into currency. Finally, women who wore jewels set in gold or silver, should pay a tax for the hands, and another for the head, while men who wore rings must suffer a like penalty.[63] Similar were the complaints against increasing expenditures for tea. Hanway, the chief opponent of it, made suggestions for the use of the money which was thus wasted:

If one of the two millions now spent in Tea, were laid out annually in Plantations, in making Public Gardens, in Paving and Widening Streets, in making Roads, in rendering Rivers navigable, or erecting Palaces, building neat and convenient Houses, where are now only Huts; draining Lands, or rendering those which are now barren, of some use; should we not be the gainers, compared with the consequences of the tea trade?[64]

Other complaints of extravagance mentioned enormous sums spent for new buildings, especially the Pantheon whose construction dissipated £60,000.[65] Young men, too, were foolish enough to give flower women half a guinea every morning for button-hole nosegays.[66] In many cases, however, the increased wealth justified larger expenditures, while the added luxuries after all eventually set a higher standard of living.[67] Thus every man of fortune now had a splendid house in town, though his forefathers had been content with a temporary lodging; while his new country estate either dispossessed the country squire or caused the latter to imitate the tastes and manners of the newcomers.[68] The genius of Sir Christopher Wren, among others, made this possible by building attractive houses for men whose incomes were as low as £200 a year.[69] If there was prodigality in the early century, it was largely confined to amounts spent on various sports and pastimes.[70] Money might have been squandered in worse ways than in the maintenance of equipages and of horses.[71] It is comforting to learn, too, that some individuals were able to acquire fortunes gracefully. In the words of a contemporary:

It is pleasant and surprising to hear how many Families have been raised from nothing, and how many more have trebled their Wealth, by one happy and well-timed Venture. But how much pleasanter it is to a virtuous Mind to know that this Indulgence of Fortune has centred on some, whose Character will do credit to their Virtues.[72]

The healthy love of show and luxury of the early century became a vice with the influx of the nabobs. The immense wealth brought in by the newcomers "bore down all barriers of economies and introduced a luxury of expense unknown to empires of vaster extent." [73] Sums unheard of before were laid out in houses and gardens and furniture. Enormous prices were paid for objects of luxury.[74] Chests filled with East Indian gold, as the one proudly exhibited by Lord Clive,[75] poured forth an endless stream to satisfy momentary whims, and to outdo London in the spirit of restlessness and change. The visitor from the metropolis, with fashion-wise suggestions, left the owner of a house with an avid desire to scrap existing equipment, and to substitute anything newer and more costly.[76] In sumptuousness of setting, in finery of display, the estate and life of the nabob surpassed all dreams of Arabian nights.[77] In public the mushroom family appeared with all the wealth of the Indies on their backs. Their pew had to be carpeted and cushioned, and

there were flowered muslins, white shawls and red shawls, white feathers and red feathers; and every now and then the young Mushroom girls pulled out little bottles and sent such a perfume around them. Nay, my old friend, their father, like a fool he was, had such a mixture of black sattin and pink sattin about him, and was so stiff and awkward in his finery, that he looked for all the world like the king of clubs, and seemed, poor man! to have as little to say for himself.[78]

More than the ostentation and extravagance of the nabob, which might be justified by the extent of his fortune, was their disastrous influence on neighbours. The latter, true to the tenets of human nature, sought to ape the vices of the wealthy Anglo-Indian. To the wives and daughters of men of moderate means things once considered comfortable or convenient now appeared disgusting. All their food and clothes were invidious by comparison with those of "Mushroom Hall." The wife and daughter of one gentleman, "alone carry the produce of ten acres on their backs," [79] for home-made muslins seemed contemptible beside custom-made garments from Bengal. Even "our barn-door fowls, we used to say, were so fat and well-tasted, we now make awkward attempts, by garlic and pepper, to turn into the form of curries and peelaws," while good old October ale gave way to Indian madeira.[80] The loss of money was a minor tragedy compared with the loss of happiness consequent upon a futile desire to emulate the splendour of the nabob.

Objects of art were avidly sought by the *nouveaux riches,* and ridiculous sums spent for their purchase. Lovers of antiquities were warned to make haste, lest "those learned patrons of taste, Lord Clive, or some other nabob, will give £50,000 for the collection, though the pictures may as yet be had for £3,000, and the antiquities for £8,000." [81] Unfortunately these expenditures were for the sake of fashion, rather than to satisfy a passion for art, and actually served only to increase their cost to real lovers of beauty.   One nabob who had purchased a splendid collection of paintings, "for a mere song," spent several hours a morning to learn his lesson in the event of callers. A commentator on the procedure said:

And yet, after all, he is sometimes mistaken about them; as last Thursday he told a gentleman that was looking at the pictures, that the half-naked woman above the chimney-piece was done for one Caroline Marrot (I suppose from the picture, some Miss no better than she should be;) whereas the gentleman, Mr. Gusto, declared it was as like Widow Renny, as one egg is like another.[82]

In fact, the reckless expenditure of the tribe of nabobs raised costs beyond reason.   According to another commentary:

You would be frightened at the dearness of everything; I build out of economy, for unless I do now, I shall not be able to afford it. I expect that a pint of milk will not be sold under a diamond, and then nobody can keep a cow but my Lord Clive. Indeed our country's fever is almost at the height every way.[83]

Competitors, then, in the mad race for display and luxury, did not hesitate to equal the nabobs in extravagance. It was feared that "unless the mob will turn reformers, and rise, or my Lord Clive sends over diamonds enough for current coin, I do not see how one shall be able soon to purchase necessaries." [84]

REFERENCES TO CHAPTER IX

[1] Brown's *Estimate*, I, pp. 152-153.

[2] The government lotteries, instituted in the reign of Anne (*The Tatler* 14/16 Sept., 1710), continued without a break until 1824 (Ashton, *History of Gambling*, pp. 229-230). See above, p. 171f.

[3] Malcolm, *Anecdotes*, II, p. 3. See also Macpherson, *Annals of Commerce*, III, p. 23, and Ashton, *Queen Anne*, I, pp. 114-116.

[4] Malcolm, *op. cit.*, II, p. 3.

[5] 8 Geo. I, c. 2.

[6] *Annual Register*, 1777.

[7] The *Times* (London), 22 July, 1795.

[8] "Bruyere" in the London *Journal* (1727); Macky, p. 189.

[9] Ashton, *History of Gambling*, pp. 90-95.

[10] *Ibid*, pp. 95, 101; Lecky, I, p. 523.

[11] *Grub Street Journal*, 2 Sept., 1736.

[12] "The Gaming Lady, or Bad Luck to Him that has Her," in *Adam and Eve Stript of their Furbelows*.

[13] Mrs. Centilevre, *The Gamester* (1705), epilogue.

[14] *Guardian*, 29 July, 1713. See also Pope, *Rape of the Lock*, Canto III, and *Gentleman's Magazine* for Jan., 1731.

[15] 12 Geo. II, c. 28.

[16] 18 Geo. II, c. 34.

[17] *Gentleman's Magazine*, V. xxvi. 564 (1756).

[18] *Ibid*.

[19] Defoe, however, states that gaming, which had formerly been scandalous, was partially abated by Acts of Parliament. *Tour*, II, p. 289.

[20] *Letter of Walpole to Sir H. Mann*, 26 Dec., 1748.

[21] *Chronicle in An. Reg.*, 1766, Feb. 8.

[22] *Letter of Walpole to Sir H. Mann*, 2 Feb., 1770.

[23] *Letter of Walpole to Hon. H. S. Conway*, 31 Dec., 1774.

[24] *Letter of Walpole to Sir H. Mann*, 16 May, 1781.

[25] *Morning Post* (London), 12 Jan., 1800.

[26] *The Times* (London), 5 Feb., 1793; 6 Feb., 1793; 2 May, 1793; 2 April, 1794, 25 June, 1794; 30 Dec., 1795, etc.

[27] *Spectator*, 16 Aug., 1711.

[28] Macky, I, p. 190.

[29] *Letter of Walpole to Sir H. Mann*, 10 July, 1774; see Malcolm, *Anecdotes*, I, pp. 374-375.

[30] *The Connoisseur*, 9 May, 1754; *Letters of Walpole to Sir H. Mann*, 19 Dec., 1750, and 10 July, 1754.

[31] Mrs. Delany, VI, p. 168.

[32] *The Spectator,* 19 July, 1714.

[33] Made possible by the Methuen treaty, 1703, with Portugal.

[34] *Parl. Hist.,* XII, 1211-1214; Macpherson, *Annals,* II, p. 639.

[35] Report of the Committee to H. M.'s Justices of the Peace for the County of Middlesex (1725) in Malcolm, *Anecdotes,* I, p. 137.

[36] In Westminster alone there were 7,044 shops where gin was sold. Read's *Weekly Journal, or Brit. Gaz.,* 24 Jan., 1736.

[37] Report of the Grand Jury of Middlesex (1729) quoted in Entick, II, p. 425.

[38] Malcolm, *op. cit.,* I, p. 169. Statistics given here show an increase of hospital cases, for 1704-1718, of 25%, for 1718-1734 of 33 1/3%, and for 1734-1749, of more than 300%.

[39] *Ibid,* I, p. 135.

[40] *Ibid,* I, p. 136.

[41] *Ibid,* I, p. 137.

[42] *Ibid.*

[43] *The Country Journal or Craftsman,* 15 May, 1736.

[44] See above, p. 178.

[45] Hanway, *Essay,* p. 312.

[46] Lecky, I, p. 480.

[47] *European Magazine,* Jan., 1783, p. 25.

[48] Hanway, *op. cit.,* p. 333.

[49] Tate, *A Poem upon Tea, with a Discourse on its Sov'rain Virtues,* p. 35.

[50] See above, Chapter III.

[51] Hanway, *Essay, passim;* see also above, p. 68.

[52] Dodd, *The Food of London,* p. 408.

[53] *Ibid,* p. 409.

[54] *Ibid.*

[55] Defoe, quoted in Dodd, *op. cit.,* p. 96.

[56] Austin, *Letters from London* (1802), p. 81.

[57] *The Weekly Journal,* 9 July, 1720.

[58] *Applebee's Journal,* 5 Aug., 1720.

[59] *The Weekly Journal,* 2 April, 1720.

[60] *Ibid,* 21 May, 1720.

[61] *The Weekly Journal or Saturday's Post,* 1 Oct., 1720.

[62] Hanway, *Essay,* p. 253.

[63] *Ibid.* See above, Chapter IV. The change of fashions was made possible in part by the introduction of cheaper silks, and the growing popularity of cheap cotton fabrics. The element of personal cleanliness and sanitation must be considered as a cause and an effect, although the money invested in clothes does not seem extravagant in consideration of increased incomes.

[64] Hanway, *op. cit.,* p. 276.

[65] See above, Chapter VII.

[66] *Letter of Walpole to Sir H. Mann,* 16 Oct., 1769.

[67] Brown, the most devastating of mid-century critics, states that in general expenditures were no more than formerly, the principal change being that money now went out of the country. *Estimate,* II, p. 73.

[68] *Ibid,* II, p. 73; Boswell, I, p. 283.

[69] Malcolm, *Anecdotes,* II, p. 365. Serious-minded American visitors were wont to call even this desire for comfort an extravagance. Austin, *op. cit.,* pp. 89-92.

[70] Chamberlayne, p. 317.

[71] Hanway, *Letters,* II, pp. 173, 197, 288.

[72] *The Wkly. Jl.,* 19 July, 1720.

[73] Walpole, *Memoirs of George III,* III, p. 198.

[74] Walpole, *Letters,* I, p. 341.

[75] Boswell, III, pp. 400-401.

[76] *The Lounger,* 8 Oct., 1785.

[77] Mrs. Delany, I, p. 218 (*Letter of Mrs. Pendarves to Mrs. Dewes,* 19 Jan., 1742).

[78] *The Lounger,* 10 Dec., 1785; see also *Letter of Walpole to Sir Horace Mann,* 26 April, 1771.

[79] *The Lounger,* 28 May, 1785.

[80] *Ibid.*

[81] This comment had reference to a splendid collection lately brought from Herculaneum, Pompeii and Sicily. *Letter of Walpole to the Countess of Ossory,* 14 Dec., 1771.

[82] *The Lounger,* 8 Oct., 1785.

[83] *Letter of Walpole to Sir Horace Mann,* 1 July, 1762; see also *ibid,* 20 July, 1767, *and to Geo. Montagu,* 7 Aug., 1767.

[84] *Letter of Walpole to Sir Horace Mann,* 25 Sept., 1766.

CHAPTER X

THE REFINEMENT OF TASTE AND MANNERS

THE extravagance and other shortcomings of the *nouveaux riches* should not blind one to the levelling of social classes and the higher standard of living which followed in the wake of the influx of wealth.[1] People of lesser importance profited by the prosperity of the nabobs and of the rich merchant aristocracy. The latter group was gradually overcoming time-old prejudice towards its character, and was winning the respect of Englishmen and foreigners.

As a writer of the time put it:

Industry, the first principle of a Citizen, is an infallible Specifick to keep the Spirits awake, and prevent that Stagnation and Corruption of Humours which make our fine Gentlemen such horrible Torments to one another and to themselves. Decency in dress is finery enough in a Place where they are taught from their Childhood to expect no Honours from what they seem to be, but from what they really are. The Conversation turns principally on the Interests of Europe, in which they are themselves chiefly concerned; and the business here is to enlarge the Commerce of their Country, by which the Publick is to gain much more than the Merchant himself. . . . In this House I have met with Merchants of as liberal Education and generous Principles, of as exquisite taste in classical Knowledge and polite Learning, as are to be found at Court or in the College.[2]

264

In emulation of the old aristocracy, the domestic retinue of the merchant prince included a cook and a house-maid, a nursery-maid, and a footman, together with a coachman and groom.[3] A duplicate staff was required for the home in the suburbs or country.[4] Here he slept on hot summer nights, and came into town after breakfast, often accompanied by his family, which would enjoy the amusements of the metropolis.   In the evening, they would return to a sumptuous repast with a handsome dessert and wines of excellent vintage.[5] Practically, then, the business man began by emulating his superiors, and ended by setting an example for them to follow. To the extent of his income, the lesser tradesman walked in the footsteps of the merchant prince. In 1700 his life was confined to the shop; by the time of George III he had two houses and spent the summer at the seaside, while his wife and daughters imitated the dress, tastes and amusements of the gentry.[6] His family gained social significance, when apprentices by living outside his home no longer shared in the social life of the household.[7] In turn this group emulated, to their modest ability, the manner of living of their masters.[8] Even clerks in the office and shop shared in the quest for a more comfortable and enjoyable life. How envied of their fellows were the fortunate shop-men of Queen Anne's reign. "They have their toilets and their fine night-gowns; their chocolate in the morning, and their green tea two hours later." [9] For this natural desire to be presentable and comfortable, they gained the reputation of effeminate foppery.   Yet a century later, such an ambition was taken as a matter of course.[10]

With the increased demand for servants came higher wages and better treatment.[11] The possibility of their leaving for other places brought about the practice of tipping, which in turn caused demoralization of domestic service.[12] At the same time, new advantages accrued to this class. A Portuguese visitor to London in 1730 comments on their improved status:

As to the common and menial servants (of London), they have great wages, are well-kept and clothed, but are, notwithstanding, the plague of almost every house in town. They form themselves into societies, or rather confederacies, contributing to the maintenance of each other when out of place, and if any of them cannot manage the family where they are entertained as they please, immediately they give notice they will be gone. There is no speaking to them; they are above correction. . . . It is become a common saying, "If my servant ben't a thief, if he be but honest, I can bear with other things," and indeed it is very rare to meet in London with an honest servant.[13]

In appearance then, during the first quarter of the century, there was little to distinguish the aristocracy from the "inferior class of men." "Titles and fine Houses, gay Chariots and splendid Equipage, with a superior Quantity of South Sea Stock are the Requisites to mark out the *Patrician Order;* and with these Qualifications he must be reverenced by the Vulgar suitable to his Rank." [14] This tendency was even more pronounced at the close of the century, when the very servant now apes and rivals her mistress in every species of whim and extravagance. All sorts of people are frequently confounded or melted down into one glaring mass of superfluity or absurdity. The lower orders are entirely lost in a general propensity to mimic the finery of the higher; and every woman we meet would seem by her gesture and apparel to possess at least an independent fortune.[15]

The sole mark of distinction was in manners,[16] for too often were the accoutrements of fashion but encumbrances to the vulgar. As Chesterfield saw fit to sum it up, a representative of the latter was even "at a loss to know what to do with his hat, when it is not upon his head; his cane (if unfortunately he wears one), is at perpetual war with every cup of tea or coffee he drinks."[17]

Yet forces were constantly at work to overcome this fault, and to improve the manners and taste of all groups of society. The amenities of metropolitan life developed a stimulating atmosphere of refinement. Here were first introduced into daily life the luxuries which followed increased commerce. Distant shores and climes were searched for commodities intended for the most delicate and exquisite uses. Coarser modes were despised when habits of higher indulgence came in. Writers bred in the environment of a "man's world," were accustomed to label this luxury "effeminacy," to consider graceful manners, as debility and languor, and to call acts of pleasurable enjoyment, mere vanity.[18]

The search for refinement, however, was not necessarily a sign of effeminacy. The desire for warm carpets under one's feet, warm hangings about him, and windows nicely jointed to prevent the intrusion of

damp winter air, splendid furniture, a long train of
attendants, an elegant and costly entertainment including "the childish vagaries of a whimsical dessert" and
delicacies from the seven seas—all of these desires
and achievements of the successful eighteenth-century
business man stamped him in the mind of his critic as
a nincompoop, a mollycoddle, a degenerate. A fairer
view, however, would be to regard such an environment as the symbol of a healthier and more refined
taste, as making less obvious the more unpleasant
mechanism of living, and above all, as a fit setting for
more polished manners and the growth of intellectual life.

Commodities from overseas improved table manners. Early in the century it was considered necessary to warn diners not to pick their teeth at table with
their forks, or to wipe utensils on the bread or
the cloth, instead of the napkin.[19] Spoons were
rarely used. Due to increased importations of silver, these implements became ordinary adjuncts of a
meal. Guide-books in etiquette, such as Defoe's
Compleat Gentleman, initiated both high and low in
a more genteel art of eating. Coffee-houses prided
themselves on the decorum of their guests. When the
demands of business deferred the dinner hour from
noon to three o'clock,[20] that meal took on added social
significance. Perfect table manners were necessary
for the encouragement of wit and repartee; the mere
eating of food must be so gracefully accomplished as
to be unnoticeable. Who could be uncouth when facing a dainty set of china, which was now a proud pos-

session of the socially ambitious?[21]   Further aids to
cleanliness were coarse doilies and napkins, fringed at
each end.[22]   Their use became common, when they
came to be manufactured of cheap cotton material.[23]

The needs of business life and the close connection
of business with social intercourse developed polite-
ness as a valuable stock-in-trade.   The visitor to London found the civility of the citizens and shopkeepers
refreshing, in comparison with the insolence of the
lower orders.   Said one of them:

"I met with complaisance and civility amongst all
the shopkeepers, whether great or little.   The tradesman sent his son or daughter to me, who often served
me as guide, after having first acted as interpreter." [24]
Elsewhere the merchant was becoming known as a
new species of gentleman.   The business men of Liverpool were "genteel in their address.   They are hos-
pitable and very friendly to strangers. . . . Their
tables are plentifully furnished, and their viands well
served up.   Their rum is excellent, and they consume
large quantities of it in punch." [25]

This improvement in manners is even more marked
by a comparison of the townsmen with members of the
rural gentry.   The country squires, like Sir Charles
Grandison of Richardson, were coarse, evil-smelling
and brutal.[26]   They were accused of wearing their
shirts half a week, of being drunk twice a day, and of
being gluttonous in the consumption of their food.[27]
This wide gulf between town and country was bridged
only by the wealth and the increase of trade from oversea commerce.

At the beginning of the century the natives of distant countries were about as different a species from those of the metropolis as the natives of the Cape of Good Hope. Their manners and dialect were entirely provincial, and their dress as far from metropolitan as Turkish or Chinese.[28] Merchants in the provinces too often acquired the manners of the country gentry. Defoe sought to "advise the rich ones among them, if they would be a little more polite and generous than they usually are, to travel . . . to London, and they will see examples worth their Imitation, as well for princely Spirit, as upright and generous Dealings." [29] With the enclosures of commons the improvement of roads [30] and the establishment in 1784 of regular mail-coach routes, access to the metropolis was made comparatively easy. As a result, town and country were knitted more closely together. The manners, fashions, amusements and vices of the metropolis made their way readily and speedily to the farthest corners of the land. Good-sized cities and innumerable small towns became miniature Londons, with their card-parties, balls, routs, and concerts by subscription, and where "reading females may hire novels from a country circulating library of one hundred volumes." [31] An observer of Manchester in particular noticed that "the vast increase of foreign trade has caused many of the Manchester manufacturers to travel abroad . . . as well as foreigners to reside in Manchester. And the town has now in every respect assumed the style and manners of one of the commercial capitals." [32]

The triumph of the merchant and of business life over the knight and the middle ages ended the practice of duelling—a decided step in the reformation of manners. Never was this dangerous pastime more prevalent than during the first two decades of the eighteenth century; to this fact the newspapers of the day bore jesting reference.[33] Indeed every gaming table, coffee-house or tavern seemed to produce its duellist. Little opportunity, indeed, did the universal fashion of wearing swords allow for the passions to subside or the reason to reflect. Even the innocent suffered, for any rake who staggered through the streets, might at will plunge a sword through an unoffending breast. Rapidly the habit of wearing swords became less common, due in part to the fashion set by Beau Nash,[34] and finally gave way to the carrying of sticks and canes, many of them of oversea origin.[35] By the opening of the following century, the sword had become obsolete except for military men, and duelling the rare exception, rather than the rule.[36] The cane, then, became an article of social embellishment, and its graceful use a matter of ritual. The fan, another oversea product, served to enhance feminine charm, to serve ably as a weapon in the new game of flirtation.[37]

Under the guidance of the incomparable Beau Nash Bath, the great melting-pot of English social life, was a powerful factor in raising the standards of manners and of social relationships. The amenities of London and suburban social life, too, inevitably improved the social graces. The coffee-house, which brought men, and in some cases women, together deserves recognition for its place in this change. The increased use of tea and coffee at social functions tended to create a respectable atmosphere in which women might appear. With new delights afforded by the added attractions of the fair sex, the party for men alone gave way in popularity to the mixed gathering. No less astute an observer than Pope credits coffee with this connective influence:

> For lo! the board with cups and spoons is crown'd,
> The berries crackle and the mill turns round;
> On shining altars of Japan they raise
> The silver lamp; the fiery spirits blaze;
> From silver spouts the graceful liquors glide,
> While China's earth receives the smoking tide;
> At once they gratify their sense and taste,
> And frequent cups prolong the rich repast.[38]

The increased gaiety of London, "where all the young people are younger than they used to be, and all the old are grown young," Mrs. Montagu attributed to the general use of tea, and to the more exquisite and subtle variety of humour found at the tea-table.[39] Incidentally, *The Spectator, The Tatler,* with other essays and magazines, formed a necessary part of every tea-equipage, and the bases for frequent discussions of the vices of the day:[40] affectation, presumption, foppery, upstart vulgarity, fashionable extravagance. Gradually, as the century wore on, the fashionable world became free and easy, as well as modish, and began to affect an agreeable negligence. It was true that conversation might still convey obscene thoughts, but at least they were clothed in modest terms and distant phrases.[41]

The admission of women to social affairs on a basis of equality meant a step upward in the refinement of manners. And, in turn, their new prominence was due to the increase of wealth and new commodities and greater leisure. With money to be freely spent, and with servants to care for household drudgery, London became a riot of frivolity for emancipated woman. In the winter, balls, concerts, operas, assemblies, masquerades, ridottos, routs, drums, and a score of other diversions seemed to critics of the day an idle waste of time. Said Defoe: "Likewise, in the Summer, there is no stirring in any Corner, without meeting with Places consecrated to Amusement, or, in plain English, driving away all Thoughts of private Oeconomy, or of public Spirit." [42] Dancing, formerly an occasional diversion, became a daily occurrence, while the mid-day hours, in earlier times free from intrusion, now offered entertainments to the pleasure-seeker.[43] Little wonder that the fastidious Chesterfield complained bitterly of the emptiness of London social life of his time.[44]

In the social sphere of the early eighteenth century woman was undoubtedly idle, unproductive, unsatisfying. She took little outdoor exercise. Swift repeatedly grumbled to Stella, advising her to reduce her consumption of claret and to buy a pair of good strong boots.[45] This criticism was generally remedied before the middle of the century, when walking in the Mall, Ranelagh and elsewhere, as well as horseback riding,

became exceedingly popular.[46]   Yet even the daily life
of the woman of Queen Anne's reign, as outlined
below, was surely an improvement over the emptiness
of former times, and a harbinger of better things to
come:

Wednesday.   From Eight till Ten, Drank two Dishes of
Chocolate in Bed, and fell asleep after 'em.

From Ten to Eleven.   Eat a Slice of Bread and Butter,
drank a Dish of Bohea, read the *Spectator*.

From Eleven to One.   At my Toilet, try'd a new Head.
Gave Orders for Veny to be combed and washed.   Mem.   I
look best in Blue.

From One till Half an Hour after Two.   Drove to the
Change.   Cheapened a Couple of Fans.

Till Four.   At Dinner.   Mem.   Mr. Froth passed by in
his new Liveries.

From Four to Six.   Dressed, paid a Visit to old Lady Blithe,
and her Sister, having heard they were gone out of Town that
Day.

From Six to Eleven.   At Basset.   Mem.   Never set again
upon the Ace of Diamonds.

Thursday.   From Eleven at Night to Eight in the Morning.
Dreamed that I punted to Mr. Froth.

From Eight to Ten.   Chocolate.   Read two Acts in *Aurenzebe* (Dryden's) abed.

From Ten to Eleven.   Tea-Table.

Rest of the Morning.   Fontange, the Tire-woman, her Account of my Lady Blithes Wash.   Broke a Tooth in my little
Tortoise-shell Comb.   Sent Frank to know how my Lady
Hectick rested after her Monkey's leaping out at Window.
Looked pale.   Fontange tells me my Glass is not true.   Dressed
by Three.

From Three to Four.   Dinner cold before I sat down.

From Four to Eleven.   Saw Company.   Mr. Froth's Opinion of Milton.   His Account of the Mohocks.   His Fancy

for a Pin-Cushion.   Picture in the Lid of his Snuff-Box.   Old
Lady Faddle promises me her Woman to cut my Hair.   Lost
five Guineas at Crimp.

Twelve a-Clock at Night.   Went to Bed.[47]

To look upon this aimless existence as an improvement surely speaks poorly for the past.   But woman
was soon to be rescued, or more exactly, to rescue herself from this purgatory.

There was at least a real joy in shopping with plenty
of leisure, a goodly stock of commodities, and the
wherewithal to spend.   Oft-times women went to gaze
upon the wares with no intent to purchase:

One of these No Customers, calls for a Set of Tea Dishes,
another for a Bason, a third for my best Green Tea, and even to
the Punchbowl; there's scarce a piece in my Shop but must be
displaced, and the whole agreeable Architecture disordered.
. . . Well, after all this Racket and Clutter, this is too dear,
that is their Aversion; another thing is Charming, but not
wanted.   The Ladies are cured of the Spleen, but I am not a
Shilling the better for it.[48]

Whatever the plaints of shop-keepers, the wealth of
the Indies and America proved for women an open
sesame to an endless variety of costume and personal
adornment, luxurious homes and delightful social
activities.   It furnished as well an escape from the
boredom and uselessness of mediæval chivalry.   Up to
this time, at least, the wife had been little more than
the best of servants; for upon marriage she lost
the power over her person, her will, and her goods,
and had to depend for the joys as well as the necessities of life on the kindness and thoughtfulness of her
husband.[49]   What a welcome relief these mornings in

the gorgeous shops must have afforded! The first glimmerings of independence, the awakening of new power must have come with the bargaining for, and the choosing of, fine handkerchiefs and silks and satins.

The gregarious instinct of woman, or possibly idle curiosity, appears responsible for the introduction of the custom of calling.[50] Sunday visiting was fashionable, and instead of leaving cards, servants were sent to ask a "How do ye?" [51] Another new institution was the "evening at home." In the opinion of a contemporary critic: "Here you will find an undistinguished and undistinguishing crowd. What is this but a well-cloathed mob, where each is entitled to a place at a Card Table?" [52] Yet at these visits, the germs of the social graces found fertile soil. The artificiality of the *nouveaux riches* in this connection was likewise condemned: "How can she get Wisdom who abhorreth books; who glorieth in dissipation, who driveth about to Silk and China Shops; who is occupied in Routs, and whose talk is of dress and masquerades?" [53]

But the time had passed when intelligence in a woman was pardonable only when accompanied by exceptional beauty or charm. Men came now to admire and even to demand in women education, the peculiar ability to act as delightful hostess, the mastery of the art of flirtation, and in general a ready wit and repartee. Fashionable schools were established to satisfy these requirements, such as a French boarding school, lately set up by a "Gentleman of Education . . . where young Ladies are taught Reading, Writing, Working and Accounts, Geography and Dancing; and instructed in all Parts of Education." [54]

"Marjory Mushroom" [55] was one of thousands who sought to escape the stigma of being termed a "country girl," by coming to the metropolis, and learning there the latest vagaries of the mode. Here she achieved the fashionable accomplishments of dancing, music and French. As a part of her education in social life, the French friseur screwed up her hair, the shoemaker pinched her toes, and the staymaker reduced the circumference of her waist to but a few inches. But she learned as well the manners of the *ton,* and such words as "ravishing, charming, divine." And most important of all, the new art of flirtation:

When I meet a gentleman in our walks, I must look full at him as I can, to shew my eyes; and laugh to shew my teeth. . . . flourish my rattan, to shew my shapes. And though in a room, I am to speak as low and mumbling as I can, to look as if I did not care whether I was heard or not; yet in a public place, I am to talk as loud and fast as possible, and call the men by their plain surnames and tell all about our last night's parties.[56]

In a word, the product fell not far short of the modern flapper.

To realize, however, that the demand for education was becoming general, rather than confined merely to fashion, one has only to note the countless schools for girls in London and nearby villages, where young ladies could be boarded and educated. Such schools necessarily followed a different plan from that of the more luxurious seminaries, for their pupils were culled from the families of tradesmen. Yet even here the girl-student was called "Miss," and the mistress of the school, a "governess." [57] The subjects included in the curriculum were French, dancing, and needlework. In this way daughters of tradesmen would be prepared for any advance in social position which their fathers might secure.

Naturally, any such aid to the levelling of class distinction would meet with opposition from the old order. What help could children thus trained be to their parents? They were unable to help their fathers in business, and were trained only to marry above their station, or to accept the alternative of ending their existence in Magdalen House. These dire predictions, of course, were not fulfilled; but the new opportunities for education were in themselves testimony to the growing freedom of women. Critics, hardly daring to denounce education itself, continued to urge its strict limitation. Schools should be kept only by discreet gentlewomen, by whom

the young people [should] be taught submission and humility towards their superiors, decency and modesty in their own dress and behaviour. That they should be instructed in all sorts of plain-work, reading, writing, accounts, pastry, pickling, preserving, and other branches of cooking; be taught to weave, and wash lace, and other linen. Thus instructed they may be of great assistance to their parents and husband . . . whereas young ladies are the most useless of God's creatures. [58]

The "Blue Stocking" parties, however, at the home of Mrs. Montagu or of Mrs. Vesey, really marked the emancipation of woman from her mediæval isola-

tion.   At these functions men and women assembled
informally to discuss freely such topics as might be of
common interest.   The freedom of meeting and of
discussion tended to end the restraint which was heretofore the rule at mixed gatherings.   "As if the two
sexes had been in a state of war," Mrs. Carter wrote
on one such occasion, "the gentlemen ranged themselves on one side of the room, where they talked their
own talk and left us poor ladies to twirl our shuttles.
. . . By what little I could overhear, our opposites
were discoursing on the old English poets, and this
subject did not seem so much beyond a female capacity, but that we might have indulged in a share of it." [59]

Class and sex distinction, however, soon melt in
informal meetings of intellectuals.   In the exclusive
constellation surrounding Mrs. Montagu were such
scintillating stars as Johnson, Burke, Richard Owen
Cambridge, and occasionally Goldsmith, besides Hannah More, Mrs. Burney, Mrs. Carter, Mrs. Vesey,
and of course Mrs. Montagu herself.[60]   The example
of substituting wit, repartee, and serious discussion for
cards and gambling came to be followed in less brilliant circles.   Hannah More exclaims enthusiastically
of this improvement in taste:

> Long was society o'er-run,
> By whist, that desolating Hun;
> Long did quadrille despotic sit,
> That Vandal of colloquial wit;
> And conversation's setting light,
> Lay half-obscur'd in Gothic night;
> At length the mental shades decline,
> Colloquial wit begins to shine;

Genius prevails, and conversation
Emerges into *reformation*.
The vanquish'd triple crown to you
Boscawen sage, bright Montagu,
Divided fell;—your cares in haste
Rescued the ravag'd realms of taste;
And Lyttelton's accomplished name,
And witty Pulteney shar'd the fame;
The men, not bound by pendant rules,
Nor ladies *precieuses ridicules;*
For polished Walpole shew'd the way,
How wits may be both learn'd and gay;
And Carter taught the female train,
The deeply wise are never vain;
And she, who Shakespeare's wrongs redrest,
Prov'd that the brightest are the best.[61]

Finally, the long succession of wars, and the continued emigration connected with English oversea expansion, in themselves brought women to a new position through the constant draining away of male inhabitants. In 1800 it was estimated that there were 450,-000 women and but 375,000 men in London.[62] The final solution of existence for this surplus of 75,000 was their admission to a position more nearly approaching equality with men. Obvious results of this chaotic composite of the new freedom with the old dependence lay in changing attitudes towards marriage. In the early century marriages were exceptionally easy. One could dispense with the formalities and expense of a public wedding by dropping into some Chapel which could marry without a license,[63] or in the Fleet and Queen's Bench prisons, where a large trade in weddings was conducted, or even at the

Ship Tavern, where the ceremony could be quickly and quietly performed.[64] When one considers the ease and lack of publicity in performing the marriage ceremony, and considerable laxity and fraud in recording, it is little wonder that one finds "polygamies, easily conceal'd, and too much practic'd." [65] Again, life after marriage was frequently none too happy, for even "good gentlemen" were prone to beat their wives, although "one of our famous Lawyers is of the Opinion that this ought to be used sparingly." [66] Equally annoying and common, though less painful physically, was the tendency of the normal husband to withhold pin-money from his spouse.[67]

Taking into consideration the large surplus of women over men, and the evils connected with marriage mentioned above, it is not strange that separations and divorces became more frequent than ever, with a corresponding increase in the number of mistresses and illegitimate children.[68] Matches made primarily for money seemingly came into prominence at the time of the South Sea affair, when the newly rich sought to marry their daughters into families of distinction by offering attractive marriage settlements.[69]

Our Marriages are made, just like other common Bargains and Sales, by the mere Consideration of Interest or Gain, without any of Love or Esteem. . . . Yet this Custom is of no ancient date in England; and I think I remember, within less than Fifty Years, the First noble Families that married into the City for Downright Money, and thereby introduced by Degrees this public Grievance, which has since ruined so many Estates by the Necessity of giving great Portions to Daughters.[70]

Marriages for money, however, could have brought no more unhappiness than the parent-made unions of earlier centuries.

As a matter of fact, while young people of both sexes boldly pretended to recoil from marriage,[71] it was attaining a new dignity never before approached in England.   Men of wealth were exhorted to encourage marriage among the poor with whom they came into contact, to employ solely married domestic servants, and to "think a little more about the increase of men for the good of their commonwealth." [72] Changes in social life were tending to make marriage a partnership, rather than a relationship between employer and employee.   The disappearance of mediæval "chivalry," in the face of education, and in the popularity of mixed gatherings, removed woman from her pedestal, and made her more the equal of man.   Here again, the "blue-stockings," by demonstrating the intellectual and social abilities of women, were chiefly responsible for winning a higher place in married life for the fair sex.   Indeed, for bringing about dissatisfaction with old conditions, and by attempting to make marriage and married life more attractive, modern feminism owes its early inception to the great social changes in eighteenth century England, produced in large measure by influences emanating from overseas.

In amusements, the coarseness of fashionable life and sentiment which prevailed during the Restoration was hardly mitigated during the first half of the eighteenth century.   The brutal exhibitions of bear-

and bull-baiting at Hockley-in-the-Hole, lewd entertainments at Mayfair, and amusements of questionable
taste at St. George's Field, where the lower classes
met to drink and smoke, leave little doubt as to the
coarseness of popular taste.[73]   The resentment of
the middle class against this type of entertainment,
coupled with the effective work of the Grand Jury of
Middlesex, made attendance at these spectacles far less
respectable.   More vital, perhaps, was the substitution, and the increased popularity of new sports, which
have been considered in another connection, the mellowing influence of Bath and other resorts, and the
higher standard for social intercourse set in London
and other great centres.[74]

The stage, too, came in for its share of criticism.
The Middlesex Grand Jury, convening at the opening
of the century, found little but condemnation for the
theatre:

The Plays which are frequently acted in the Play-houses in
Drury-lane and Lincoln's-Inn-Fields in this Country are full
of prophane, irreverent, lewd, indecent, and immoral expres-
sions, and tend to the great displeasure of Almighty God, and to
the corruption of the auditory both in their principles and their
practices.[75]

From the pulpit and press came emphatic exclama-
tions against the blasphemy, immorality and obscenity
of the stage.   An order from the Queen, proclama-
tions by the Lord Mayor and Aldermen of London,
and the work of the Grand Jury aided considerably
in lessening these evils during the first decade of the
century.[76]   A mid-century author objected to the

theatre only on the ground that its entertainment was "piffling," and too trifling to give constructive satisfaction to the auditor.[77] In maintaining a clean stage women must share the credit. Many of the fair sex objected to hearing or seeing in public what they would not countenance in their own homes. In the belief that the real means of correcting abuses lay with women of distinction, the following advice was given:

Go to these immoral, or lewd plays, and you support them. Absent yourselves, show your dislike by not appearing at them, they will be corrected, or never performed, and consequently fall into oblivion.[78]

REFERENCES TO CHAPTER X

[1] *The Lounger,* 5 Aug., 1758.

[2] "Bruyere" in the *London Journal,* 7 May, 1727.

[3] Hanway, *Letters,* II, p. 173.

[4] *Ibid;* see above, p. 193.

[5] Malcolm, *Anecdotes,* II, pp. 416-417.

[6] Boswell, I, p. 283; *Annual Register,* 1766, pp. 205-207; 1767, p. 168; 1768, pp. 202-203.

[7] *Letters on the Present State of England* (1772), pp. 227-228; Wales, *My Grandfather's Pocket-book from 1701-1796,* p. 171.

[8] *Ibid.*

[9] *The Female Tatler,* 1709.

[10] Malcolm, *op. cit.,* I, p. 235.

[11] Defoe, *Behaviour of the Servants of England,* p. 12.

[12] *The Spectator,* 30 May, 1711; Defoe, *Behaviour of the Servants of England,* p. 12; *Gent. Mag.,* 1731, pp. 249 ff.

[13] Pinkerton's *Travels,* II, p. 95.

[14] *The Wkly. Jl.,* 29 Oct., 1720.

[15] *European Magazine,* Apr., 1784, p. 245.

[16] *The Wkly. Jl., or Sy.'s Post,* 15 Oct., 1720.

[17] Chesterfield, *Letters to his Son,* 27 Sept., 1749.

[18] Brown's *Estimate,* I, pp. 157-158.

[19] Defoe, *Compleat Gentleman.*

[20] Malcolm, *Anecdotes,* II, pp. 229, 237; *The Tatler,* No. 263.

[21] Mrs. Delany thought nothing unusual of sending an assortment of these aids to refinement to a friend in the country. In the box were included, 'three japan bords, six forks and spoons with French silver saltsellers and a pair of china ones, which you may think old-fashioned but it is the *new mode,* and all saltsellers are now made in that manner." *Mrs. Pendarves to Mrs. Anne Granville,* 5 Oct., 1727, in Mrs. Delany, I, pp. 74-75.

[22] Mentioned by Swift in his *Journal to Stella.*

[23] See above, Chapter IV; see also Le Blanc, *Letters,* I, p. 329.

[24] Grosley, p. 66. This visitor commented most favourably on English punctuality in keeping appointments—a sign that time was now an important factor in the successful transaction of business. *Ibid,* p. 84.

[25] Samuel Derrick's account of his visit to Liverpool (1760) cited in Baines, *History of Liverpool,* p. 427; see also Fox Bourne, *English Merchants,* II, p. 57.

[26] Richardson, *Sir Charles Grandison.* See also, Goldsmith, *The Life of Richard Nash of Bath, Esq.*

[27] *The Tatler,* 19 May, 1709.

[28] *Annual Register,* 1761, p. 205.

[29] Defoe, *Tour,* II, p. 307; *The British Journal,* 21 Sept., 1723.

[30] 452 Acts were passed between 1762 and 1774, for the improvement of highways. Traill, V, p. 347.

[31] *Annual Register,* 1761, pp. 206-207.

[32] *Ibid,* 1796, p. 142.

[33] "People sicken and die at an uncommon rate in and about this city and suburbs; and there is a sad outcry raised (especially by ancient females) of a plague and pestilence, and what not which has occasioned abundance of people to leave the town and fly to the country for refuge." *Orig. Wkly. Jl.,* 22 May, 1719.

[34] Goldsmith, *Life of Beau Nash,* p. 60.

[35] See above, pp. 96-97.

[36] Malcolm, *Anecdotes,* I, pp. 261-262.

[37] See above, pp. 86, 98. The proper use of the fan could only be acquired by constant practice. In the words of a contemporary advertiser: "I have erected an Academy for the training up of young women in the Exercise of the Fan, according to the most fashionable airs and motions that are now practiced at Court. . . . A Woman of tolerable Genius who will apply herself diligently to her exercise for the space of one-half year, shall be able to give her fan all the graces that can possibly enter into that modish little machine." *The Spectator,* 27 June, 1711.

[38] Pope, *Rape of the Lock,* Canto III.

[39] *Letter to Her Sister,* 30 Oct., 1724.

[40] These publications people took seriously, and they wielded a healthy influence on social conduct. *The Weekly Register,* 14 Feb., 1731; *The Templar,* 16 Feb., 1731, and *Gentleman's Magazine,* Feb., 1731.

[41] Brown's *Estimate,* I, p. 37.

[42] Defoe, *Tour,* II, p. 165.

[43] *Ibid,* II, p. 166. See also *The Female Spectator,* quoted in Hill, p. 15.

[44] *Letter to His Son,* Apr. 22, 1752.

[45] Swift, *Journal to Stella,* No. 23.

[46] See above, Chapter VII.

[47] *The Spectator,* 11 March, 1712.

[48] *Ibid,* 27 March, 1712.

[49] Chamberlayne, pp. 304-305.

[50] Chesterfield, in Stanhope, *Queen Anne,* p. 566.

[51] Swift, *Works,* III, p. 82.

[52] Hanway, *Essay on Tea,* p. 250.

[53] *Ibid,* p. 251.

[54] *The Country Journal, or the Craftsman,* 12 Feb., 1732.

[55] The sister-in-law of a typical nabob.

[56] *The Lounger,* 30 Dec., 1786.

[57] "How would a foreigner be astonished at the opulence of a country where the meanest tradesmen kept governesses for their daughters!" *Annual Register,* 1759, p. 425.

[58] *Ibid,* 1759, p. 426. See also Burnet, *History of His Own Times,* II, p. 653.

[59] *Letters from Mrs. Elizabeth Carter to Mrs. Montagu* (Ed. 1817), III, p. 68. See also Huchon, *Mrs. Montagu and her Friends,* pp. 263-294.

[60] *Ibid,* pp. 268-269.

[61] Hannah More, V, pp. 316-317.

[62] Austin, p. 60.

[63] Misson, p. 221.

[64] *The Postman,* 28/31 Aug., 1703; *The Guardian,* 21 July, 1713; Ashton, *Queen Anne,* pp. 38-45.

[65] Misson, p. 221.

[66] *The Spectator,* 9 Sept., 1712; *The Tatler,* 18 July, 1710.

[67] *The Spectator,* 7 Feb., 1712.

[68] Brown's *Estimate,* II, pp. 57-59.

[69] See above, pp. 147, 149.

[70] Sir William Temple, *Works,* I, p. 268.

[71] Anon, *A Sunday Ramble,* p. 82.

[72] Hanway, *Essay on Tea,* pp. 351-352.

[73] See above, p. 222f. See also Malcolm, *Anecdotes,* II, pp. 129-134.

[74] See above, Chapter VII.

[75] *Presentment of the Grand Jury of Middlesex* (4 June, 1701), quoted in Malcolm, *Anecdotes,* II, pp. 116-117.

[76] *The Tatler,* 18 April, 1709.

[77] *Annual Register,* 1758, p. 446.

[78] Hanway, *Essay,* pp. 30-31.

CHAPTER XI

THE AWAKENING OF A PHILANTHROPIC SPIRIT

THE attitude of the middle class of the nineteenth century toward their fellow-men is now a matter of history. Its evolution is marked by the ruthless struggle between the early factory-owners and their employees, a contest largely devoid of the humanitarian spirit. With victory assured, the industrial capitalist became complacent, even benevolent, toward the conquered, literally showering them with an almost living wage, passable working conditions, and with paternal kindness, education and the ballot. Strikingly similar reads the story of the eighteenth century capitalist. He alone was to share in the first fruits of victory, which were often squandered in showy and expensive amusements, costumes and equipages. The poor, the indigent, the frail—the downtrodden in general who comprised a considerable part of England's population—were passed by as unworthy of notice, or else were condemned and dismissed as liabilities sapping the vitality of a great and prosperous world-empire. Far happier was the lot of the heathen in distant lands, who were either left alone in blissful savagery, or were instructed in the teachings of the Gospel, and in the refinements of an unsurpassable civilization. As the century went on, the position of the new bourgeoisie in social and political life became assured.   With a sigh of relief they could now turn a kindly and paternal attention towards their less fortunate brethren.   The seamen, who made this wealth possible, were discovered to be suffering the tortures of the damned; thousands in town and country districts were found to be living under unbearable conditions; the children of the poor were literally crying for immediate relief from suffering.   Philanthropic and charitable schemes by the hundreds emanated from the ample brains of the newly thoughtful, and strangely enough, some of them might actually be turned to the profit of the state. Men of affairs finally withdrew some of their attention from the benighted heathen, who showed surprisingly little gratitude toward their saviours, and opened their purses in a genteel and well-ordered manner to those at home who had already lost their souls in trying to keep their bodies together.

And yet English citizens of wealth were more deeply imbued with charity and the humanitarian spirit than their cousins on the continent.   One writer, indeed, was convinced that the commencement of the century was remarkable for a great effort of charity, referring to

the schools established by one divine impulse in every quarter of the metropolis, and when he compares the chaos of ideas which must have composed the minds of the poorest classes of children, previous to the existence of these institutions.[1]

Below it will be seen that there was a catch even in this innocent scheme, whose chief contributors were the leading tradesmen of London.[2]   The testimony of Defoe at all events would indicate that England was far ahead of the continental countries:

The innumerable Alms-Houses, which are to be seen in almost every Part of London, make it certain that there is no City in the World can show the like Number of Charities from private Hands, there being not less than 20,000 People maintained of Charity, besides the Charities of Schooling for Children, and besides the Collections at the annual Feasts of several Kinds.[3]

If one suspects that Defoe looked at this problem through rose-tinted glasses, Sir John Fielding may be called on for corroboration:

One should imagine that scarce a distress should arise to the poor, but there is a hospital, infirmary, or asylum to relieve; yet alas, how short-sighted is the eye of man! for behold a new Charity makes it appearance . . . a Dispensary for the benefit of the infants of the industrious poor . . . who have frequently large families, which they may indeed subsist, but numbers of these sort of children are precipitately snatched from the fond mother's embrace by sudden diseases. The lives of children hang on a slender thread, and their diseases, though few, require immediate and able assistance. . . . And how objects so essential to the community should have been so long overlooked by the ingenious and benevolent is very surprising.[4]

Here is apparent in one instance at least a genuine awakening of a kindly feeling towards the most helpless of all unfortunates: the children of the poor. From all accounts the success of the Armstrong Dispensary in treating little patients was remarkable.[5] As this institution seemed to be a lone exception, however, it is easy to imagine the lot of sick children of the poor in general. Still another writer, one usually critical of his times, is sympathetic towards the growing spirit of charity:

The many noble Foundations for the Relief of the Miserable and the Friendless; the large Annual Supplies from voluntary Charities to these Foundations; the frequent and generous Assistance given to the Unfortunate, who cannot be admitted into these Foundations; all these are such indisputable Proofs of a national Humanity, as it were the highest Injustice not to acknowledge and applaud.[6]

It is not a difficult matter to perceive how limited the extent of private charity in the early part of the century was. The gifts in 1713, for example, were believed to be "considerable," [7] but could not be accurately ascertained; although in this year it was a matter for boasting that the charity children were drawn up for review, and inspected by distinguished characters! In 1714 the King gave his sheriffs £1,000 for the relief and discharge of poor prisoners for debts; [8] during the next two years the only gift of significance was 400 chaldrons of coal donated by Mr. Feast, a brewer, for the freezing poor who were out of work.[9] In 1716 it was estimated that there were in England 1,221 charity schools imparting instruction to 30,000 children. One hundred and twenty-one of these institutions were in London.[10] In December of the same year, the Prince Regent gave £1,000 to the sufferers from a fire in the Limehouse district, "which laudable example was promptly followed by others to a considerable amount." [11]

So far gifts were few, and comparatively small in

extent, and in large part donated by members of the
royal family.   On the other hand 1720 marks a new
era in the annals of philanthropy.   In this year vast
sums were made overnight by speculation in South Sea
stock.   The winners in the gamble were eager to
spend part of their gains in any manner which might
attract the public eye: in costume, equipage, splendid
estates—and in philanthropy.   To their credit perhaps
should be placed a natural feeling of sympathy with
those who were less fortunate.   The sum of £2,645
was donated to the Society for the Relief of Widows
and Children of Clergymen.   A large legacy went
towards the foundation of Bethlehem Hospital for in-
curable lunatics, "which has since flourished with so
much success;" 12 and the year closed with the generous
contribution of Mr. Guy, who had made a large
fortune in South Sea Stock, for the foundation of the
hospital which has immortalized his name,13 and with
the liberation of 350 men imprisoned for debt. Among
many instances of charity cited in the papers of the
day, there was at least one man who did not wish to
gain fame through his charitable gifts:

. . . An unnamed but prominent Gentleman of London
who has acquired a prodigious fortune in South Sea, that he
has relieved a great many unhappy Persons from Prisons, contributed large Sums to unfortunate Clergymen, lent money to
Decaying Tradesmen, without the least Prospect or Expecta-
tion of Repayment, and is now actually about building a *Char-
ity-School* for the poor Children of his own Ward.14

From this date to 1760, however, gifts to charity
were inconsiderable, when one takes into consideration

the need for amelioration of the poor and the unprecedented prosperity of the wealthy.

This attitude was due in part to the growing conviction that indiscriminate charity was not an unmixed
blessing. Early in the century, Defoe argued that
giving alms was not charity.[15] Later it was held that:

some acts of beneficence, are productive of great mischiefs. We
feed many who can work, and suffer some to perish who cannot. What a reproach it is to a nation, that the Aged, the
Blind, the Married, or Sickly, should disgrace human Nature,
by being exposed in our streets. Either these objects wickedly
impose upon the humanity of the passenger, and ought to be
corrected by the civil magistrates; or they are in real distress,
and yet are suffered to pine in want and misery.[16]

This lack of interest in humanity was in evidence even
among the poor themselves and the public was warmly
urged to increase revenues of the Foundling Hospital,
to "prevent millions of infants falling victims to the
carelessness and intemperance of those who bring them
into the world." [17]

While indiscriminate alms-giving was decried as
defeating its own ends, a new spirit of kindliness
coupled with generosity was awakened in the second
half of the century. In large part this change was
due to patent sufferings from the protracted struggle
with France for colonial and commercial supremacy.
That this feeling was genuine humanitarianism, rather
than a mere outburst of patriotism, is shown by a
popular subscription, taken up in 1760, when a sum of
£1,782 was raised for the relief of French prisoners
of war, and by a poem written in honour of the occasion:

Cowards to cruelty are still inclin'd,
But generous pity fills each Briton's mind.
Bounteous as brave; and tho' their hearts are steel'd,
With native intrepidity, they yield
To Charity's soft impulse: this their praise,
The proud to humble, th' oppressed to raise,
Nor partial limits can their bounty know:—
It aids the helpless alien, though a foe.
Hear this, ye French, who urge the insidious strife,
That arms the Indian with murdering knife;
Who, to your foes less cruel, leave your own
Starving in sad captivity to groan. . . .
. . . . and ye Britons
Nor needed yet this bounteous act to prove
Your wide humanity, and social love:
All, all who want it, your protection find;
For Britons are the friends of all mankind.[18]

Similarly, when a few years later a number of stranded
Germans from the devastated Palatinate were lying
in the open fields near London, without coverings,
money, or other necessaries of life, Londoners contributed £1,200 to their relief, of which £800 was
raised at "Batson's Coffee-House." [19] Incidentally the
King granted to the indefatigable Wachsel, who
directed this relief work, a large tract of land in
South Carolina.[20]

The rising spirit of philanthropy was fostered, too,
by those merchants and bankers who became wealthy
in oversea business. Those of Liverpool were particularly alive to the sufferings of the poor, and
generous in their attempts to alleviate their misery.
They contributed extensively to the Liverpool Infirmary, and to the Charity "Blue-coat" School.[21] That

the religious element was present is shown by the founding of Warrington Academy, in 1775, which served as a liberal school for the training of Unitarian ministers.[22]   Sir John Gladstone, who made his fortune in American grain, and in Jamaican sugar and rum, became a leader in the great philanthropic movement of the nineteenth century.[23]   William Rathbone, who died in 1809, left a record distinguished for benevolence as well as for honesty.[24]   James Cropper was the founder of several orphan schools, and was an influential leader in the movement to abolish negro slavery.[25]   Among other Liverpool merchants who made their fortunes in oversea trade, and were renowned for benevolences, should be included Thomas Leyland and William Ewart.[26]

The great bankers of London whose funds were tied up in oversea investments were equally active in generous deeds.   Henry Hoare, who died in 1725, left £2,000 to charity schools and workhouses, and an equal sum for distribution of Bibles, prayer-books and other religious works, besides several smaller amounts for various benevolent purposes.[27]   David Barclay was an even more princely philanthropist, and among other things was responsible for founding a House of Industry, which he finally made self-supporting.   Owner of a great estate in Jamaica, he refuted the charge that negroes were too ignorant and barbarous for freedom, by emancipating his slaves.[28] When instructed in trades and handicrafts, "the members of this community prospered under the blessing of his care, and lived to show that the black skin enclosed hearts full of gratitude, and minds as capable of improvement as the proudest white." [29]　Francis Baring, East India proprietor and banker, with all his associates, became interested in philanthropy,[30] while Joseph Paice, who was considered the "finest gentleman of his time," spent his entire fortune in charitable deeds.[31]　The first Sir Robert Peel, who had gained his wealth in calico-printing, was one of the few and the first factory owners to better the conditions of white slaves in English mills.[32]　Jonas Hanway, himself a merchant, was the original proposer of the Marine Society, became governor of the Foundling Hospital (1758), and until his last illness in 1786, was active in supporting and promoting charitable institutions.[33]　Of all this group, John Taylor was alone accused of "never having done one generous action" in his entire life.[34]

By the close of the century, this wave of humanitarianism, which had been fostered by the merchant and banker princes of oversea wealth, became so general that particular instances no longer need receive especial attention.　As a writer of 1807 phrased it:

We have now arrived at a period within the recollection of most of my readers; it will not therefore be necessary to notice every Institution existing at present, the result of recent exertion; they are numerous beyond all former example.　From the temporary relief afforded during severe winters, and the charities even to passing mendicancy, with that to individuals advertising for assistance, up to the incorporated Societies for constant duration, all are successful, and none more so than the Patriotic Fund, established for relieving and rewarding military and naval sufferings and merits.[35]

On this last point it should be said that throughout the century both the army and the navy were almost unceasingly at work, fighting, convoying or transporting.   Neither service, however, was popular, in spite of the comparatively generous wages, and it was necessary to fill in the ranks by impressment.   Able seamen were in great demand, and as merchant ships returned from America or the Indies, and their sailors were looking forward after the long voyage to seeing their wives and children, it was common for men-of-war to lie in wait, board the returning vessels and press their sailors into service, often for long terms.[36]   This practice was legal and had been common from the beginning of the century.[37]   Great numbers of young men in London and other large centres were kidnapped by agents in the service, and were confined in secret and under circumstances of the utmost cruelty, until they could be quietly slipped aboard.[38]   The East India Company was one of the worst offenders in this regard.[39]   Every means was tried to enlist men for the navy or merchant marine, and a bribe was held out, which provided for the discharge of every male prisoner for debt (under £20), who should enlist either in the army or the navy.[40]

It is little wonder, then, that healthy and ambitious young men refused to enter willingly into the low company which made up the man-of-war.   Nor is it surprising that

the hideous influences to which they were exposed, beginning at a very tender age, spoilt all but a few of them, and turned them into ruffianly boors; capable enough as seamen, but abso-

lutely unfit to associate even with moderately decent people
on shore. . . . There's not a vice committed on shore but is
practiced here; the scenes of horror and infamy on board a
man-of-war are so many and so great, that I think they must
rather disgust a good mind than allure it.[41]

That sanitary conditions alone must have been abomi-
nable is attested by casualty reports for the campaign
ending in 1763, in which 1,152 men were killed in
action, while 133,708 were said to have perished by
disease, or were reported missing.[42]

Service in the army was no less unpopular. Here,
too, impressment was the order of the day and several
acts were passed, granting insolvent debtors liberty if
they enlisted in the service, and allowing criminals in
general who were undergoing sentence to pass into the
army.[43] When one considers the condition of the
English jails, this privilege was undoubtedly a sheer
act of humanity, in that the victim had in the service
at least a fighting chance to escape. Yet the press-
gangs found the greatest difficulty in enlisting men
for the American war. In 1776 the press for sailors
had been particularly severe, when eight hundred were
seized in London alone within a single month.[44]
Earlier in the century hard labour in England had
given way to transportation to the colonies.[45] Now it
occurred to the government to employ able-bodied
criminals in the coercion by land and sea of the revolted
colonies. There is every reason to believe, therefore,
that large numbers of criminals, of all but the worst
category, passed at this time into the English army
and navy.[46] If immorality was prevalent in the fight-

ing forces, the presence therein of large numbers of the criminal classes must bear the responsibility.[47]

Since enlistment in the service, or transportation was preferable to languishing in English jails, kindly disposed individuals demanded and achieved an amelioration in conditions.   By the middle of the century the military service had been rid of some of its worst evils, and was considered "more grossly vicious in Queen Anne's reign than at present," [48] although the refined and effeminate vices which remained were still regarded as inimical to the best interests of the state.   At the same time other steps were taken to protect the interests of the helpless recruits who had been forcibly enlisted.   One suggestion was:

to pay our soldiers and seamen regularly in money, or by Tickets, to bear an interest, and to provide them regularly with such Clothing, such Food and Air, as experience teaches to be proper, that if possible not one of these valuable men may perish by noxious air, avoidable sickness, or inclemency of weather.[49]

As early as 1728, Parliament took up the evils of naval service, and sought to make conditions so favourable that men "might be invited, rather than compell'd into the Service of their Country." [50]   Other measures to improve the condition of seamen may be enumerated as follows:

1729, Half pay granted to retired senior surgeons.
1732, Corporation for the Relief of Poor Widows of Sea Officers; King's gift to this organization.
1740, Reorganization of Sick and Hurt Office; impressment of men over 50 and under 18 forbidden.
1747, Establishment of rank and uniform for officers.[51]

Prior to this time, Defoe states that provision had been made for crippled veterans, and for the widows of men who had died in the royal service.[52] In 1747, moreover, Parliament passed "An Act for the Relief and Support of maimed and disabled Seamen, and the Widows and Children of such as shall be killed, slain, or drowned in the Merchants' Service." To achieve this purpose, a corporation was established "of considerable merchants to purchase land for a hospital, and to render relief to those deserving it." [53] The scheme, however, was not purely charitable, for all seamen aboard merchant ships were taxed 6d. each month, in order to be entitled to the benefits of this Act.[54] Those in the service of the East India Company were alone exempted, "being already sufficiently provided for by their respective Masters." [55]

The lamentable lack of generosity toward these makers and saviours of empire is shown by the fact that for the first half of the century there was but one home in all England for superannuated soldiers and sailors, and for "Merchants that by Piracy, or Shipwreck, are reduced to Necessity"; and that this establishment, through lack of funds, was forced to limit the number of its residents to eighty.[56] The founding of the Marine Society in 1756, therefore, was a belated act of humanity. It was considered excellent, in that it rescued a number of wretched boys from lives of crime and misery—and incidentally relieved the public of the results of their crimes—that it gave added relief to distressed seamen and their relatives, and that it tended to alleviate the evils of impressment.[57] Evidently the majority of merchants were still too busily engaged in their own schemes of charity, and the general public too indifferent, effectively to hear this cry of distress, or to seek to remove its causes.[58]

On the other hand, at a time when the rural districts of England and the continental capitals were callous and neglectful, commercial London began to open its purse-strings in aid of the sick of the community.[59] The hospital movement dates properly from the days of the Restoration, when Chelsea-College, or the Royal Hospital for Disabled Soldiers, the Greenwich Hospital and Bethlehem's, St. Thomas' and St. Bartholemew's were founded by Charles II. This enthusiasm soon subsided, and by the opening of the eighteenth century, their quarters had become filthy and unsanitary, as well as insufficient for the needs of a larger metropolis.[60] In the second decade, however, after the old St. Thomas' Hospital had been torn down, voluntary subscriptions were solicited for a larger and more commodious structure. Evidently response was slow, for by 1766 only three of the quadrangles had been completed. Besides its beds accommodating almost five hundred patients, this establishment took care of a number of out-patients.[61] Similarly, St. Bartholemew's hospital had become so dangerous that in 1729 subscriptions were taken up for a new building, which by 1766 was three-quarters completed. This was chiefly a haven for distressed soldiers and sailors.[62] In like manner was Greenwich

Hospital largely rebuilt and redecorated in "a most elegant taste for the entertainment of superannuated and disabled seamen in the king's service." [63]

In view of the cruel treatment of lunatics, it was perhaps not so fortunate that two additional wings to the Bethlehem Hospital were constructed about 1730.[64] A handsome brick and stone wall, with a pair of fine iron gates, together with "two images or statues in a reclining posture, one representing raving, the other melancholy madness," may have served to cheer, if not to clear, "those cloudy intellects."

Perhaps the greatest achievement by one individual was the founding and endowment of Guy's Hospital. Its chief donor gained a fortune in the South Sea affair, as did Mr. Hunt who made a handsome donation towards its completion.[65] This hospital furnished accommodation for 435 patients and their attendants.[66] In 1758, on the site of the old London Infirmary, was founded the Magdalen, surrounded by a high wall, to "prevent the prying curiosity of the public." As the title implies, "the objects of this foundation are women, who, having been seduced and plunged into ruin by temptation to which their youth and personal advantages had exposed them, repent of their lewd way of life." [67] In the attempt to reconstruct the lives of its inmates, they were given separate beds and chests for clothes and linen, were permitted to register under false names if desirous of concealing their identity, were given uniforms of light grey, plain and neat, and were required to work according to their individual ability.[68]

Perhaps the model institution of the century was the new London Hospital, founded in 1740. "Here," Defoe affirms, "the best order is observed, the best Medicines dispensed, and the best Assistances given, as well by Physicians, as Surgeons and Apothecaries, to all who are admitted into these Charities." [69] It was unique, too, in willingness to accept cases, whether recommended or not, at any hour of the day or night. Supported entirely by voluntary contributions, it relieved over 150,000 distressed patients between 1740 and 1766.[70]

Most unfortunate, perhaps, were the victims of that dread disease originally from overseas—smallpox, which was both epidemic and endemic during this century; for all hospitals prudently excluded the contagion from their precincts. In 1746 charitably inclined Londoners furnished two houses, in airy situations and at due distance from other habitations, for the reception of the miserable victims of the disease. One house was for inoculation, the other for "the reception of patients in the natural way." [71] About this time provision was finally made for another group of unfortunates: expectant mothers of the poor. It was a well-known fact that, by advertising in the papers, expectant mothers, or those with newly-born babes, could receive relief through the charitably inclined of a great metropolis.[72] It was equally a fact, however, that countless others who shunned publicity perished through starvation or lack of medical attention.[73] Through the efforts of certain philanthropists, the old Shaftesbury house was transformed into a charity lying-in hospital, and this pitiable condition was tardily remedied (1750).[74]

Other instances of the growth of a charitable spirit, are the Charter House, or Sutton's Hospital, and an infirmary for clergyman's sons.[75]   The most potent appeal for relief, however, came from the most helpless: the children who were deserted by their parents. In 1739 there was established by royal charter a hospital for the maintenance and education of exposed and deserted children.[76]   The founder, a retired sea captain, was most industrious in soliciting subscriptions, and in seeing the idea through to completion.   Evidently this institution was calculated to produce seamen for the future, as the foundlings were named after such heroes as Drake, Blake and Norris.[77]   It served as a model for later establishments of the sort and was considered preferable to "putting-out" foundlings to parish nurses—a custom which people felt simply reënacted the tragic scene of Herod's cruelty.   The new foundling-hospitals were wise and humane, in that they insured their wards sufficient food and clothing, imparted to them a minimum of education, and taught them a trade, so that they might not be thrown helpless on the world.[78] Such institutions were favoured by mercantilists, and received Parliamentary aid,

which at several times has applied considerable sums of the nation's money to promote the national benefit that may be continually reaped from this institution; where children that might otherwise have been murdered, or left by their parents as a burden upon society, are preserved and brought up for the service of His Majesty's Navy; and the girls to be servants and useful members of Society."[79]

By 1760, then, the hospitals of London were so considerable in number and size, that they could accommodate 15,000 patients annually, and "scarce any persons are so destitute of friends, but they can procure admission to one or other of them."[80]   As we have seen, it was now customary for the substantial man of affairs, the grave and sedentary citizen, to give freely to all charitable instiutions. On the other hand, the *bon vivant* responded to appeals at feasts and entertainments, when the mind, the heart and the purse were most likely to dilate most generously. It was hoped that this method of "filling the chasms of more disinterested benevolence will prevail till such methods are unnecessary."[81]

In consideration of the poor, economics took precedence over the humanitarian spirit, which was now trying to assert itself in many laudable directions. Much attention had been given to pauperism after the "Glorious Revolution."   Several bad seasons in succession, heavy war expenses, interrupted commerce, were all factors contributing to the increase in the number of the poor.   It had been estimated that approximately one-quarter of the entire population of England was dependent on parochial relief, while in 1685 the total poor-rates were said to be £665,000, or as much as was required to maintain all the expenses of government in times of peace.[82]   Mercantilists, accordingly, sought to reduce this drain on the resources of empire, and to turn the liability of idle-

ness into assets of production.   Cary [83] advocated
work-houses for the poor of both sexes and all ages,
but Mackworth's plan introduced in the House of
Commons, to establish a factory in every village, was
dropped in the upper chamber, because of the opposition of Defoe.

Defoe, who represented the prevailing school of
mercantilism, blamed the distresses of the poor on
idleness, but warned his countrymen that the poor
must not compete with "legitimate" industry, but must
seek new fields:

> Suppose now a workhouse for the employment of poor chil-
> dren sets them to the spinning of worsted. For every skein of
> worsted these poor children spin, there must be a skein the less
> spun by some poor person or family that has spun it before. . . .
> If these worthy gentlemen, who show themselves so forward to
> relieve and employ the poor will find out some new trade, some
> new market, where the goods they make shall be sold, where
> none of the same sort were made before; if they will send them
> to any place where they shall not interfere with the rest of that
> manufacture, or with some other made in England, then indeed
> they will do something worthy of themselves.[84]

It is true that a considerable portion of the poor-
rates was wasted in litigation between parishes as to
the responsibility for the support of undesirable dependents. The simplest solution was to diminish the
accommodations for possible paupers; and the open
war waged against cottages resulted in serious rural
over-crowding, while "permission to marry was as
strictly controlled by the parish authorities as it had
been among the mediæval villains." [85] The worker's
search for employment elsewhere was seriously

hampered by an Act providing for the seizure of his property by the parish for the support of dependents.[86] By the Law of Settlements parish officers were empowered to force newcomers to move elsewhere. Adam Smith complained that "there is scarce a poor man in England, over forty years of age, who had not in some part of his life felt himself cruelly oppressed by the Law of Settlement." [87] On the other hand, the naturally lazy could remain *in statu et loco quo,* and be content to receive their dole from society. Certainly in this attitude there was little, if any, of the humanitarian spirit. This condition Henry Fielding blamed, and perhaps justly, on ignorance:

The sufferings of the Poor are indeed less observed than their misdeeds; not from any want of compassion, but because they are less known; and this is the true reason why we hear them so often mentioned with abhorrence, and so seldom with pity.[88]

In the latter half of the century, mercantilists attained more enlightened economic knowledge, and eventually a more sympathetic understanding of the poor. The fundamental cause of pauperism was now held to be, not indolence, but want of employment, sickness or accident.[89] In rural England, the swallowing-up of small holdings by the enclosure movement and the application of capital to farming made agricultural life subject to the fluctuations suffered by other industries.[90] In many cases the peasant was severed from the soil, or had to cultivate his small holdings, under old and slovenly methods, or was forced to accept work as a day-labourer.[91] Writers agreed that in any case his lot had become insufferable,

and that he should be considered an object of com-
miseration.[92]   While the domestic system remained,
the peasant might seek by-employment in weaving or
spinning, but with the coming of the Industrial Revolution this opportunity ceased.[93]   This great change,
itself a result in greater or less degree of the wealth
procured through the acquisition of India and of new
markets and sources of raw material there and elsewhere overseas, offered a partial solution to the problem.   There followed an increasingly large migration
from rural parishes to market towns, and finally to the
great manufacturing centres, where at least there was
opportunity for employment.[94]   During this transition, it was said, "there is no country in Europe in
which man changes his residence as often as in England." [95]   It was estimated that in London, and the
great industrial centres, three-quarters of the inhabitants were strangers.[96]

From an understanding of the causes of pauperism
to a real sympathy with its victims was but a short
step—and herein lay the real hope for solution.   The
monumental work of Eden in itself and the frequent
studies of the problem by Parliament show the trend
of opinion.   Even earlier it had found expression:

At a time when happiness and prosperity crown our nation,
it is not amiss to go into the case of the poor. . . . They are
fellow-creatures and fellow-Christians, made of the same blood,
and heirs of the same glory: nay, and in a political light, it
certainly merits our most attentive consideration how best to
provide for the lower, but most useful members of this society;
for, owe we not to them all the ease and elegance of superior
life? Owe we not to the painful hand of industry and labour
all the comforts and conveniences of more elevated stations? [97]

The Industrial Revolution with its new set of tyrants postponed a happy ending, but the spirit of humanity for humanity's sake was awakened.   In Charity Schools for the education of poor children and in the Sunday School of the later century enthusiastic efforts were made to prepare and direct the younger generation for useful and self-supporting occupations.[98]   It was believed that the name "work-house" carried with it the idea of correction and punishment.   The Quaker merchants of Philadelphia, in the true spirit of kindliness, had called their home "The Bettering House." [99] In this case oversea influence appears to have won for the homes of the poor in England the names of "House of Maintenance," "House of Protection," [100] or "House of Industry." [101]

The results of this scheme proved it to be a step in the right direction:

The poor men, women and children according to their different abilities are constantly and regularly employed; chiefly in hempen works, and in spinning, according to the direction of the managers. . . . It was pleasing and affecting to see little children, who could scarce speak, plying their reels, or performing their tasks, with an assiduity that could scarce be expected. . . . The industry which every able inhabitant is obligated to exert, has much diminished the number of lazy and troublesome poor in the different parishes within their hundreds; the worthy and deserving poor are comfortably provided for; no beggars are seen or allowed within the district, and very large savings must necessarily be made in the poor's rates throughout the parishes.[102]

It is unfortunate, certainly, that the humanitarian spirit should thus be exploited by unscrupulous manufacturers.   The important fact, however, is that the dormant sympathy for suffering and the sense of duty towards one's fellow-men had finally been awakened and was to become a permanent and effective contribution to English national character.

Undoubtedly the foulest blots on England of the eighteenth century were the condition of its prisons and the treatment of the prisoners. The number of punishable offences and the severity of the penal code kept the jails pitiably overcrowded, and huddled innocent debtors with the most hardened and degenerate offenders. Writers throughout the early decades of the century continually exposed these evils, but failed to ameliorate them. As late as 1766 Newgate Prison —the county jail for Middlesex—was a dismal hole and so overcrowded that it was "seldom clear of a dangerous infection, which is called the gaol distemper." Ten years of effort were required to persuade the authorities to install a single ventilator in the roof of the building.[103] Infinitely worse were the country prisons. One reads of debtors most cruelly treated because of their inability to pay the gaoler's fees, having to catch mice for subsistence, being dragged on hurdles, dying of starvation and malaria, covered with boils and blains, or imprisoned in underground dungeons.[104] These conditions were confirmed by the comprehensive visits of John Howard, who wrote:

the gaols are generally close and confined, the felons' wards nasty, dirty, confined and unhealthy . . . and small, no way proportioned to the number of persons confined there. Many others are the same; as Gloucester, Warwick, Hereford, Sussex, etc. . . . The poor unhappy creatures are ever confined within doors without the least breath of air.[105]

The awakening of the humanitarian spirit, here, as in the case of the poor, was due to the appalling economic loss caused by their non-productiveness. According to a statement of 1759:

We live in an age of commerce and computation; let us, therefore, coolly enquire what is the sum of evil which the imprisonment of debtors brings upon our country. . . . What shall we say of the humanity or the wisdom of a nation that voluntarily sacrifices one in every three hundred to lingering destruction?[106]

Furthermore, each of the men in prison gave trouble to at least one or two others, thus multiplying distress. Estimating the inaction, or cost of idleness, of prisoners at one shilling a day, the annual loss to the state amounted to £300,000. Besides, disease and corruption yearly put an end to the life of one prisoner in every four. So 150,000 perished every generation in the jails. "That in every century, a nation eminent for science, studious of commerce, ambitious of empire, should willingly lose in noisome dungeons 500,000 of its inhabitants, a greater number than has ever been destroyed at the same time by the pestilence and sword!"[107] seemed incredible. Inefficient, too, was the presence in prison of a number equal to that of England's armed forces and men who, it was felt, should be propagating their species.

The work of John Howard linked economic considerations with the humanitarian spirit. He believed that the reasons for the necessity of prison reform would appeal alike to merchant, statesman, and humanitarian: sickness (especially jail-fever and small-pox), slackness in caring for the sick, air so close that prisoners could not stand the smell of their clothes, the appalling lack of a water supply (but three pints a day were allowed each prisoner for purposes of drinking and cleanliness), the absence of a sewer system, of bedding and food, the hoarding together of old and young and men and women, the fleecing of prisoners by their jailers, the prevalence of gambling, and the utter lack of medical or religious attention.[108] Conditions in prisons were so intolerable that they prevented

our sending healthy useful lads to our Colonies as transports out of our gaols; they become infectious, sickly, miserable objects, half of whom die on their passage; and many of those that arrive at the places of their destination infect the families they enter into. I saw lately in your paper, what I knew our Colonies complained of from Philadelphia: "An Act passed to prevent infectious diseases being brought into that Province." [109]

While earlier efforts had achieved nothing of permanence, the results of Howard's crusade were tangible.[110] In particular was this true of the introduction of the penitentiary plan, which sought by hard labour and religious instruction to reform prisoners and to train them in habits of industry.[111] Groups of individuals were spurred to renewed activity in aid of certain unfortunate cases; [112] and the Parliamentary Inquiry of 1779 succeeded in bettering the state of transported convicts by insisting on clean decks, shoes and stockings, and clean and sufficient bedding and provisions.[113] Howard, in later visits to prisons (in

1779 and 1782) found that their condition had been bettered, though there was still room for improvement: [114]

> The results of the visits thus announced have long been before the public, and that infinite improvement followed must be admitted; yet much still remains to be done, merely to obtain that order and cleanliness which the Legislature has at various periods declared should be maintained in each prison throughout the Kingdom.[115]

The good work had been started at any rate, and the death of Howard proved the occasion for its continuance by Jeremy Bentham, Wilberforce and other practical philanthropists.[116]

If Englishmen were slow to awaken to the distresses of their fellow-beings, they had already developed a real kindness towards animals.[117] It is true that in 1700 there were still defendants of bull and bear-baiting, but the influence of essay-writers continued to discountenance them, and to foster a warm regard for the sufferings of lower animals. Affection for monkeys and dogs was universal; it hardly seems logical to credit the plea of the critic who stated that England was considered "the best country in the world for women, and the worst for horses." [118] The writer who made this statement complains bitterly that

> cruelty is shown to all the animated works of the Almighty, except half a dozen birds, and as many four-footed beasts. Betty and John are considered as inferior beings to Tabbey and Pompey. The costly chicken is ordered for the cat or dog by her who never thinks of giving a morsel of bread to relieve the hunger of a man. This is strange, but it sometimes

happens to those who permit their affections to take a wrong bias.[119]

The quotation is typical of the awakening spirit of kindliness, which lacked only a definite objective. This was afforded by the practice of vivisection which had become very popular among scientists since the discovery of the circulation of the blood. A real sympathy was awakened for the unfortunate animals used for experimental purposes.[120]   Gay's poems, especially the one on field sports, showed a great compassion for animals, while Dr. Johnson dwelt bitterly on useless barbarities which were practiced, such as the nailing of .dogs to tables and mutilating them, "to examine whether burning irons are felt more acutely by the bone or tendon, and whether the more lasting agonies are produced by poison forced into the mouth, or injected into the veins." [121]

This exposure of cruelties awakened the public conscience to such mistreatment of animals. It was agreed that preachers should discourse, particularly at Shrovetide, on the duty of clemency to dumb brutes.[122]   A practical result of this feeling was the establishment of homes for animals.

The difference between the halting contributions of the early century and the generous outpourings of thought and money in its last years has been pointed out. It is significant that the leaders of philanthropy in the days of its unpopularity were wealthy merchants of London and Liverpool, men who were never far removed in sympathy from the lower orders whence they sprang. Through their efforts ignorance, indifference and misunderstanding of man's less fortunate fellow-creatures were at least partially dispelled. More direct influences from lands overseas fostered the feeling of humanity towards man and beast. The benevolence of the Quakers in America has already been noticed.[123] At a time when colonists in the islands of Nevis and St. Christopher were suffering severe losses from French invasions the government set an example for private individuals to follow, in appropriating the sum of £103,000 for distribution among the sufferers.[124] A later Act provided for a low rate of interest and cancellation of the repayment of the principal.[125] In particular the humane conduct of the American colonists during the Revolution could hardly fail to be felt in England. For example, in the instructions of Franklin to Paul Jones (in 1779) the latter was ordered not to follow the example of the English in burning defenceless towns, and in all cases to give sufficient notice as would enable the inhabitants to remove the women and children, the sick and aged, to places of safety.[126] Again it was Franklin who, on the occasion of a desolating storm in the West Indies in 1780, issued orders that provision ships should pass unmolested to the British as well as to the other islands.[127] On the other hand, contributions were actually raised in England for the relief of the Americans during the Revolution. Among them were £100 contributed by the "Constitutional Society" at Cornhill, for the relief of widows, orphans, and aged parents of those who were "MURDERED by the KING'S troops at or near Lexington and Concord, in the province of Massachusetts." [128]

In the softening manners of the late century benevolence and philanthropy became fashionable. Hannah More refers to the "age of benevolence" not as an evangelical movement or as evidence of Christianity, but rather as a substitute for the deadened formalism in the older churches of the time.[129] Philanthropic endeavours also opened up a new occupation or profession for unmarried women, a group which formerly had only to live an idle and useless existence.[130] The great era of constructive philanthropy was yet to come, just as one still awaits the abolition of poverty, disease and crime. But the old feeling of lethargy, of indifference to one's fellow-creatures, had largely died out. In its place had awakened a new sense of responsibility towards those who could not help themselves. The new philanthropy, if not ideal, if only partially effective, was at least current among self-respecting citizens, and helped to promote a greater degree of happiness in society.

REFERENCES TO CHAPTER XI

[1] Malcolm, *Anecdotes*, I, p. 19.
[2] See below, p. 295; *The Weekly Miscellany*, 19 May, 1733.
[3] Defoe's *Tour*, II, p. 121.
[4] Quoted in Malcolm, *Anecdotes*, I, pp. 75-76.
[5] London *Chronicle* (1770), p. 62.
[6] Brown's *Estimate*, I, pp. 21-22.
[7] Malcolm, *op. cit.*, I, p. 19.
[8] *Ibid*, I, p. 20.
[9] *Ibid*.
[10] *Ibid*, p. 22.
[11] *Ibid*.
[12] *Ibid*, pp. 24-25.
[13] Cunningham, *Lives*, IV, pp. 120-121.
[14] *The Wkly. Jl. or Sy.'s Post*, 9 July, 1720.
[15] Eden, *The State of the Poor*, I, p. 257.
[16] Hanway's *Journal*, p. 162.
[17] *Ibid*, p. 163.
[18] Quoted in Malcolm, *Anecdotes*, I, pp. 52-53.
[19] *Ibid*, I, pp. 65-70.
[20] *Ibid*, I, pp. 70-71.
[21] Fox Bourne, *English Merchants*, II, p. 65. The careers of these men, most of whom had risen from penniless boys to merchant princes, have been considered in another connection. See above, Ch. V. The spirit of their example was contagious, and aroused in their equally fortunate countrymen elsewhere the dormant feeling of philanthropy.
[22] Fox Bourne, *op. cit.*, II, p. 65.
[23] *Ibid*, II, pp. 293-295.
[24] Baines, *History of Liverpool*, p. 538.
[25] *Ibid*, p. 658; Fox Bourne, II, p. 293.
[26] *Ibid*, II, p. 295.
[27] Forbes, W., *Memoirs of a Banking House*, pp. 2-9; Hoare, R. C., *Pedigrees and Memoirs of the Families of Hore and Hoare*, II, pp. 26-30.
[28] Fox Bourne, II, pp. 135-137.
[29] *Morning Chronicle* (London), 6 June, 1809.
[30] *Gent. Mag.*, lxxx, pt. ii, p. 382; Fox Bourne, II, p. 240.
[31] *Ibid*, II, p. 241.
[32] *Ibid*, II, pp. 162-164.
[33] Cunningham, *Lives*, V, p. 384.
[34] Smiles, *Lives of Boulton and Watt*, p. 232.
[35] Malcolm, *Anecdotes*, I, p. 85.

[36] *Annual Register,* 1770, p. 147.

[37] *The Flying Post,* 4/7 Apr., 1702; *The Daily Courant,* 4 Mar., 1703.

[38] *Ann. Reg.,* 1767, p. 82.

[39] Lecky, III, p. 536.

[40] This shows the condition of the poor debtors who were asked to exchange prison for the inferno of a man-of-war. I Anne, 19.

[41] Testimony of Captain Edward Thompson (1756) quoted in Traill, V, p. 216. See also, Brown's *Estimate,* I, p. 101; II, pp. 175-176.

[42] Traill, V, p. 214. For an exposure of the horrors of life on men-of-war, see Smollett, *Roderick Random,* and Lind's *Essay on the Health of Seamen.*

[43] Clode, *Military Forces of the Crown,* II, pp. 12-15.

[44] Walpole, *Last Journals,* II, pp. 75, 77, and 81.

[45] See above, pp. 142-145.

[46] Lecky, III, p. 540.

[47] *Chatham Correspondence,* IV, p. 420; Walpole, *Last Journals,* I, p. 459; Franklin, Benjamin, *Life,* p. 401.

[48] Brown's *Estimate,* II, p. 172.

[49] Hanway, *Essay,* p. 353.

[50] *The Wkly. Jl. or Brit. Gaz.,* 3 Feb., 1728.

[51] Traill, V, pp. 207-208.

[52] Defoe, *Tour,* II, p. 120.

[53] *Ibid,* II, p. 121.

[54] *Ibid.*

[55] *Ibid,* II, p. 122.

[56] Macky, p. 163. For hospitals, see below, p. 301f.

[57] Brown's *Estimate,* II, p. 180.

[58] See above, p. 288.

[59] The hospitals, homes and schools of Liverpool have been considered in another connection. See above, p. 294f.

[60] For the superiority of London charities over those of continental cities, see above, p. 289, and Defoe, *Tour,* II, p. 116. The neglect of rural England is emphasized by the fact that outside of London, there were but fourteen hospitals in the country. Malcolm, *Anecdotes,* I, p. 54.

[61] Entick, IV, pp. 380-381.

[62] "There have yearly been received in here many maimed and sick seamen and soldiers, with other diseased persons, from divers parts of the king's dominions, and some from foreign parts, and many cured, and relieved with money, and other necessaries, at their departure, besides their diet and lodging during their care. *Ibid,* IV, p. 254.

[63] *Ibid,* IV, p. 443.

[64] *Ibid,* IV, pp. 69-70.

[65] Cunningham, *Lives,* IV, pp. 120-121.

[66] Entick, IV, p. 384.

[67] *Ibid*, IV, p. 311.

[68] *Ibid*, IV, pp. 314-315.

[69] Defoe, *Tour*, II, p. 119.

[70] Entick, IV, p. 437.

[71] *Ibid*, III, p. 12; Defoe, *Tour*, II, p. 120.

[72] Malcolm, *Anecdotes*, I, p. 64.

[73] *Ibid*, I, p. 64.

[74] Entick, III, pp. 342-343.

[75] Defoe, *Tour*, II, p. 119-120.

[76] *Ibid*, II, p. 120.

[77] Malcolm, *Anecdotes*, I, p. 11; Entick, III, p. 13.

[78] "We should so augment foundling hospitals to support all the children under a certain age, of parents who cannot, or being wicked will not, support their own offspring. If, by the good conduct of these hospitals, we can introduce a less vicious race of working people, the next generation will lessen the numbers in that hospital, and in time the disease will cure itself." Hanway, *Essay*, p. 241. "Christ's Hospital is lately further improved by entertaining a master to teach the boys drawing, some skill in which art is useful to many, or most mechanical trades, as besides painters, those of seamen, carpenters, joiners, plumbers, carvers, masons, bricklayers, etc." Entick, IV, p. 177.

[79] *Ibid*, IV, p. 429.

[80] Malcolm, I, pp. 54-55.

[81] *Ibid*, I, pp. 56-57. For these gifts, see *Ibid*, II, p. 133.

[82] D'Avenant, *Balance of Trade*, in *Works*, II, p. 184.

[83] *Essay Towards Regulating the Trade, and Employing the Poor of This Kingdom* (1700).

[84] Defoe, "Giving Alms no Charity," in *Works*, II, p. 434. For the arguments in favor of establishing charity workhouses see Eden, I, pp. 259-265.

[85] Cunningham, *Growth of Industry and Commerce*, II, p. 381.

[86] 9 Geo. I, c. 7. In the 6 Geo. II laws were passed to indemnify parishes for the charges arising from illegitimate children, and the father was thrown into jail until he promised to support his offspring or to relieve the parish of responsibility. Eden, I, p. 290.

[87] Quoted in Eden, I, p. 297.

[88] Quoted in Eden, I, p. 329.

[89] Massie, J., *A Plan for the Establishment of Charity Houses*, p. 50.

[90] *Ibid*, p. 99.

[91] *Ibid*, p. 63; Eden, I, p. 168.

[92] Harte, *Essays on Husbandry*, p. 205; Young, *A Farmer's Letters*, p. 114.

[93] Cunningham, *Ind. & Com.*, p. 389. Economists now criticized the

parochial system of relief, in that movements of labour were inevitable, and the Elizabethan Poor Law, because the poor were deterred from leaving the parish. Massie, *op. cit.,* p. 63.

[94] *Ibid,* p. 99.

[95] Eden, I, p. 298.

[96] *Ibid,* p. 299.

[97] *Annual Register,* 1761, p. 193.

[98] Eden, I, pp. 287-288. See also the reprint of Mandeville, *Fable of the Bees* (1723), with an *Essay on Charity Schools.* That charity schools only served to increase poverty, by hindering manufacturing and agriculture, and depriving parents of the aid of their children, was roundly denied by its supporters: "The Children are not kept in the School longer than till they are of Age and Strength to perform the principal Parts of it, or to bear constant Labour in it; and even whilst they are under this Course of Education, . . . they shall never be hinder'd from working in the Fields, or being employ'd in such Labour as they are capable of . . . for the Support of their Parents and themselves." *London Journal,* 27 July, 1723.

[99] Eden, I, p. 285, n. 1.

[100] *Ibid,* I, p. 285.

[101] *Annual Register,* 1761, p. 193.

[102] *Ibid,* pp. 194-195.

[103] Entick, IV, p. 183.

[104] Malcolm, I, p. 80; Ashton, *Queen Anne,* II, pp. 248-249.

[105] Letter of John Howard to *London Chronicle,* 6 March, 1774.

[106] *Annual Register,* 1759, p. 429.

[107] *Ann. Reg.,* 1759, p. 430.

[108] Howard, *The State of the Prisons in England and Wales* (1777), pp. 3-34.

[109] *Letter of John Howard to London Chronicle,* 7 May, 1774.

[110] In 1728 the Society for the Promotion of Christian Knowledge had forced a feeble enquiry by Parliament. Traill, V, p. 483. For the founding of Georgia as a refuge for debtors, see above, p. 139, and below, p. 329. In 1772 a society was formed for the relief of persons confined for small debts. Nichols, II, pp. 689-706.

[111] Malcolm, I, p. 82; 19 Geo. III, c. 74.

[112] Malcolm, I, p. 83.

[113] Howard, *op. cit.*

[114] *Ibid.*

[115] Wilberforce, *Life,* pp. 59-61.

[116] The attention of the Government had been called much earlier in the century to the need for better treatment of prisoners-of-war. Entick, II, p. 490, footnote. The growth of the humanitarian spirit is evidenced by the adoption of the honour system at Magdalen for in-

mates of superior education or behaviour. *Ibid,* IV, pp. 313-316, footnotes; see also above, p. 302.

[117] See above, p. 235.

[118] Hanway's *Journàl,* p. 71.

[119] *Ibid,* p. 70.

[120] See Coventry's *Pompey the Little,* pt. III, ch. xi. Pope also spoke of the practice with detestation. Spence's *Anecdotes,* section viii.

[121] *The Idler,* 5 Aug., 1758.

[122] *Annual Register,* 1761, p. 198.

[123] See above, p. 309.

[124] 10 Anne, c. 34.

[125] Macpherson, *Annals,* III, p. 14.

[126] *American Diplomatic Correspondence,* III, p. 78.

[127] *Parl. Hist.,* XXII, p. 221.

[128] Reid, *Memoirs of the Public Life of John Horne Tooke,* p. 25.

[129] Hannah More, *Works,* XI, pp. 87-91.

[120] Wilberforce, *Life,* I, p. 238.

CHAPTER XII

In the previous chapter the slow awakening of the eighteenth century Englishman to a realization of human suffering at home has been observed. As knowledge of deplorable conditions became diffused, occasional acts of charity became merged into a more insistent and consistent sympathy and the development of a true humanitarian spirit. Similarly, as people came to understand the significance of a vast empire, sentiments of pity and responsibility were aroused towards native peoples in remoter parts of the world. In no sense, however, did the English feel the crusading spirit of the Spaniards, and to a lesser degree of the French, whose expansion overseas was inspired by a desire to spread the true faith as well as for economic motives. Generally speaking it is safe to say that the foremost consideration of British empire-builders had been the acquisition of territory, trade and wealth. Among other things, however, the trial of Warren Hastings drew the attention and the sympathies of Englishmen to a race somewhat strange to them, "and the peasant of Cornwall or Cumberland had learned to thrill at the suffering of a peasant of Bengal." [1] Similar interest was caused by the discov-

eries of Captain Cook.[2] Furthermore, the tales of
heathen folk which confronted readers of magazines
and newspapers, and the appearance of their representatives in Britain from time to time tended to promote the idea of conversion,[3] and of inculcating in
distant regions the blessings of Christianity and a
higher form of civilization.

While the Church of England as a whole was not
interested in missionary endeavours, it felt a responsibility to care for its own members wherever they
might be. It sought to provide for the needs of colonists in new countries, while feeling but little responsibility for the religious welfare of natives. Where
economic reasons were paramount, practical difficulties seriously checked missionary efforts on a large
scale. In the case of India, there was the fear, to a
considerable extent justifiable, that the introduction of
Christianity would serve only to unite the believers of
native faiths in a stand against the European. Thus
England's hold on India might become more precarious than it then was. In the New World the very
existence of the colonists seemed to depend on the
extermination of the Indian, or at least on his expul-
sion. With either of these policies systematic conversion was incompatible. Finally, in the case of the
negroes, the controversy as to whether conversion to
Christianity would necessarily bring emancipation, was
the determinant in a *laissez-faire* attitude. As one
critic observed:

Sentiment ought never to rise higher than permanent condition. Hence why teach the negro the Christian religion? You

only fire him with indignation, and give him a weapon which ought to slay yourself. . . . Then how absurd to teach the Christian duties one day, which politically must be counteracted the six following.[4]

It was best, therefore, to let alone the regions populated by this race. According to another commentator:

Happily for the people of West Africa, the climate of their country is a safeguard against foreign invasion, more certain and effectual than armies or fortification could ever be. We cannot, however, consider them as altogether safe from foreign disturbance so long as we have plans proposed for the civilization of Africa. Let, then, the generous nations of Europe allow the Africans to enjoy their barbarism a few centuries longer. . . . Natives everywhere are rapidly diminishing in numbers from the ravages of European diseases, and the despotism of self-interested and fanatical missionaries.[5]

Yet the missionary spirit suggested by conditions overseas was not entirely lacking. The responsibility of caring for the religious needs of the heathen appealed in some measure at least to members of various evangelical denominations as well as to Englishmen who had come under the spell of the humanitarian spirit. This new spirit accounted for the founding of the "Society for the Promotion of Christian Knowledge" and the "Society for the Propagation of the Gospel in Foreign Parts."[6] Then, too, as the evils of the slave trade were exposed to view, it was realized with horror that through apathy alone this great curse had been allowed to reach staggering proportions. With the movement to remove the blot of the slave-trade and of slave holding itself came a new sense of responsibility toward all the natives of far-flung lands. In general, those who pitied the sufferings of unhappy slaves were now most eager in missionary efforts.

In India the propagation of the Gospel was confined for the greater part of the century to the desultory efforts of chaplains in the service of the East India Company.[7] The charter of 1698 and that of the United Company (1708) required that "there should be provided in every garrison or superior factory one minister and one decent and convenient place for divine service only." These ministers were expected to learn Portuguese and the language of the natives, "the better to instruct the Gentoos that shall be servants or slaves of the Company and of their agents in the Protestant religion." [8] Throughout the century the attitude of the Directors was certainly favourable enough to missionary efforts. In 1752, and again in 1774, they gave hearty assistance to the Society for Promoting Christian Knowledge, which before now had turned its attention to India. Its missionaries were to have the use of a church at Cuddalore and one at Madras.[9] To encourage this work, the Directors of the Company wrote to their servants, empowering them to donate, at any time they thought proper, "any sum of money not exceeding 500 pagodas," and finally, "to give us from time to time an account of the progress made by them in educating children and increasing the Protestant religion, together with your opinion of their conduct in general, and what further encouragement they deserve." [10]

Unfortunately, the servants of the Company in India were not only too engrossed in the pursuit of wealth to be interested in missions, but felt that too fervid an attempt to introduce Christianity, by uniting members of native faiths, might render untenable their only too precarious foothold in India.[11]   Occasionally, of course, chaplains sent to minister to English residents and troops in India sought to arouse interest among the natives.[12]   Among them may be mentioned Henry Martyn (1781-1812), and "three Scotchmen" who dared "going without support and without protection to India to make converts to Christianity."[13] These endeavours, however, were possible only after the intervention of the Government in Indian affairs and serve to emphasize the lack of religious instruction throughout the greater part of the century.   The difficulties appealed to the philanthropists of the late century; and, with the revision of the Company's charter in 1813, Wilberforce, who had already aroused public opinion, carried a motion, after making an eloquent appeal in Parliament, for allowing missionaries to proceed to India without hindrance.[14]   In like manner, the uncertain foothold of the Hudson's Bay Company excluded any sustained missionary effort in its field of operation.[15]

The problem of the English Church in the New World was indeed complicated, for here was found an unusual medley of faiths.   While the Church was established by law in the southern colonies, the Catholics predominated in Maryland, the Quakers in Pennsylvania, the Presbyterians and Baptists in New Jersey, various Calvinistic sects in New England, while Lutherans and Moravians from Germany abounded in the Carolinas and Georgia. The visit of Dr. Thomas Bray, a celebrated divine and philanthropist, to Maryland (1695) exposed the poverty and lack of knowledge of the clergy who were sent, or were likely to be sent, to America. His ardent desire to remedy this condition encouraged him to raise subscriptions, and to become the main founder of the Society for the Promotion of Christian Knowledge, in 1698.[16] While its original design was "to propagate Religion in the Plantations, and to secure the pious and useful Education of the Poor here at home," [17] its activities were largely confined to the latter purpose. The crying needs of lands overseas were met by an offshoot, also sponsored by Dr. Bray, The Society for the Propagation of the Gospel in Foreign Parts, which was incorporated in 1701. By voluntary subscriptions this group proposed to "transmit the Gospel, pure and incorrupt, to those dark regions of the Earth . . . by sending divers Ministers into the Province of North America, the Leeward Islands, etc., where they are most wanted, with a laudable yearly Maintenance, and other suitable Encouragements of Books, etc." [18] In spite of a limited income, which never exceeded £6,000 in any year, missions were gradually established, on the American continent (1702), Newfoundland (1703), the West Indies (1732), Nova Scotia (1749), and Western Africa (1752),[19] for the dual purpose of converting the heathen and administering to Christian emigrants.

Another religious-philanthropic manifestation took form in a third group, founded about 1724, which came to be known as "The Associates of the Late Rev. Dr. Bray." [20] This body became interested in exposing flagrant abuses in prisons, in securing ameliorative legislation, and in releasing debtors from confinement.[21] They became associated, too, with other earnest reformers, such as Oglethorpe, Lord Percival, Robert Hucks, Rogers Holland, John Laroche and others. At the meetings of the Associates in 1730-1732 the idea of colonizing Georgia rapidly took form.[22] This enterprise was philanthropic, rather than religious; its *entrepreneurs* [23] were in many cases identical with those philanthropists who secured prison reform and were instrumental in establishing foundling hospitals.[24] In 1737 the Associates announced that they had erected at home, and abroad, "twenty-three libraries, larger and smaller." [25] This work has been continued without cessation to the present time, when the Associates maintain nearly one hundred and seventy libraries overseas, besides supporting several negro schools in the Bahamas.[26]

The general apathy towards missionary effort which prevailed in the continental colonies was due in part to the pressure of physical limitations which have been mentioned above. Here the work of conversion was carried on largely by the Methodists and the Moravians. The work of the Wesleys created a momentum which was not permitted to die down; [27] and in 1732 the Moravians from Silesia, moved by a simple pietism, satisfied their strong crusading impulse by extending their influence to distant fields.   In Pennsylvania and in Georgia, where some had joined Oglethorpe's colony, they pushed beyond the frontier, where their efforts rivalled the zeal of the Jesuits among Indian tribes.[28]   In the previous year, the Gospel society had sent out three missionaries to convert the Indians on the borders of New England.[29]

The same humanitarian spirit which prompted the founding of Georgia forbade by charter the importation of slaves, and achieved a practical result in diminishing the atrocities of Indian wars.[30]   In this colony many missionary efforts were centred, where

> One driven by strong benevolence of soul,
> Shall fly like Oglethorpe from pole to pole.[31]

Georgia became the scene of the labours, not only of the Moravian sect, but of the Wesleys and Whitefield, the founders of Methodism.   Like the Moravians, to whom they owed so much, they had a fervent missionary spirit.   In this frontier of empire their itinerant ministers were spreading the Gospel and gaining inspiration for the awakening of elements of faith at home which had long been neglected.[32]

Till the coming of the Moravians missions in Jamaica had been futile.   West India planters generally opposed the conversion of negroes, lest it might lead to their demand for freedom.[33]   Complaints were common, too, that "the Clergy here are of a Character so vile, that I do not care to mention it; for, except a few, they are generally the most finished of all Debauchees." [34]   The religious needs of white settlers were none too satisfactorily satisfied, while the slaves, with few exceptions, were left in heathen darkness. In 1754, however, the Moravians sent four missionaries who entered upon their work with unsurpassed devotion.[35] By 1787 the number of converted negroes under their care was estimated at 16,045.[36] Toward the close of the century the missionary spirit was revived in the churches at home, and "Jamaica became a scene of anxious solicitude for many." But the visits of Dr. Cook, with two other Wesleyan missionaries, in 1789, 1791, 1792 and 1793, still met with the hostility or indifference of planters,[37]—a feeling which could no longer be openly displayed.

In this connection must be mentioned the ill-fated plan of Bishop Berkeley in 1728 to found a Christian university in Bermuda for the civilization and conversion of America. Verbal enthusiasm, it is true, was aroused on its behalf; but the failure of Walpole, among others, to pay their subscriptions compelled Berkeley to abandon his plan and return from Rhode Island to Ireland.[38] The real reason for its failure is that it came half a century before its time. In the New World it was only by the end of the century that feeble and desultory missionary efforts grew into a militant Christianity and communicated a crusading spirit that was to revitalize the spiritual and moral life as well of Old England.[39]

From the middle of the century to 1800 missionary activities continued to expand. In 1792 Carey, destined to be one of the greatest of Indian missionaries, prevailed on his fellow-members of the Baptist sect

to establish missions in the East and West Indies, West
Africa, and China.[40]   Three years later the Congregationalists established the London Missionary Society, which sent its emissaries to India, South Africa,
the West Indies, the Pacific and Madagascar.   In
the same year sixteen clergymen, moved by the lack of
missionary effort in the continents of Asia and Africa,
formed the Society for Missions to Africa and the East.
The title of this body was soon changed to that of
Church Missionary Society for Africa and the East.[41]
Missionary endeavours were furthered by two other
groups of enthusiasts: the Religious Tract Society, and
the British and Foreign Bible Society, founded in 1799
and 1802, respectively.[42]   This sudden revival of missionary enthusiasm is ascribed to the interest aroused
by the thrilling tales of Captain Cook's voyages and
discoveries.[43]   To the new sympathy with the inhabitants of the Pacific Islands the London Missionary
Society also owed its inception.[44]   This body, composed at first of Congregationalists, soon came to
include members of all religious bodies, and imposed
no form of church government on its converts.[45]
Through the efforts of Wilberforce the government
provided a chaplain to care for the needs of the convict colony established in Australia in 1787.   Here the
chief work of missionary societies was confined to the
education of the unfortunate children of the convicts
and of other settlers.[46]

As already observed,[47] the awakening of sympathy
for human suffering at home and the increasing desire
to save the souls of the heathen in distant lands, cou-

pled with a widespread knowledge of the horrors of
the African slave-trade, served to arouse a degree of
indignation which was almost national in scope, and
finally awakened a humanitarian spirit to active aid in
behalf of unfortunate human beings of all races and
classes. The slave-trade itself, of course, was not a
product of the eighteenth century, for between 1680
and 1700 alone English merchants tore from their
tribes in Africa about 300,000 negroes—an average
of about 15,000 a year.[48] A greater period of prosperity for the traffic, however, arrived with the Asiento
treaty of 1713, giving a monopoly to the British for
the supply of slaves to the Spanish colonies.[49] From
this time on, the maintenance and expansion of the
trade, both to the Spanish and to the English colonies,
became a fixed object of English commercial policy.[50]

Because of the enormous profits accruing from the
traffic capital flowed into it freely. Officially and otherwise mercantilists sought to protect and encourage
their investments. In 1750 it was estimated that 46,-
000 negroes were sold annually in the British colonies
alone.[51] From 1752 to 1762 over 70,000 of them
were brought to Jamaica;[52] from 1759 to 1762, over
40,000 to Guadeloupe.[53] By 1776 the English had supplied the French, Spanish and English colonies with
no fewer than three million African slaves; and to
the number must be added more than a quarter of a
million who perished on the long voyage.[54]

Up to this time the conscienceless forces of capital-
ism had kept the English public ignorant of the horrors of the "Middle Passage," as the voyage of slave-

ships from Africa to their destination in the New
World came to be known.   Possibly their exposure
would have mattered little, for the principle of slavery
was not looked upon as abhorrent.   In fact, many
warm-hearted Christians believed that contact with
European civilization would be of practical benefit to
the heathen Africans.   The mercantilists approved
slavery, because in their judgment colonial areas supplied with slave-labour would never become industrial,
and thus rival the mother country.[55]   The institution
indeed had crept into England, at least in the case of
body-servants who were brought thither by their masters.   Newspapers of the early century teem with
advertisements of fugitives, *e.g.*:

An Indian Man, aged about 21 Years, named Jasper, his
Hair cut close on the top of his Head, and hath some Bunches
on his Face, went away on Sunday last, from his Master,
Capt. Whitwell . . . having Robb'd him of Money and
Cloaths. Whosoever speedily secures him, and brings him to
his Master aforesaid shall have 10s. reward.[56]

Run away from on Board the Lusitania, an East India
young man, by name Cæsar, aged about 17 Years, speaks English very plain. Reward 3 g. for Return.[57]

Negro. 22 Years—run away—middle Size, with stammer-
ing Speech; cut on Forehead; Jerusalem Arms, West Indies,
1706, on Left Arm; 1 guinea for Return, or voluntary Pardon.[58]

There were even slave-marts where the human commodity was bought and sold.   One advertiser, a resident of Holborn, paired for sale "a chestnut gelding,
and a well-made, good-tempered black boy," [59] while in
Liverpool negroes were sold in batches.[60]

That the pure air of freedom should be thus defiled

was intolerable to the liberty-loving Englishman. Finally, in a test case brought before the King's Bench in 1772 it was decided that a slave was free when he touched English soil.[61] The joy felt by the public at the ending of slave-holding in England, is fancifully depicted by Cowper:

> Slaves cannot breathe in England: if their lungs
> Receive our air, that moment they are free;
> They touch our country, and their shackles fall.
> That's noble, and bespeaks a nation proud
> And jealous of the blessing. Spread it then
> And let it circulate through ev'ry vein
> Of all your Empire, that where Britain's pow'r
> Is felt, mankind may feel her mercy, too.[62]

True, before this time, opponents of slavery had begun to express their views. [63] Defoe, perhaps, was the first, followed by Thomson, Savage and Shenstone, and supported by noted divines, such as Heylin, Warburton and Paley, and philosophers like Hutcheson, Adam Smith and Beattie. Walpole was strongly opposed to slavery,[64] and Johnson abhorred the evil.[65] The latter, indeed, was unsympathetic towards the American colonies, because, as he asked: "How is it we hear the loudest yelps for liberty among the drivers of negroes?" [66] This growing aversion to slavery, however, was not yet reflected in politics, where planters and traders, as well as mercantilists in general, were convinced of the importance of their cause to the British Empire. Efforts to bring up the question in Parliament received little attention.

Undoubtedly the growth of anti-slavery sentiment

owed its origin and inspiration to America.   The
Quakers were the most consistent opponents of the
institution.   As early as 1727 they censured the African trade; [67] and in 1754 "publickly testified their
sentiments upon the subject, declaring that to live in
ease and plenty by the toil of those whom fraud and
violence had put into their power, was neither consistent with Christianity, nor common justice." [68] Thereupon many Quakers liberated their slaves, and in 1763
branded those who were engaged in this nefarious
traffic as criminals. [69]   The English members of the
sect reflected this attitude in favouring general emancipation, in enquiring of their members if they were
concerned in the African trade, in appointing a committee to obtain general information on the subject,
and finally by petitioning Parliament for interference. [70]
John Wesley, also, in his experience in Georgia, had
come into contact with slavery and vehemently denounced the system to his fellow-countrymen. [71]

By the middle of the century the force of public
opinion had aroused Parliament sufficiently to make it
adopt measures to prevent the forcible seizure of
natives in Africa. [72]   That this sop to the awakening
spirit of humanity failed is shown by the fact that in
one year alone (1768), 97,000 slaves were taken from
Africa, obviously not of their own accord. [73]   The
American Revolution crippled for a time the British
slave-trade; various measures, too, were taken by the
Continental Congress (1776), [74] and later by England, [75] in restricting trade between the British West
Indies and America, the latter to British ships. [76] These

circumstances, coupled with hurricanes and famine, served only to accentuate the unfortunate plight of the negroes, killing off no fewer than 15,000 of their number.[77]

An unprecedented revival of the slave-trade followed the close of the American Revolution, with its activities now centred in Liverpool. In the decade 1783-1793 Liverpool ships carried from Africa to the West Indies 303,737 slaves and in the period 1795-1804, 323,777; whereas London ships took only 46,405, and Bristol vessels, 10,718.[78] This business, remunerative to the extent of £300,000 annually, became bound up with the prosperity of the town;[79] and in its merchants, as well as in the West India planters, was centred the most determined opposition to the increasing national abhorrence of the slave-trade.

At last the horrors of this nefarious traffic aroused the conscience of the British public, showing that the earlier attitude of the Quakers and of literary opponents had had effect. After the restoration of peace with the United States, also, general attention was called to the subject by swarms of American negroes,—who had been emancipated in one way or another, by the events of the war, penniless and starving, begging in the streets for employment and food.[80] It is stated that in

1787 about 700 of these destitute blacks were collected for the purpose of being sent out in government transports to Sierra Leone; and although a large proportion of them died, or deserted, or had to be discharged as unmanageable, before the

vessels sailed, about 400 of the number were actually con-
veyed to Africa, where, however, the settlement that was thus
attempted to be formed did not prosper.[81]

The actual abolition movement in England seems to
have been started by a woman: the wife of Sir Charles
Middleton, who had been the commander of a man-of-
war stationed in the West Indies. Aroused by the
cruelties suffered by slaves in the Middle Passage, she
appealed to Wilberforce to take action.[82]   Other eye-
witnesses, too, sought to interest humanitarians in the
cause of the negro.[83]   Granville Sharpe, at one time
resident of Jamaica,[84] continued his pioneer work,
after being instrumental in securing the Somerset
decree.[85]   General Walpole, who had studied conditions in the West Indies, denounced their horrors from
his seat in Parliament.[86]   The first authentic account
of the conditions of slavery was given to the public in
1766 by James Ramsay, whose residence of twenty
years in the West Indies qualified him to speak.[87]
Two years later (1768), inquiries regarding the Middle Passage were made of African merchants and
received full replies, for at this time the subject of
abolition was not discussed sufficiently to alarm them.[88]

After nearly twenty years of further agitation, in
May 1787 the first meeting of a self-appointed board
of twelve was held under the chairmanship of Granville Sharpe.   The majority of the members were
London merchants, and all but two of them, Quakers.[89]
Realizing that "the trade had struck its roots too
deeply amongst the commercial interests of the country to fall before a single blow," this body sought

instead to arouse the general moral feeling of the nation.[90]   Contributions for the cause were solicited, and authors and preachers were requested to spread its propaganda in pamphlets and from the pulpit.   A steadily growing literature during the next few years strove to convince the public of the cruelty and iniquity of the traffic in slaves.[91]   From the pulpit an increasing number of ministers appealed to their congregations as men, as Britons, and as Christians, to end the traffic,[92] although the majority of the Bishops still supported the slave-trade.[93]

With the awakening of the public conscience Wilberforce now took his case to Parliament. In Pitt he found a vehement and eloquent friend of abolition as a moral duty, although his hands were tied by the political strength of Liverpool merchants and West India planters.[94]   It should be remembered, however, that the West India planters were now largely represented in England by rich and absentee owners,[95] while others, such as Sir Philip Francis, opposed the slave trade despite the efforts of rich relatives in the West Indies to silence him.[96]   An important step forward was secured by the passage of the Act of 1788, which sought to mitigate the evils of the Middle Passage, by limiting the number of slaves to each vessel.[97]   In the following year Wilberforce brought the question of abolition before the House, pronouncing the slave trade a national iniquity, but without practical results.[98] In 1792, William Pitt, in perhaps the greatest speech of his career, demanded immediate abolition. Unfortunately fear of the spread of French revolutionary

principles [99] postponed a decision, while conditions
during the next few years were too upset to risk Parliamentary defeat.[100] When certain of the French
and Dutch colonies passed to England, under mercantilist banners, the slave-trade indeed became more
active than ever before.[101]

By 1804, several changes had occurred; and Wilberforce felt encouraged to renew his struggle. The
French democracy had assumed the more attractive
form of despotism; England's safety on the seas was
assured, and the West India planters were now willing to suspend the trade for a period of from three to
five years. The new lands were more fertile than the
old for the cultivation of sugar, the demand was
greater than the supply, and the fear of over-produc-
tion, rather than a sense of justice, brought about a
changed attitude.[102] The bill passed by an over-
whelming majority in the Commons, but was defeated
in the Upper House, despite its approval on the part
of the public. In September, 1805, however, an Order
in Council seriously checked the slave trade, by forbidding English ships to bring slaves into the Dutch colonies.[103]

Further progress was made by William Fox. As
early as 1791 he had urged the boycott of West India
rum and sugar until slavery was abolished.[104] In this
stand he was backed by scores of lecturers and pam-
phleteers, who urged an adoption of this procedure
until Parliament should remedy the cruelties of slavery.[105] That this boycott reached national proportions was conclusive proof of public interest and con-

victions, and as such, a source of satisfaction to its sponsor. Said he:

> It cannot but afford a peculiar pleasure, to the truly benevolent mind, to hear that so many families, public societies, and thousands of individuals have at last aimed at the abolition of the Slave Trade, by their determined resolution to abstain from West India sugar and rum.[106]

The conclusion of this remarkable outburst of humanitarianism takes one into the following century. Charles James Fox, in fact, made the abolition of the slave trade a main object of his policy. In a speech he declared:

> If it was a trade founded in violence and injustice, Great Britain ought to wash her hands of it at any rate; nor was the practice of other countries anything at all to the question. . . . Mere gain was not a motive for a great country to rest on as a justification of any measure; it was not the first purpose of a well-regulated government; honour was its superior as much as justice was superior to honour. . . .
>
> As the first nation in Europe, we ought to set the example, and in the cause of justice and humanity, to claim the post of honour—of danger, if there were any.[107]

In 1806 British subjects were not only forbidden to supply foreign powers, whether hostile or neutral, with slaves, but the employment of British vessels, seamen and capital in the foreign slave-trade, was prohibited, and foreign slave-ships were not allowed to be fitted out in British harbours.[108] Finally, in 1807, a bill for total abolition of the traffic was carried in both houses of Parliament.[109]

The significance of the abolition movement is obvious. The perseverance of a small band of Quakers in the New World, the ceaseless efforts of a few London merchants, the denunciations by press and pulpit of intolerable treatment of one's fellow human beings, the arousal of the conscience of the public to the obligations, as well as the profits, of national wealth and strength, and the enforcement of their wishes upon reluctant politicians—all served to develop a new and remarkable attribute of British character: the ideal of the brotherhood of man and the idea of protection of the weak by the strong. Thus the wells of human sympathy, which had once been tapped to aid a helpless and deeply-wronged race, needed little encouragement in later years to remedy evils near at home. The humanitarian spirit in turn was to grapple with, and to mitigate, the evils of the factory system, the problem of pauper apprentices, of child and of woman, labour in the factory and the mine, of hours of labour, of working and housing conditions, and finally of the perplexities of modern industrial, civic and national life.

REFERENCES TO CHAPTER XII

[1] Green, *History of the English People,* IV, p. 276.

[2] Creighton, *Missions, Their Rise and Development,* p. 67.

[3] The philosopher of the seventeenth century was inclined to look upon the simple and innocent natives of foreign lands as better off without interference on the part of representatives of a higher civilization. See the *People of Madagascar* (1698) in *Harleian Miscellany,* XI, p. 534; see also below, p. 237.

[4] Austin, p. 43.

[5] Howison, *op. cit.,* I, pp. 99-100.

[6] Creighton, *op. cit.,* p. 144.

[7] Tucker, *The English Church in Other Lands,* p. 165.

[8] Tucker, *op. cit.,* p. 13; Willson, *Ledger and Sword,* p. 51.

[9] Willson, pp. 108-109.

[10] *Ibid.*

[11] Creighton, p. 75. The character of the nabobs in general, as described in Chapter V, bears out this attitude toward "mere religion."

[12] Willson, *op. cit.,* p. 51.

[13] *Letter of Bishop Porteus to Mrs. More,* 16 Jan., 1797, in *Works,* II, p. 4; Creighton, p. 75.

[14] Creighton, p. 76.

[15] Tucker, p. 40.

[16] Chamberlayne, p. 335.

[17] *Ibid.*

[18] *Ibid,* p. 334.

[19] Tucker, p. 14.

[20] Crane, "The Philanthropists and the Genesis of Georgia," in *The American Historical Review,* XXVII, No. 1, p. 63.

[21] *Ibid,* p. 65.

[22] *Ibid,* p. 67.

[23] The list of Associates, is published in *Biographia Britannica* (1748), II, p. 976, footnote.

[24] Crane, *op. cit.,* pp. 67-68.

[25] Nichols, II, p. 119.

[26] *Report for the Year 1920 of the Association Established by the Late Dr. Bray and His Associates for Libraries for the Clergy, with an Account of a Trust for Supporting Negro Schools and Brief Notes on the Life of Dr. Bray.*

[27] See below, p. 330.

[28] Lecky, I, p. 545.

[29] *Gentleman's Magazine,* Jan., 1731, p. 25.

[30] This "mistake" was later "rectified." Anderson, III, pp. 188-189.

[31] Pope, *Imitation of Horace,* Ep. ii.

[32] Lecky, I, p. 545.

[33] Gardner, p. 199.

[34] *British Empire in America,* II, p. 374.

[35] Gardner, p. 200.

[36] Edwards, II, pp. 171, 178.

[37] Gardner, pp. 345-347.

[38] *Georgian Era,* I, pp. 219-220; Lecky, I, p. 541.

[39] Foakes-Jackson, *Social Life in England,* 1750-1850, Lecture 1.

[40] Tucker, p. 15.

[41] *Ibid,* p. 16.

[42] Lecky, VI, p. 275.

[43] Creighton, *Missions,* p. 67. Cf. above, p. 19f.

[44] Creighton, p. 67.

[45] *Ibid.*

[46] *Ibid,* pp. 154-155.

[47] See above, Chapter XI.

[48] Macpherson, *Annals,* II, p. 638.

[49] Egerton, p. 127; Anderson, III, p. 55; see above, p. ...

[50] Walpole, *George III,* pp. 227-228.

[51] Macpherson, *Annals,* III, p. 403.

[52] *Ibid.*

[53] Admiral Rodney, in *Grenville Correspondence,* II, p. 12.

[54] Bancroft, *History of the United States* (ed. 1885), III, pp. 411-412.

[55] Postlethwayt, *The African Trade,* p. 4.

[56] *The Post-Man,* 1/3 April, 1703.

[57] *Ibid,* 19/22 Jan., 1712.

[58] *The Daily Courant,* 29 Mar., 1712.

[59] *London Gazetteer,* 18 April, 1769; for other instances see Gardner, p. 266.

[60] Williamson's *Advertiser,* 12 Sept., 1766.

[61] The famous Somerset decree. See Hargrave, *An Argument in the Case of Jas. Sommersett, a Negro.* For the attitude of slave-traders and slave-owners, see Estwick (a West-India planter) in *Considerations on the Negro Cause.* He opposed the decision of the King's Bench on the ground that negroes were property, and trade in them as such was sanctioned by English law.

[62] Cowper.

[63] Defoe, *The Reformations of Manners,* and *Life of Col. Jacque.*

[64] *Letter of Walpole to Sir Horace Mann,* 25 Feb., 1750.

[65] Boswell, II, Appendix B, p. 478.

[66] *Ibid.*

[67] Clarkson, *An Essay on the Slavery and Commerce of the Human Species, particularly the African* (1786), p. 7.

[68] *Ibid*, p. 22.

[69] Clarkson, *History of the Abolition of the Slave Trade*, I, pp. 112-116.

[70] Ibid, *An Essay on the Slavery*, etc., p. 26.

[71] Wesley, J., *Thoughts on Slavery*.

[72] 23 Geo. II. c. 31. See also Edwards, II, p. 251, and *Letter of Walpole to Sir Horace Mann*, 25 Feb., 1750.

[73] Macpherson, *Annals*, III, p. 484.

[74] Lecky, VI, p. 284.

[75] Rose, *Diaries*, I, p. 38; Bancroft, *op. cit.*, III, pp. 393-414.

[76] Macpherson, *Annals*, IV, pp. 17-20.

[77] Edwards, VI, ch. iv.

[78] *Ibid*, II, p. 260. For other statistics of the slave trade see Gardner, pp. 144-153, and Roscoe, *op. cit.*, p. 114, footnote 2.

[79] Baines, *Hist. of Liv.*, p. 719.

[80] Craik, III, p. 111.

[81] *Ibid*.

[82] *Life of Wilberforce*, p. 63.

[83] Sharpe, *Law of Liberty* (1776).

[84] Gardner, pp. 216-217.

[85] See above, p. 334.

[86] Gardner, pp. 235-237.

[87] *Ibid*, p. 218. See also, Ramsay, *An Essay on the Treatment and Conversion of African Slaves in the British Sugar Colonies* (1784). A reviewer of this work commented: "If planters have any conscience, they cannot but feel the might of the arguments used in this performance; and in the eye of the public, they will appear to bear an exact proportion to the value which it sets upon the prosperity and happiness of upwards of half a million (*sic*) of our fellow-creatures." *European Magazine*, June, 1784, p. 448.

[88] The results of this investigation were embodied in Clarkson, *An Essay on the Slavery*, etc.

[89] *Life of Wilberforce*, p. 66.

[90] *Ibid*, p. 67.

[91] The following is a partial list of tracts and pamphlets describing the slave trade and conditions of its victims. All agree on the conditions under which slaves were captured, sold and treated in servitude: Ramsay, James, *Objections to the Abolition of the Slave Trade with Answers* (1788); *Ibid, Examination of the Rev. Mr. Harris's Scriptural Researches on the Licitness of the Slave Trade* (1788); Wilberforce, W., *A Letter on the Abolition of the Slave Trade;* Beaufoy, *Speech in a Committee of the Whole House on a Bill for Regulating the Conveyance of Negroes from Africa to the West Indies* (1789); Falconbridge, A. (late Surgeon in the African Trade), *An Account of the Slave Trade on the Coast of Africa*

(1788) ; Robinson, R., *Slavery Inconsistent with the Spirit of Christianity* (1788) ; Thomson, A., *Substance of Speech Delivered to Edinburgh Society for Abolition of Slavery;* Harris, R., *Scriptural Researches on the Licitness of the Slave Trade* (1788) ; Beatson, J., *A Sermon Occasioned by That Branch of British Commerce Which Extends to the Human Species* (1789) ; Liddon, J., *Cruelty the Natural and Inseparable Consequence of Slavery, and Both Diametrically Opposite to the Doctrine and Spirit of the Christian Religion* (1792) ; also works quoted above.

[92] See Dore, *A Sermon on the African Slave Trade* (1788), and Booth, A., *A Sermon Preached in Little Prescot Street, Goodman's Fields* (1792).

[93] Hammond, *Charles James Fox,* p. 235.

[94] Lecky, V, pp. 64-65.

[95] Hammond, *Fox,* p. 233.

[96] *The Georgian Era,* I, p. 338.

[97] *Life of Wilberforce,* pp. 70-71.

[98] *Ibid,* p. 79.

[99] *Ibid,* p. 259.

[100] *Ibid,* p. 258.

[101] See above, p. 336, and *Edinburgh Review,* July, 1808 (Coleridge).

[102] *Life of Wilberforce,* p. 259.

[103] Lecky, V, p. 66.   For the course of the abolition movement to 1799, see the *Annual Register* for that year.

[104] Fox, Wm., *An Address to the People of Great Britain on the Propriety of Abstaining from West India Sugar and Rum* (14th ed., 1791).

[105] See Crafton, *A Short Sketch of the Evidence Delivered Before a Committee of the House of Commons for the Abolition of the Slave Trade* (1792), and *No Rum—No Sugar! or, The Voice of Blood, Being Half an Hour's Conversation Between a Negro and an English Gentleman Shewing the Horrible Nature of the Slave Trade* (1792).

[106] Fox, Wm., *A Second Address to the People of Great Britain.* 1792.

[107] Fox, C. J., *Speeches,* IV, p. 402.

[108] *Annual Register,* 1806, p. 90; Clarkson, *Hist. of the Abol. of the Slave Trade,* II, pp. 503-506.

[109] *Life of Wilberforce,* p. 284; Lecky, V, p. 68.

BIBLIOGRAPHY

The student who is interested in eighteenth century problems will never lack an abundance of source and secondary material. The stirring events of the reign of Anne and of the Hanoverian Era encouraged not only the professional writer to discuss in serious or satirical vein the interesting topics of the day, but inspired hundreds of other contemporaries to record intimate and seemingly trivial details of their public and private lives. Newspapers, essays, magazines, diaries, memoirs, autobiographies, reminiscences and letters furnish a mine of information which has only begun to be utilized by students of succeeding generations. While the ambitious task of compiling a complete and connected story of English society of the eighteenth century has not yet been attempted, numerous treatises on social life in the several reigns have been written, as have many on such special topics as dress, furniture, food, pottery and porcelain, etc. As the books in the last-mentioned groups have failed for the most part to trace the causes of the century's changes, or to connect them with the growth of empire, they have been of little service in the preparation of this treatise.

This writer, therefore, has been confronted with the task of selecting from an almost inexhaustible source of material. Although his bibliography is by no means complete, it is at least representative of the several kinds of authors and works which may reasonably be expected to reflect changes in social life. In this attempt to choose material which is relevant, and to exclude the rest, invaluable help has been rendered by Gillespie's *The Influence of Oversea Expansion on England to 1700,* and by Lecky's monumental *History of England in the Eighteenth Century.* As suggested above, the general political and social histories of England, as well as the histories of colonization, were not particularly helpful. For questions of economic import, the works of Anderson, Macpherson, D'Avenant, Adam Smith, Joshua Gee and William Wood were invaluable, in the order named. Special treatises on food-stuffs and beverages, on dress, furniture, and pottery and porce-lain were of assistance only in conjunction with contemporary works of a more general nature. For various aspects of social life, the works of Addison, Steele, Swift, Defoe, Walpole, Johnson, as translated into print by the ever-faithful Boswell, Goldsmith, Chesterfield, Hannah More, Wilberforce and Eden, furnished the bulk of information contained in this treatise. This writer, too, was fortunate in being able to peruse the splendid collection of newspapers of the eighteenth century, in the British Museum.

This bibliography includes only material of considerable value in describing and co-ordinating various aspects of English society in this period with influences emanating from overseas. In-cluded in the source are all works which, by reprinting contem-porary documents, throw a light upon conditions of the eighteenth century.

SOURCES

Chronological Table and Index of the Statutes to the End of the Session 50 Victoria 1886. London, 1887.

COBBETT, WILLIAM, *Parliamentary History of England, 1066-1803.* 36 vols. London, 1806-20.

Finance Reports, 1797, 1798; Proceedings thereupon, 1798-1803. 7 vols. London, 1797-1803.

The Official List published by Authority of the Registrar-General of Births, Deaths and Marriages . . . .corrected to March 1, 1899. London, 1899.

PICKERING, DANBY, *The Statutes at Large.* Cambridge.

BOYER, ABEL, *The Political State of Great Britain.* Vols. I-LIV, Jan., 1711, to Dec., 1737. Vols. LVI-LX; July, 1738, to Dec., 1740. London, 1711-1740.

CHAMBERLAYNE, EDWARD and JOHN, *The Present State of England.* London, 1704 and 1748.

CHAMBERLAYNE, EDWARD, *The New Present State of Great Britain.* London, 1770.

PETTY, SIR WILLIAM, *Political Arithmetick, or a Discourse concerning the Value of Lands, People, et cetera.* London, 1690 and 1691. Glasgow, 1751. London, 1877.

Fortescue MSS. (containing the Grenville Family Papers). *The MSS. of J. B. Fortescue, Esq., preserved at Dropmore.* Published by the Historical Manuscripts Commission in 9 vols. London, 1892-1915.

Harleian Manuscripts, in the British Museum. Catalogued in 1808, *et seq.*

Harleian Miscellany: A Collection of Scarce, Curious and Entertaining Pamphlets and Tracts . . . found in the late Earl of Oxford's Library. 12 vols. London, 1808-1811.

Marchmont Papers. *A Selection from the Papers of the Earls of Marchmont* (in the possession of the Rt. Hon. Sir G. H. Rose), *illustrative of Events from 1685 to 1750.* 3 vols. London, 1831.

The Norris Papers, ed. by Heywood, T. Manchester, 1846.

Portland Manuscripts. *Report on the Manuscripts of His Grace the Duke of Portland, preserved at Welbeck Abbey.* Published by the Hist. Mss. Comm. 8 vols. London, 1891-1907. (Vol. V., Norwich, 1899.)

CONTEMPORARY PERIODICALS

(*Printed in London if not otherwise stated*).

The Annual Register: A Review of Public Events at Home and Abroad. 1758-1800.

(Applebee's) *Original Weekly Journal.* (British Museum.)

The British Apollo; or Curious Amusements for the Ingenious. To which are added the most material occurrences, Foreign and Domestick. (British Museum.)

The Connoisseur by Mr. Town, Critic, and Censor-General

(written chiefly by George Colman and Bonnell Thornton).

The Country Journal or the Craftsman. (Brit. Mus.)

The Daily Advertiser. (Brit. Mus.)

The Daily Courant. (Brit. Mus.)

The Daily Post. (Brit. Mus.)

The Edinburgh Review. Edinburgh, 1755-1756. Largely a book review, edited by W. Robertson and Adam Smith among others.

The Edinburgh Review, or Critical Journal. Edinburgh, 1802-1829.

European Magazine and London Review. 1782-1822.

The Examiner, or Remarks Upon Papers and Occurrences. 1710, *et seq.*

The Female Tatler, ed. by Mrs. Manley. 1709. (Brit. Mus.)

The Flying Post; or the Post-Master. 1696-1703 f. (Brit. Mus.)

Gentleman's Magazine; or Monthly Intelligencer. Vol. I-V, 1731-1735. After the latter year, name was changed to *The Gentleman's Magazine and Historical Chronicler.* Vols. VI-LXXVII, 1736-1807.

The Guardian. 1713. (Brit. Mus.)

The Humours of a Coffee-House: A Comedy as It Is Daily Acted, etc. 1707. (Brit. Mus.)

The Idler (by Samuel Johnson and others). 2 vols. 1761.

The London Chronicle. 1757-1823. (Brit. Mus.)

The London Gazette. 1703. (Brit. Mus.)

The London Journal. 1727. (Brit. Mus.)

The London Spy. 1709. (Brit. Mus.)

The Lounger. Edinburgh, 1785-1786.

Memoirs of the Society of Grub-Street. 2 vols. 1737. (Brit. Mus.)

The Mirror. Edinburgh, 1779-1780.

Mist's Weekly Journal, 1728. (Brit. Mus.)

The Morning Post. (Brit. Mus.)

The Observator. 1724, *et seq.*

The Post-Boy. (Brit. Mus.)

The Postman and the Historical Account of the Publick Transactions of Christendom. 1695-1703, and 1710. (Brit. Mus.)

The Protestant Mercury. (Brit. Mus.)

Public Characters. 1799-1809. (Brit. Mus.)

(Read's) *Weekly Journal or British Gazetteer.* (Brit. Mus.)

The Spectator. 1711-1714.

The Tatler. 1709-1711.

The Templar; or Monthly Register of Legal and Constitutional Knowledge. 1789. (Brit. Mus.)

The Times. 1791 ff. (Brit. Mus.)

The Weekly Journal or Saturday's Post. (Brit. Mus.)

The Weekly Miscellany, giving an Account of the Religion, Morality, and Learning of the Present Times. 2 vols. 1736-8. (Brit. Mus.)

The Weekly Register and Political Magazine. 3 vols. 1810.

Williamson's Liverpool Advertiser. Liverpool.

The World.

CONTEMPORARY LITERATURE

I. *Drama*

BAKER, T., *Tunbridge Walks; or, The Yeomen of Kent; a Comedy.* London, 1703. (Brit. Mus.)

BROWN, THOMAS, *The Dispensary; a Farce.* In Vol. III of his collected works. London, 1744. (Brit. Mus.)

COVENTRY, F., *The History of Pompey, the Little; or, The Life and Adventures of a Lap-dog.* London, 1751. (Brit. Mus.)

CUMBERLAND, RICHARD, *The Choleric Man; a Comedy.* London, 1775. (Brit. Mus.)

GAY, JOHN, *The Beggar's Opera.* London, 1728.

GAY, JOHN, *Polly; an Opera* (in three acts) *being the Second Part of the Beggar's Opera.* London, 1729.

GAY, JOHN, *Trivia; or, the Art of Walking the Streets of London.* London, 1716(?).

JOHNSON, C., *The Gentleman Cully; a Comedy.* London, 1702. (Brit. Mus.)

SHADWELL, THOMAS, *Epsom Wells* (a comedy in five acts). London, 1673 and 1704. (Brit. Mus.)

II. *Fiction*

DEFOE, DANIEL, *Life of Colonel Jacque.* London, 1722.

DEFOE, DANIEL, *Moll Flanders.*

DEFOE, DANIEL, *Robinson Crusoe.* London, 1719.

FIELDING, HENRY, *Amelia.* London, 1751.

RICHARDSON, SAMUEL, *The History of Sir Charles Grandison.* London, 1754-6.

SMOLLETT, TOBIAS G., *The Expedition of Humphrey Clinker.* London, 1766 and 1794.

SMOLLETT, TOBIAS G., *The Adventures of Roderick Random.* London, 1748.

SWIFT, JONATHAN, *Gulliver's Travels.* London, 1726.

III. *Poetry*

CANTILEVRE, MRS., *The Gamester.* London, 1705.

COWPER, WILLIAM (1731-1800), Poems. London, 1905.

DEFOE, DANIEL, *The Reformation of Manners; a Satyr.* London, 1702.

GAY, JOHN, *The Fan; a Poem.* London, 1714.

POPE, ALEXANDER, *Imitation of Horace.* London, 1738.

POPE, ALEXANDER, *The Rape of the Lock.* London, 1712.

SOUTHEY, ROBERT, *Botany Bay Eclogues.* No. 1, Elinor. Oxford, 1794.

SWIFT, JONATHAN, *The Bubble, a Poem,* and *The City-Shower, a Poem.* London, 1721 and 1710, respectively.

IV. *Biographies, Correspondence, Diaries, Memoirs and Speeches*

ANGELONI, BATTISTA, *Letters on the English Nation.* London, 1755.

AUSTIN, WILLIAM, *Letters from London Written During the Years 1802 and 1803.* Boston, 1804.

LE BLANC, M. L'ABBE, *Letters on the English and French Nations.* London, 1746.

BOARDMAN, JAMES, *Bentleyana: or, a Memoir of T. Bentley . . . with Extracts from His Correspondence.* Liverpool, 1851.

BOSWELL, JAMES, *Life of Johnson.* 6 vols. Oxford, 1897.

BURKE, EDMUND, *Correspondence.* London, 1844.

CARTER, MRS. ELIZABETH, *Memoirs.* London, 1808.

CHESTERFIELD, EARL OF, *Letters to His Son.* New York, 1857.

COXE, WILLIAM, *Memoirs of John, Duke of Marlborough.* London, 1820.

COXE, WILLIAM, *Memoirs of the Life and Administration of Sir Robert Walpole, Earl of Orford. With original correspondence and authentic papers never before published.* London, 1800.

DELANY, MRS., *Autobiography and Correspondence.* 2 vols. Boston, 1880.

FRANKLIN, BENJAMIN, *The Autobiography of Benjamin Franklin.* London, 1850.

FRASER, ALEXANDER C., *Life and Letters of George Berkeley.* Oxford, 1871.

FOX, CHARLES J., *The Speeches of the Rt. Hon. Charles James Fox, in the House of Commons.* 6 vols. London, 1815.

GOLDSMITH, OLIVER, *The Life of Richard Nash, of Bath, Esq., extracted principally from his Original Papers.* London, 1762.

HOARE, R. C., *Pedigrees and Memoirs of the Families of Hore and Hoare.* Bath, 1819. (Brit. Mus.)

METEYARD, ELIZABETH, *The Life of Josiah Wedgwood from His Private Correspondence and Family Papers.* 2 vols. London, 1865-6.

MONTAGU, LADY MARY WORTLEY, *The Letters and Works of* (ed. by her grandson). 3 vols. London, 1837.

MORE, HANNAH, *Works*. 8 vols. London, 1853.

MUIRHEAD, JAMES P., *The Life of James Watt with Selections from His Correspondence*. London, 1858.

PITT, WILLIAM, Earl of Chatham, *Correspondence*. 4 vols. London, 1838.

REID, W. H., *Memoirs of the Public Life of John Horne Tooke, Esq*. 2 vols. London, 1812.

ROBERTS, W., *Memoirs of · the Life and Correspondence of Mrs. Hannah More*. 2 vols. New York, 1834.

ROSE, THE RIGHT HON. GEORGE, *The Diaries and Correspondence of, containing Original Letters of the Most Distinguished Statesman of His Day* (ed. by L. V. Harcourt). 2 vols. London, 1860.

SPENCER, A. (ed.), *Memoirs of William Hickey, 1749-1775*. 3 vols. London, 1919.

SWIFT, JONATHAN, *Journal to Stella*. London, 1710-1713.

TEMPLE, RICHARD, Earl of Grenville, 1711-1779, *The Grenville Papers: being the Correspondence of Richard and George* (ed. by W. J. Smith). London, 1852-3.

TEMPLE, SIR WILLIAM, *Works*. 4 vols. London, 1770.

THORESBY, RALPH, *Diary* (1677-1724). London, 1830.

VOLTAIRE, FRANÇOIS, M. A. DE, *Letters Concerning the English Nation*. London, 1733. (Edited by P. Cunningham.)

WALPOLE, HORACE, *Letters*. 9 vols. London, 1891.

WALPOLE, HORACE, *The Last Journals of Horace Walpole during the Reign of George III*. London and New York, 1910.

WALPOLE, HORACE, *Memoirs of the Reign of King George III*. 4 vols. London, 1845.

WALPOLE, HORACE, *Memoirs of George II*. Vols. VI and VII of *Works*. London, 1798-1825.

WHARTON, FRANCIS, *The Revolutionary Diplomatic Correspondence of the United States*. Washington, 1889.

V. Critical Accounts of English Manners and Customs by
Contemporary Travellers and Observers

ANON., *Narrative of the Journey of an Irish Gentleman Through England in 1752.* London, 1869.

ANON., *St. James' Park, a Satyr.* London, 1709. (Brit. Mus.)

ANON., *A Modern Sabbath, or a Sunday Ramble in and about the Cities of London and Westminster.* London, 1807.

ANON., *A Trip Through London: containing Observations on Men and Things. . . .* London, 1727.

BBOWN, J., *Estimate of the Manners and Principles of the Time.* 2 vols. London, 1757.

BURNET, BISHOP, *History of His Own Times.* 2 vols. London, 1734.

DEFOE, DANIEL, *The Compleat Gentleman* (ed. by Karl Bulbring). London, 1890.

DEFOE, DANIEL, *The Great Law of Subordination Consider'd, or the Insolence and Insufferable Behaviour of the Servants of England Duly Enquired Into.* London, 1724.

DEFOE, DANIEL, *A Tour Through the Whole Island of Great Britain.* 4 vols. London, 1748.

ENTICK, JOHN, *A New and Accurate History and Survey of London, Westminster, Southwark and Other Places Adjacent.* 4 vols. London, 1776.

GROSLEY, PIERRE J., *A Tour to London, or New Observations on England and Its Inhabitants.* 2 vols. London, 1765.

KALM, P., *Account of His Visit to England on His Way to America in 1748.* (Tr. by J. Lucas.) London, 1892.

Letters Concerning the Present State of England. Particularly Respecting the Politics, Arts, Manners and Literature of the Time. (Brit. Mus.) London, 1772.

MACKY, JOHN, *Journey Through England.* London, 1714 and 1724.

MAC RITCHIE, W., *Diary of a Tour Through England in 1795.* London, 1897.

MAITLAND, WILLIAM, *The History of London from Its Foundation by the Romans to the Present Time . . . with the Several Accounts of Westminster, Middlesex, Southwark, etc.* 2 vols. London, 1775.

MALCOLM, JAMES P., *Anecdotes of the Manners and Customs of London During the Eighteenth Century.* 2 vols. London, 1808.

MILLER, SAMUEL, *Brief Retrospect of the Eighteenth Century, a Sketch of the Science, Arts and Literature During That Period.* New York, 1803.

MISSON, HENRI, *Memoirs and Observations in His Travels Over England.* (Tr. by Mr. Ozell.) London, 1719.

NICHOLS, JOHN, *Literary Anecdotes of the Eighteenth Century; comprising Biographical Memoirs of W. Bowyer, and Many of His Learned Friends, etc.* 9 vols. London, 1812-5.

NICHOLS, JOHN, *Illustrations of the Literary History of the Eighteenth Century, consisting of Authentic Memoirs and Original Letters of Eminent Persons, and Intended as a Sequel to the Literary Anecdotes.* 8 vols. London, 1817, *et seq.*

RUMFORD, SIR BENJAMIN T., *Essays, Political, Economical and Philosophical.* Boston, 1798-1804.

SILLIMAN, B., *A Journal of Travels in England, Holland and Scotland in 1805 and 1806.* London, 1810.

SPENCE, JOSEPH, *Anecdotes, Observations and Characters of Books and Men Collected from the Conversations of Mr. Pope and Other Eminent Persons of His Time.* London, 1820.

WARD, E., *The Gaming Lady, or Bad Luck to Him That Has Her,* in *Adam and Eve Stript of Their Furbelows: or, The Fashionable Virtues and Vices of Both Sexes Exposed to Public View.* London, 1710(?).

WATSON, BISHOP, *Anecdotes of His Life.* 2 vols. London, 1818.

WEST, J., *A Trip to Richmond in Surrey.* London, 1787.

ECONOMIC WORKS

I. *Agriculture*

HARTE, WALTER, *Essays on Husbandry.* London, 1764.

HOLT, JOHN, *General View of the Agriculture of the County of Lancaster.* London, 1795.

Report of the Committee of the Board of Agriculture Appointed to Extract Information from the County Reports, and Other Authorities, Concerning the Culture and Use of Potatoes. London, 1795. (Brit. Mus.)

TULL, JETHRO, *The New Horse-Houghing Husbandry, or an Essay on the Principles of Tillage and Vegetation.* London, 1733-40.

YOUNG, ARTHUR, *The Farmer's Letters to the People of England, containing the Sentiments of a Practical Husbandman, etc.* London, 1767.

YOUNG, ARTHUR, *General View of the Agriculture of the County of Essex.* London, 1807.

YOUNG, ARTHUR, *General View of the Agriculture of Hertfordshire.* London, 1804.

YOUNG, ARTHUR, *General View of the Agriculture of the County of Lincoln, drawn up for the Consideration of the Board of Agriculture and Internal Improvement.* London, 1799.

YOUNG, ARTHUR, *Norfolk.* London, 1804.

YOUNG, ARTHUR, *A Six Months' Tour Through the North of England, containing an Account of the Present State of Agriculture, Manufactures, and Population in Several Counties of This Kingdom, etc.* 4 vols. London, 1770-71.

YOUNG, ARTHUR, *Suffolk.* London, 1797.

II. *Commerce and Industry*

ANDERSON, ADAM, *History of Commerce. An Historical and Chronological Deduction of the Origin of Commerce, from the Earliest Accounts. Containing an History of the Great Commercial Interests of the British Empire. To which is prefixed an Introduction exhibiting a View of the Ancient and Modern State of Europe; of the Importance of our Colonies; and of the Commerce, Shipping, Manufacturing, Fisheries, etc., of G. B. and Ireland; and their Influence on the Landed Interest.* 4 vols. London, 1787-89.

BOULTON, MATTHEW, *Memorial Relative to Assaying and Marking Wrought Plate at Birmingham, etc.* London, 1773. (Brit. Mus.)

CAMPBELL, R., *The London Tradesman.* London, 1747.

D'AVENANT, CHARLES, *The Political and Commercial Works of That Celebrated Writer, Charles D'Avenant, relating to the Trade and Revenue of England, the Plantation Trade, the East-India Trade.* Collected and revised by Sir Charles Whitworth. 5 vols. London, 1771.

DEFOE, DANIEL, *The Anatomy of Exchange Alley; or a System of Stock-Jobbing, by a Jobber.* London, 1719.

FORBES, W., *Memoirs of a Banking House.* London, 1860.

GEE, JOSHUA, *The Trade and Navigation of Great Britain Considered.* Glasgow, 1731.

HUTTON, WILLIAM, *History of Birmingham.* Birmingham, 1781.

Liverpool Memorandum Book; or Gentlemen's, Merchants' and Tradesmen's Daily Pocket-Book for . . . 1753, etc. Liverpool, 1752. (Brit. Mus.)

MACPHERSON, DAVID, *Annals of Commerce.* 4 vols. London, 1805.

MACPHERSON, DAVID, *The History of the European Commerce with India.* London, 1812.

The New Bristol Guide: *Containing Its Antiquities . . . Historic Annals . . . and Other Particulars . . . also*

Accounts of the Hotwells and Clifton . . . Brief Biography of Some Eminent Natives of Bristol, etc. Bristol, 1799. (Brit. Mus.)

NOLTE, V., *Fifty Years in Both Hemispheres, or Reminiscences of a Merchant's Life.* London, 1854.

POLLFEXEN, SIR HENRY, *A Discourse of Trade, Coyn and Paper Credit.* London, 1697.

POSTLETHWAYT, MALACHI, *The African Trade.* London, 1745.

POSTLETHWAYT, MALACHI, *Historical State of the South Sea Company.* London, 1757.

POSTLETHWAYT, MALACHI, *Universal Dictionary of Trade and Commerce.* 4th ed. London, 1774.

ROSE, GEORGE, *A Brief Examination into the Increase of the Revenue, Commerce, and Manufactures of Great Britain from 1792 to 1799.* London, 1799.

SMITH, ADAM, *Inquiry into the Nature and Causes of the Wealth of Nations.* 2 vols. New York, 1878.

STEELE, RICHARD, *The Female Manufacturer's Complaint,* bound with *Town Talk* and Other Essays. Dublin, 1790. (Brit. Mus.)

TEMPLE, SIR WILLIAM, *A Vindication of Commerce and the Arts.* London, 1758. (Brit. Mus.)

TUCKER, JOSIAH, *Cui Bono, or an Inquiry What Benefits Can Arise Either to the English or the Americans or the French, Spaniards or Dutch from the Greatest Victories?* Gloucester, 1781.

WOOD, WILLIAM, *Survey of Trade.* London, 1718.

III. *Colonies*

BROWN, DR. PATRICK, *Civil and Natural History of Jamaica.* London, 1789.

BURKE, EDMUND, *An Account of the European Settlements in America.* 2 vols. London, 1770.

CARROLL, BARTHOLEMEW, *Historical Collections of South*

Carolina, embracing Many Rare and Valuable Pamphlets, etc. New York, 1836.

DOUGLASS, WILLIAM, *A Summary Historical and Political of the Planting, Progressive Improvements, and Present State of the British Settlements in America.* Boston, 1749.

EDWARDS, BRYAN, *The History, Civil and Commercial, of the British Colonies in the West Indies.* 4 vols. Philadelphia, 1806.

FORCE, PETER, *Tracts and Other Papers, Leading to the Origin, Settlement, and Progress of the Colonies in North America, from the Discovery of the Country to the Year 1776.* 4 vols. Washington, 1836-46.

Importance of British Plantations in America. London, 1731.

JONES, HUGH, *Present State of Virginia.* London, 1724. (Brit. Mus.)

LONG, EDWARD, *The History of Jamaica.* 3 vols. London, 1774.

OLDMIXON, JOHN, *The British Empire in America.* 2 vols. London, 1768.

RAYNAL, GUILLAUME, T. F., *Histoire Philosophique et Politique des Establissements, et du Commerce des Européens dans les Deux Indes.* 8 vols. Geneva, 1780. (English translation, published in 8 vols. in London, 1783.)

WHITE, GEORGE, *Historical Collections of Georgia.* New York, 1854.

WYNNE, J. H., *A General History of the British Empire in America.* 2 vols. London, 1770.

FOREIGN TRAVEL, VOYAGES AND DISCOVERIES

COOK, CAPT. JAMES, and KING, CAPT. JAMES, *A Voyage to the Pacific Ocean, Undertaken by the Command of His Majesty, for Making Discoveries in the Northern Hemisphere, to Determine the Position and Extent of the West Side of North America; Its Distance from Asia; and the Practicability of a Northern Passage to Europe, Performed Under the Direction of Capts. Cook, Clarke and Gore, in H. M.'s Ships, the Resolution and the Discovery in the Years 1776-1780.* 3 vols. (Vols. I and II by Cook, Vol. III by King.) London, 1784.

DALRYMPLE, ALEXANDER, *Collection of Voyages to the South Seas.* London, 1770.

DAMPIER, WILLIAM, *A Collection of Voyages.* 4 vols. London, 1729.

ELLIS, W., *An Authentic Narrative of a Voyage Performed by Capt. Cook and Capt. Clarke, in H. M.'s Ships, the Resolution and Discovery, During the Years 1776, 1777, 1778, 1779, 1780, in Search of a Passage Between the Continents of Asia and America. Including a Faithful Account of All Their Discoveries and the Unfortunate Death of Capt. Cook; Illustrated with a Chart and a Variety of Cuts.* 2 vols. London, 1782.

JOHNSON, SAMUEL, *A Journey to the Western Islands of Scotland.* London, 1775.

PARK, MUNGO, *Travels in the Interior Districts of Africa; Performed Under the Direction of the African Association in the Year 1795, 1796 and 1797 with an Appendix Containing Geographical Illustrations of Africa by Maj. Rennell.* (Ed. by Bryan Edwards.) London, 1799.

PINKERTON, JOHN, *A General Collection of the Best and Most Interesting Voyages and Travels in All Parts of the World, etc.* 17 vols. London, 1808-14.

PHILANTHROPY AND HUMANITARIANISM

CARY, JOHN, *Essay Toward Regulating the Trade and Employing the Poor of This Kingdom.* London, 1700.

COLQUHOUN, PATRICK, *A Treatise on the Police of the Metropolis.* 5th ed. London, 1797. (Brit. Mus.)

DEFOE, DANIEL, *Givnig Alms No Charity.* London, 1704.

EDEN, SIR FREDERICK M., *The State of the Poor.* 4 vols. London, 1797.

FIELDING, HENRY, *On the Late Increase of Robbers.* London, 1751.

FIELDING, SIR JOHN, *On the Police.* London, 1753.

HANWAY, JONAS, *Letters on the Importance of the Rising Generation of the Labouring Part of Our Fellow-Subjects.* 2 vols. London, 1767.

HEBERDEN, WILLIAM, *Observations on the Increase and Decrease of Different Diseases and Particularly of the Plague.* London, 1801.

HOWARD, JOHN, *State of the Prisons in England and Wales.* London, 1777.

LIND, JAMES, *An Essay on the Most Effectual Means of Preserving the Health of Seamen in the Royal Navy.* London, 1757.

MANDEVILLE, BERNARD, *The Fable of the Bees; or Private Vices, Public Benefits with an Essay on Charity and Charity Schools, etc.* London, 1723.

MASSIE, JOSEPH, *A Plan for the Establishment of Charity-Houses for Exposed or Deserted Women and Girls. Observations Concerning the Foundling Hospital. Considerations Relating to the Poor and Poor Laws. Also, a New System of Policy . . . for Relieving the Poor, etc.* London, 1758.

SHORT, THOMAS, *A Comparative History of the Increase and Decrease of Mankind in England and Several Countries Abroad.* London, 1767. (Brit. Mus.)

THE SLAVE-TRADE

BEATSON, J., *A Sermon Occasioned by That Branch of British Commerce Which Extends to the Human Species.* London, 1789.

BEAUFOY, HENRY, *Speech in a Committee of the Whole House on a Bill for Regulating the Conveyance of Negroes from Africa to the West Indies.* London, 1789.

BOOTH, A., *A Sermon Preached in Little Prescot Street, Goodman's Field.* London, 1792.

CLARKSON, THOMAS, *An Essay on the Slavery and Commerce of the Human Species, Particularly the African.* London, 1786.

CLARKSON, THOMAS, *History of the Rise, Progress and Ac*

complishment of the Abolition of the Slave Trade by the British Parliament. New York, 1836.

CRAFTON, W., *A Short Sketch of the Evidence Delivered Before a Committee of the House of Commons for the Abolition of the Slave Trade.* London, 1782.

DORE, J., *A Sermon on the African Slave Trade.* London, 1778.

ESTWICK, SAMUEL, *Considerations on the Negro Cause.* London, 1772.

FALCONBRIDGE, A., *An Account of the Slave Trade on the Coast of Africa.* London, 1788.

FOX, WILLIAM, *An Address to the People of Great Britain on the Propriety of Abstaining from West India Sugar and Rum.* 14th ed. London, 1791.

FOX, WILLIAM, *A Second Address to the People of Great Britain, Containing a New and Powerful Argument to Abstain from the Use of West India Sugar.* London, 1792.

HARGRAVE, FRANCIS, *An Argument in the Case of Jas. Sommersett, a Negro, etc.* London, 1772.

HARRIS, R., *Scriptural Researches on the Licitness of the Slave Trade.* London, 1778.

LIDDON, J., *Cruelty the Natural and Inseparable Consequence of Slavery, and Both Diametrically Opposite to the Doctrine and Spirit of the Christian Religion.* London, 1792.

No Rum! . . . No Sugar! or, The Voice of Blood, Being Half an Hour's Conversation Between a Negro and an English Gentleman, Shewing the Horrible Nature of the Slave Trade. London, 1792.

RAMSAY, JAMES, *An Essay on the Treatment and Conversion of African Slaves in the Sugar Colonies.* London, 1784.

RAMSAY, JAMES, *Examinations of the Reverend Mr. Harris's Scriptural Researches on the Licitness of the Slave Trade.* London, 1788.

RAMSAY, JAMES, *Objections to the Abolition of the Slave Trade with Answers.* London, 1788.

ROBINSON, R., *Slavery Inconsistent with the Spirit of Christianity.* London, 1788.

SHARPE, G., *Law of Liberty*. London, 1776.

THOMPSON, ANDREW, *Substance of a Speech Delivered at the Meeting of the Edinburgh Society for the Abolition of Slavery; on October 19, 1830*. Edinburgh, 1830.

WESLEY, JOHN, *Thoughts on Slavery*. London, 1774.

WILBERFORCE, WILLIAM, *Letter on the Abolition of the Slave Trade Addressed to the Freeholders of Yorkshire*. London, 1807.

WILBERFORCE, ROBERT and SAMUEL, *Life of William Wilberforce*. (Abridged from the London edition, by Caspar Morris.) Philadelphia, 1839.

FOOD AND COOKING

An Enumeration of the Principal Vegetables, etc., That May Be Substituted in Place of Wheat and Other Bread-Corn. London, 1796.

HANWAY, JONAS, *An Essay on Tea*. London, 1756.

MOSELY, A., *A Treatise Concerning the Properties and Effects of Coffee*. London, 1785.

RUNDELL, MRS. HELENE, *A New System of Domestic Cookery Formed Upon Principles of Economy*. 3d ed. Exeter, 1808.

SMITH, E., *The Compleat Housewife; or, Accomplish'd Gentlewoman's Companion; etc.* London, 1734.

TATE, N., *A Poem Upon Tea, with a Discourse on Its Sov'rain Virtues*. London, 1702.

GARDENING

AITON, W., *Hortus Kewensis, or a Catalogue of the Plants Cultivated in the Royal Botanic Garden at Kew*. 3 vols. London, 1789.

CHAMBERS, SIR WILLIAM, *A Dissertation on Oriental Gardening*. London, 1772.

CHAMBERS, SIR WILLIAM, *Plans, Elevations, Sections and Perspective Views of the Gardens and Buildings at Kew, Seat of the Princess Dowager of Wales*. London, 1763.

COWELL, JOHN, *A True Account of the Aloe Americana, or Africana, now in Blossom. . . . Also Two Other Exotic Plants Called the Sereus or Torch-Thistle.* London, 1732.

EHRET, GEORGE D., *Of a New Peruvian Plant Lately Introduced into the English Gardens.* London, 1767. (Brit. Mus.)

ELLIS, JOHN, *Directions for Bringing Over Seeds and Plants from the East Indies and Other Distant Countries in a State of Vegetation.* London, 1770.

HALPENNY, J., *Rural Architecture in the Chinese Taste, Being Designs for the Decoration of Gardens, etc.* 4 parts. London, 1750. (Brit. Mus.)

MILLER, PHILIP, *The Gardener's and Florist's Dictionary, or a Complete System of Horticulture.* 2 vols. London, 1724.

PULLEIN, SAMUEL, *Observations Toward a Method of Preserving the Seeds of Plants in a State of Vegetation During Long Voyages.* London, 1760. (Brit. Mus.)

PULTENEY, RICHARD, *Historical and Biographical Sketches of the Progress of Botany in England from Its Origin to the Introduction of the Linnæan System.* 2 vols. London, 1790.

WALPOLE, HORACE, *Essay on Modern Gardening.* Strawberry Hill, 1785.

SECONDARY ACCOUNTS

GENERAL

HUNT, WILLIAM, *The History of England from the Accession of George III to the Close of Pitt's First Administration (1760-1801).* London and New York, 1905.

KNIGHT, CHARLES, *The Popular History of England.* Vol. V, 1733-1783. London, 1832.

LEADAM, ISAAC S., *The History of England from the Accession of Anne to the Death of George II (1702-1760).* London and New York, 1909.

LECKY, WILLIAM E. H., *History of England in the Eighteenth Century*. 8 vols. New York, 1878-1890.

MASSEY, RT. HON. WILLIAM N., *A History of England During the Reign of George III*. 4 vols. London, 1855-1863.

MAY, THOMAS E., *The Constitutional History of England Since the Accession of George III, 1760-1860*. 2 vols. London, 1861. *Ibid,* 3d ed. 3 vols. London, 1871.

OLDFIELD, THOMAS H. B., *The Representative History of Great Britain and Ireland; being a History of the House of Commons and of the Counties, Cities, and Boroughs of the United Kingdom, from the Earliest Period*. 6 vols. London, 1816.

PORRITT, A. G. and EDWARD, *The Unreformed House of Commons*. 2 vols. Cambridge, 1903.

STANHOPE, EARL, *History of England, Comprising the Reign of Queen Anne (1710-1713)*. 7 vols. London, 1870.

TREVELYAN, GEORGE M., *England Under the Stuarts*. 5th ed. New York, 1912.

WRIGHT, T., *Caricature History of the Georges*. London, 1877.

SOCIAL HISTORIES

ASHTON, JOHN, *Social Life in the Reign of Queen Anne, Taken from Original Sources*. 2 vols. London, 1882.

FOAKES-JACKSON, FREDERICK J., *Social Life in England, 1750-1850*. New York, 1916.

HUCHON, R., *Mrs. Montagu and Her Friends, 1720-1800*. London, 1907.

KNIGHT, CHARLES (ed.), *The Land We Live In. A Pictorial and Literary Sketch-Book of the British Empire*. 4 vols. London, 1842.

LOCKITT, C. H., *The Relations of French and English Society (1763-1793)*. London, 1920.

ROSCOE, E. S., *The English Scene in the Eighteenth Century*. New York, 1912.

TRAILL, HENRY D., *Social England*. Vols. IV and V. New York, 1901.

ECONOMIC WORKS

I. *Agriculture*

HAMMOND, BARBARA and JOHN L. LE B., *The Village Labourer*, 1760-1832. London and New York, 1911.

JOHNSON, ARTHUR H., *The Disappearance of the Small Landowner*. Oxford, 1909.

PROTHERO, ROWLAND E., *English Farming, Past and Present*. London and New York, 1912.

PROTHERO, ROWLAND E., *The Pioneers and Progress of English Farming*. London and New York, 1888.

II. *Commerce and Industry*

BAINES, SIR EDWARD, *History of the Cotton Manufacture in Great Britain; with a Notice of Its Early History in the East and in All the Quarters of the Globe*. London, 1853.

BAINES, SIR EDWARD, *History of Liverpool*. Liverpool, 1852.

BRISCO, NORRIS A., *The Economic Policy of Robert Walpole*. New York, 1907.

BROOKE, L., *Liverpool as It Was During the Last Quarter of the Eighteenth Century*. London, 1853.

CRACE-CALVERT, DR. F., *Dyeing and Calico Printing*. Manchester, London and New York, 1876.

CRAIK, GEORGE L., *The History of British Commerce*. London, 1844.

CUNNINGHAM, WILLIAM, *The Growth of English Industry and Commerce In Modern Times*. Vol. II. Cambridge, 1907.

FAIRBAIRN, SIR WILLIAM, *Iron, Its History, Properties, and Processes of Manufacture*. 3d ed. Edinburgh, 1869.

FOX BOURNE, H. R., *English Merchants; Memoirs in Illustration of the Progress of British Commerce*. 2 vols. London, 1866.

GASKELL, P., *The Manufacturing Population of England; Its Moral, Social, and Physical Conditions, and the Changes Which Have Arisen from the Use of Steam Machinery; with an Examination of Infant Labour.* London, 1833.

GILLESPIE, JAMES E., *The Influence of Oversea Expansion on England to 1700.* New York, 1920.

HAMMOND, BARBARA and JOHN L. LE B., *The Town Labourer,* 1760-1832. London, 1917.

MELVILLE, LEWIS, *The South Sea Bubble.* London, 1921.

MURPHY, J. A., *Treatise on the Art of Weaving.* Glasgow, 1844.

URE, ANDREW, *The Cotton Manufacture of Great Britain Investigated and Illustrated.* 2 vols. London, 1861.

USHER, ABBOTT P., *An Introduction to the Industrial History of England.* New York, 1919.

WILLSON, BECKLES, *The Great Company.* New York, 1900.

WILLSON, BECKLES, *Ledger and Sword, or the Honourable Company of Merchants Trading to the East Indies.* London, New York and Bombay, 1903.

III. *Colonies*

BANCROFT, GEORGE, *History of the United States.* 6 vols. New York, 1885.

CUNDALL, FRANK, *Studies in Jamaica History.* London, 1900.

EGERTON, H. E., *The Origin and Growth of the English Colonies and of Their System of Government.* Oxford, 1903.

EGERTON, H. E., *A Short History of British Colonial Policy.* London, 1897.

GARDNER, W. J., *A History of Jamaica.* London, 1873.

JEFFREY, R. W., *The History of the Thirteen Colonies of North America, 1497-1763.* London, 1908.

MILL, JAMES, *History of British India.* 10 vols. London, 1858.

WHITMORE, WILLIAM H., *The Cavalier Dismounted.* Salem, 1864.

WOOD, G. A., *The Discovery of Australia.* London, 1922.

BIOGRAPHIES

CUNNINGHAM, G. E., *A History of England in the Lives of Englishmen*. 8 vols. London, 1853.

Dictionary of National Biography. London, 1887.

EDWARDS, E., *Lives of the Founders of the British Museum, 1570-1870*. Vol. I. London, 1870.

The Georgian Era: Memoirs of the Most Eminent Persons, Who Have Flourished in Great Britain from the Accession of George I to the Demise of George IV. 4 vols. London, 1833.

HAMMOND, J. L. LE B., *Charles James Fox*. London, 1903.

MALCOLM, JOHN, *Life of Robert, First Lord Clive*. 3 vols. London, 1836.

SMILES, SAMUEL, *Lives of Boulton and Watt*. London, 1865.

THURSFIELD, J. R., *Peel* (in *Twelve English Statesmen* Series). London, 1891.

TREVELYAN, GEORGE O., *The Early History of Charles James Fox*. London, 1880.

TROTTER, L. J., *Warren Hastings* (in *Rulers of India* Series), Oxford, 1890.

WILSON, WALTER, *Memoirs of the Life and Times of Daniel Defoe*. 3 vols. London, 1830.

WORKS ON SPECIAL TOPICS

ANDREWS, ALEXANDER, *History of British Journalism from the Foundation of the Newspaper Press in England to 1855*. London, 1859.

ASHTON, JOHN, *History of Gambling in England*. Chicago, 1899.

BEVAN, G. P., (ed.), *British Manufacturing Industries*. Vol. VII, on pottery, furniture and woodwork. London, 1876.

BOULTON, W. B., *Amusements of Old London*. 2 vols. London, 1901.

BRADLEY, ROSE M., *The English Housewife in the Seventeenth and Eighteenth Centuries*. London, 1912.

CANDOLLE, ALPHONSE L. P. P. DE, *Origine des Plants Cultivées*. Paris, 1883.

CECIL, E., *A History of Gardening in England*. New York, 1910.

CLODE, CHARLES M., *The Military Forces of the Crown; Their Administration and Government*. 2 vols. London, 1869.

CLOUSTON, R. S., *English Furniture and English Furniture Makers of the Eighteenth Century*. London, 1906.

CREIGHTON, L., *Missions, Their Rise and Development* (in *Home University Library*). New York, 1912.

DODD, G., *The Food of London*. London, 1856.

FAIRHOLT, F. W., *Costume in England*. London, 1846.

GRANT, JAMES, *The Newspaper Press: Its Origin, Progress and Present Position*. 3 vols. London, 1871-2.

A Guide to the English Pottery and Porcelain in the Department of British and Mediæval Antiquities. London, 1910.

HAZLITT, W. C., *Old Cookery Books and Ancient Cuisine*. London, 1902.

HEATON, J. A., *Furniture and Decoration in England During the Eighteenth Century*. 2 vols. London, 1889-92.

HILL, GEORGIANA, *History of English Dress from the Saxon Period to the Present Day*. New York, 1893.

LECKY, WILLIAM E. H., *History of the Rise and Influence of the Spirit of Rationalism in Europe*. 2 vols. London, 1865.

LENYGON, FRANCIS, *Furniture in England from 1660 to 1760*. London, 1914.

LOUDON, J. C., *An Encyclopædia of Gardening*. London, 1826.

MAHAN, ALFRED T., *The Influence of Sea Power Upon History, 1660-1783*. Boston, 1890.

MURRAY, D., *Museums, Their History and Their Use*. Glasgow, 1904.

PHILLIPS, HENRY, *History of Cultivated Vegetables*. 2 vols. London, 1827.

PHILLIPS, HENRY, *Pomarium Britannicum: An Historical and Botanical Account of Fruits Known in Great Britain.* London, 1820.

SINGLETON, ESTHER, *The Furniture of Our Forefathers.* New York, 1916.

SMITH, JOHN, *A Dictionary of Popular Names of Plants Which Furnish the Wants of Man, in All Matters of Domestic and General Economy, Their History and Uses.* London, 1882.

TUCKER, HENRY W., *The English Church in Other Lands; or the Spiritual Expansion of England.* London, 1886.

ENCYCLOPÆDIAS

CHAMBERS' *Encyclopædia of Current Knowledge.* Philadelphia, 1867.

Encyclopædia Britannica. 11th ed. Cambridge, 1910.

INDEX